D1214319

THE LEEDS UNITED STORY

THE LEEDS UNITED STORY

Martin Jarred and
Malcolm Macdonald

breedon **books**
PUBLISHING

First published in Great Britain in 1992 by
The Breedon Books Publishing Company Limited
Breedon House, 3 The Parker Centre,
Derby, DE21 4SZ.
This edition 2002

ISBN 1 85983 341 1

Printed and bound by Butler & Tanner, Frome,
Somerset, England.

Cover printing by Lawrence-Allen Colour Printers,
Weston-super-Mare, Somerset, England.

Contents

The Birth of Soccer in Leeds

SOCCER took a quarter of a century to become firmly established in Leeds, where rugby was the dominant winter sport during the Victorian era. An apathetic Leeds public preferred the handling code and early attempts to introduce them to 'socker', as it was called in those days, were greeted with indifference.

Yet only 35 miles further south, in Sheffield, football was growing in popularity each year. Sheffield FC, reckoned to be the oldest club in the world, was formed in 1857. And Sheffield Wednesday, the fifth oldest club in the Football League, were formed as The Wednesday in 1867, the same year that the Sheffield FA was formed.

As the game continued to make great strides in the steel city, further north in Leeds the sporting public were blissfully unaware of the game. Thus, Leeds owe their South Yorkshire neighbours a great debt, as the first soccer match believed to have been played in Leeds was organised by soccer pioneers from Sheffield.

It was arranged by Fred Sanderson, president of the Sheffield Association, who took two teams from Sheffield to play an exhibition match at Holbeck Recreation Ground on Boxing Day 1877.

They turned up with all their kit, a ball, umpires and even a set of posts, like missionaries spreading the soccer gospel.

Despite a bitterly cold wind the game attracted a good crowd and the Sheffield visitors reckoned they had covered their expenses – until they discovered that most of the spectators were Holbeck Rugby Club season-ticket holders who had got in without paying.

With so many rugby folk at the ground it was not surprising that soccer was given a lukewarm reception by people who 'reckoned nowt to it'.

On the outskirts of Leeds, however, there was more interest, with both Rothwell and Oulton having teams. Fred Waterhouse, a player and administrator with Rothwell School, was anxious to see the game expand and made another attempt to show the Leeds public what soccer was all about.

In 1881, Rothwell fixed up a match with Blackburn Rovers at the Holbeck Recreation Ground, but once again it failed to generate much interest.

Leeds, though, could not resist soccer for much longer and the first club in the city was formed at Kirkstall in 1885 and called simply 'Leeds'.

The club's founder was Leonard Cooper, later to become head of a well-known firm of Leeds construction engineers, and he managed to persuade several well-known players of the day to join in the new venture. They included R.W. Burrows (Old Foresters), E.Cautley (Old Carthusians), T.R.H.Cook (Swifts), S.G.Smith and J.V.Smith (Notts County), and H.S.Spark and T.W. Strother (Old Carthusians).

The new Leeds club arranged its first match against Hull Town at Armley cricket ground in Armley Park on 3 October 1885, but the visitors failed to turn up, a common occurrence in those days.

Leeds played at both the cricket ground and on a field adjoining the Star and Garter pub at Kirkstall, but failed to attract decent attendances at either and after two years folded.

In 1888, two new clubs emerged – Leeds and Leeds Albion. The Leeds club, like the first club of that name, also played on the Star and Garter field at Kirkstall where they kicked-off their life with a 2-2 draw with Staincross.

Like their predecessors, Leeds found it difficult to attract a crowd of any size. Players were still struggling to play the game properly and spectators had to watch some dreary exhibitions.

Football as we know it today sprang up from the 'mob' game of early England. No doubt Leeds, like most other towns, had some form of street football in medieval times. It survives today, in places like the Derbyshire town of Ashbourne where they play an annual Shrovetide match between 'Uppards' and 'Downards'.

Early Struggles

Even the visit of a Preston North End XI to play Leeds at Cardigan Fields attracted only about 2,000 spectators. Leeds Albion, meanwhile, formed at the works of Wilson and Mathiesons, Armley, had a strong Scottish contingent. Soccer was popular north of the border and the firm, which came to Leeds in 1888, brought many Scots workers with them.

Albion rented a ground in Brudenell Road and played their first game at Harrogate on 20 October 1888 when they won 3-1.

Leeds met Albion in the first soccer derby in the city on 10 November with Leeds running out 3-1 winners. Both clubs struggled financially in their first year but continued in 1889-90, although Albion moved from Brudenell Road to Armley.

Again they embarked on a series of friendlies and, as there was still no local cup competition, both clubs entered the Scarborough and East Riding Cup.

Even these cup-ties, though, failed to attract spectators and coverage by local newspapers was scant with even the results failing to get a mention.

At the end of the season Leeds folded, but as they disappeared over the horizon a new club, Leeds Steelworks, had been formed in the Hunslet area of the city in October 1889.

Leeds Steelworks was made up of men in that industry and they played largely for fun, whilst Leeds Albion went into the 1890-91 season determined to improve their standing.

They moved once again, this time from Armley to Cardigan Fields, which had become available as Leeds St John's Rugby Club had transferred their headquarters to Headingley.

Albion became the first Leeds side to play in the FA Cup and hoped a good run in the national competition would create much-needed interest in the city.

But in the first qualifying round, at Derbyshire club Belper Town on 25 October 1890, they lost and the dream of spreading the soccer gospel soon ended.

The following season, Albion beat Rothwell 2-0 in the FA Cup at Cardigan Fields in a qualifying-round replay.

In the next round Leeds Albion were due to travel to Darlington on 14 November 1891, but Albion were unable to make the journey north and withdrew from the competition.

The writing was on the wall. Unable to build up funds through gate receipts, Albion, like Leeds, succumbed to the inevitable. The people of the city were still too engrossed in rugby to switch their allegiance to soccer.

By 1891 soccer was virtually dead in Leeds but was revived by a split in the ranks of the handling code. The rugby world was divided over the question of professionalism. The Rugby Union refused to acknowledge the paid player and in 1895 the clubs which opted for professionalism formed the Northern Union (the present Rugby League).

The division in the rugby world gave soccer a new opportunity to establish the dribbling code. Soccer pundits recognised that spectators wanted to see a more competitive edge to matches.

The Visit of Mighty Preston

In the early 1890s, virtually all soccer games were friendlies but the formation of the West Yorkshire

League in 1894 gave the game the competitive boost it needed.

At last soccer was able to gain a foothold in the area as Leeds, Hunslet, Rothwell, Castleford, Altofts, Pontefract, Normanton, Oulton, Featherstone, Pontefract Garrison and Ferrybridge entered the new league.

The new Leeds club had no connection with the two previous organisations of the same name, although their secretary, Robert Mason, had been a driving force behind the defunct Leeds Albion.

Leeds were formed on 22 February, at a meeting at the Cardigan Arms, four days before the West Yorkshire League was founded.

Hunslet, meanwhile, were the old Leeds Steelworks team and played on the Wellington Ground in Low Road.

Soon after the season began, Mr M.Nicholson, president of the West Yorkshire League, persuaded mighty Preston North End to play an exhibition match against a West Yorkshire League representative side.

The Football League's president, John Bentley of Bolton, realised this was an ideal opportunity for soccer to make an impact in Leeds and ensured that Preston fielded a strong team which included internationals Francis Becton and Bob Holmes.

Preston, the first ever Football League Champions in 1888-9, were among the elite sides of the day and their visit to the West Riding Ground in Meanwood Road on 28 November 1894 pulled in a crowd of 5,000, easily the biggest to see a soccer match in Leeds.

The spectators, many of whom had only seen a crude amateur version of soccer, were enthralled as Preston unveiled their skills in a 5-0 win. For the record the teams were:

West Yorkshire League: Couch (Pontefract Garrison), Ellison (Leeds), Burr (Altofts), Daniels (Rothwell), Betteridge (Castleford), Taylor (Rothwell), Richardson (Hunslet), Boyes (Oulton), Deeley (Pontefract), Gettings (Normanton), Fernside (Pontefract).
Preston North End: Trainer; Dunn, Holmes, Sharp, Orr, Sanders, Gordon, Cunningham, Barr, Becton, Henderson.

The experiment had been a tremendous success and the Football League gladly sanctioned a friendly between Leeds and Everton at Harehills Road three months later. A powerful Everton side, which included England international centre-forward Fred Geary, won 7-0 in front of a 3,000 crowd.

It was a momentous season for the new Leeds club. They won the inaugural West Yorkshire League, the Leeds Workpeople's Hospital Cup and the Scarborough and East Riding Cup.

Their success in the latter sparked a tremendous controversy. Leeds met Scarborough in the Final at the Scarborough Recreation Ground on 30 March 1895 and before the kickoff both captains agreed that in the event of a draw, extra-time of ten minutes each way should be played.

The game finished at 1-1 but Leeds refused to play on, despite being given five minutes by Sheffield referee Fred Bye to make up their minds.

Leeds dug in their heels, the referee awarded the match to Scarborough and the trophy was duly presented to them. Leeds lodged an appeal on the grounds that there was no rule compelling them to play extra-time. Scarborough then said they felt uncomfortable holding a trophy they had actually not won and both clubs agreed to a replay.

This time Leeds won 2-1, after extra-time, at Scarborough and in a game controlled by the same referee.

In the West Yorkshire League, Leeds won 18 of their 20 games to finish eight points clear of Castleford and added the Leeds Workpeople's Hospital Cup to their trophy haul on Easter Monday 1895 by beating Castleford 3-1 at Headingley.

Midway through the season the committee running the Leeds club had decided to move from their ground at Harehills Lane to join the Leeds Cricket, Football & Athletic Club at Headingley.

Headingley had the best facilities in the city and, to cap a season of great progress for soccer, it hosted the FA Amateur Cup Final and a semi-final.

In the semi-final, Old Carthusians and South Bank fought out a 1-1 draw before a 3,000 crowd. Two weeks later, Old Carthusians returned to Headingley for the Final but went down 2-1 to Middlesbrough.

Both matches were prestigious affairs but neither had pulled in the size of crowd soccer administrators had hoped, which was a major blow to the Leeds club, who had switched to Headingley in an effort to generate more support.

Despite that disappointment, soccer had clearly made great strides and with junior clubs like Pudsey, Leeds St Luke's, Leeds Northern and Rothwell White Rose springing up, the prospects looked rosy.

Hunslet's 'Twinklers'
Although Leeds retained the Scarborough and East Riding Cup by beating Pickering in the 1896 Final, the city side did not dominate the local scene as they had the previous season.

This time it was Hunslet who were the team of the moment, sharing the West Yorkshire League title with Bradford and enjoying a tremendous run in the FA Amateur Cup.

They had moved from the Wellington Ground

to the Laburnum Ground at Parkside, only a narrow strip of land separating it from the Hunslet Rugby Ground.

The change of scenery seemed to inspire them as Hunslet eliminated West Hartlepool, Loftus and Buxton in the Amateur Cup before entertaining powerful Old Etonians in the second round proper on 15 February 1896.

It was the big event of the season with few giving Hunslet, known locally as 'The Twinklers' much chance. Those fears seemed to have substance when Hunslet went 2-0 behind after only seven minutes. But a stirring fightback brought a 3-2 win, one of the goals coming from 'Tipper' Heffron, a winger who was to play for Leeds City in the club's early days.

It was a memorable milestone but in the quarter-final, Hunslet went out against Darlington and finished the season £35 in the red – an indication of how difficult it was to make soccer pay.

In 1897-8 there was no fully organised league in the Leeds area, the West Yorkshire League having folded after just a couple of seasons, so five members of the West Yorkshire Association joined the new Yorkshire League which was promoted by the Sheffield and Hallamshire Association.

The Yorkshire League comprised Leeds, Hunslet, Bradford, Huddersfield, Halifax, Mexborough, Barnsley St Peter's, Doncaster Rovers Reserves, Sheffield United Reserves and Sheffield Wednesday Reserves.

Leeds moved back to Headingley after their sojourn at Meanwood Road for what would be their last season in existence.

Once again they were involved in a furore with Scarborough in the Scarborough and East Riding Cup Final. The Final, at Pickering, was drawn and a replay was fixed for 9 April by the Cup Committee. Amazingly Scarborough refused to play because they had already arranged a match with Ossett on that date.

The trophy was awarded to Leeds, whilst Scarborough were 'suspended for the day' so they could not play their game against Ossett either.

Furious Scarborough withdrew from their local association and did not re-enter the competition again until 1900 as Scarborough Utopians.

Leeds also reached the Final of the Leeds Workpeople's Hospital Cup against Hunslet and the two clubs fought out a 2-2 draw on 16 April before 7,000 spectators on the Leeds Parish Church Ground at Crown Point.

A fortnight later, Hunslet won the replay which was held on the same ground before the Leeds Elementary Schools Cup Final between York Road and Bewerley Street.

It was the last time Leeds played. The move to Headingley had been unsuccessful and failure to attract consistently good crowds meant the club continued to run at a loss.

The soccer section had an uneasy alliance with the directors of the Leeds Cricket, Football & Athletic Club, who owned the Headingley ground next to the famous cricket arena.

They told the Leeds soccer section to come up with a scheme which would ensure they could meet their expenses at the Headingley ground from gate receipts.

When only three people turned up at the club's annual meeting on 22 June 1898 to discuss the problem, the men behind the Leeds soccer club decided enough was enough and the club folded.

Although Leeds had fallen by the wayside, rivals Hunslet were in the ascendancy. They won the West Yorkshire Cup Final on 23 April 1898 by beating Harrogate 1-0 in the first soccer match ever to be played on the current Elland Road ground.

Hunslet were the rising soccer power in Leeds and were the forerunners of the Leeds City side which gained entry to the Football League in 1905.

They won the West Yorkshire Cup for a fourth successive time in 1900 and lifted the Leeds Workpeople's Hospital Cup for the fourth time in the same year by beating Huddersfield Town 2-1 after two drawn games.

Cup kings Hunslet even held Blackburn Rovers to a 1-1 draw in a friendly at Crown Point on Easter Tuesday 1900, although the game attracted only a 3,000 crowd.

Star man for Hunslet in those days was goalkeeper Harold Lemoine, who became one of the best goalkeepers in amateur football. When he left Hunslet he played for Shepherd's Bush and Clapton, winning English amateur honours in 1908-09 against Ireland and Belgium and in the 1909-10 season against Denmark.

It was Hunslet who led a deputation to the West Yorkshire Association, urging them to form leagues for the scores of new soccer clubs which were springing up around the area.

But the West Riding's best clubs continued to play under the wing of the Sheffield and Hallamshire Association until 1902.

Smaller clubs, however, did thrive in the Leeds League which was formed in 1898-9 and comprised church and chapel teams from Salem, Stourton United, St Silas, Beeston Hill Congs, Woodville, Burley, Holbeck Unitarians, St Jude's Mission, St Patrick's, Leeds Acme and Hunslet Parish Church.

Other notable sides that began to emerge included Woodville, Leeds Clarendon and Armley Christ Church.

Homeless Hunslet Fold

Despite the increasing number of players, discipline on the field was sometimes poor with authorities adopting a lenient attitude to offenders in case they drove players away from the game.

There were several cases when teams walked off in protest because one of their men had been sent-off.

The increase in teams put pressure on open space within the city and many clubs had to share grounds.

Hunslet had a constant problem finding a permanent home and during summer 1902, club officials scoured South Leeds looking for a suitable ground ready for the relaunching of the new West Yorkshire League which had folded in 1898.

Although Hunslet were regarded as the premier club in Leeds, they had always struggled to find a ground of their own. When they were forced to quit their Nelson ground in Low Road, they were unable to find a new headquarters in time to line-up alongside the other 13 teams in the West Yorkshire League.

They were scheduled to open the season at Dewsbury Celtic on 13 September 1902, but homeless Hunslet reluctantly decided not to embark on the new season and the club died.

Through the family tree of Leeds soccer, Hunslet were undoubtedly one of the true pioneers of the game in the city.

Under their former name, Leeds Steelworks, they were formed in 1889 and played their first game against the second Leeds club on 26 October. When they joined the West Yorkshire League in 1894 they changed their name to Hunslet.

Although Hunslet folded in 1902, a new club arose out of their ashes – Leeds City, forerunner of the current Leeds United.

Leeds City and Election to the Football League

DESPITE the failure of Hunslet, the men behind that club were convinced that Leeds could support first-class soccer. Soon after Hunslet's demise they met and vowed to create another club, one big and strong enough to support League football.

Driving forces behind the new Leeds City club were chairman John Furness, secretary Frank Jarvis and treasurer Mr M.Myercroft.

Soccer was enjoying a boom period and Leeds, the largest city in England without representation in the Football League, was in danger of getting left behind.

From the shell of Hunslet, the Leeds City club was formed and entered the West Yorkshire League for the 1904-05 season.

Even then, a place in the Football League seemed light years away as the club had no permanent base.

Ironically, the problem of a headquarters was solved by the demise of Holbeck Rugby Club, which folded after failing to beat St Helens in a play-off for a place in Division One of the Northern Union in 1904.

They decided not to continue with the lease at Elland Road, site of the current stadium, because of the expense, so an eager Leeds City moved in.

That soccer should replace the 'old enemy' rugby at Elland Road illustrated how much soccer had caught the imagination of the Leeds public.

But there was no gloating in soccer circles at Holbeck's closure, for the rugby club had done much to lay down the foundations at Elland Road.

Holbeck used to play half a mile further down Elland Road at Holbeck Recreation ground. It was perched on the top side of Holbeck Moor where the streets known as 'The Recreations' now stand. It extended from the Waggon and Horses pub to Brown Lane, from Top Moor Side along Elland Road to the Neville Works in Brown Lane. On one side of the ground stood a grandstand that had once stood at the old Leeds Racecourse in Pontefract Road.

The facilities at Holbeck made it the best sporting arena in Leeds prior to the development at Headingley, and staged rugby, soccer and cricket matches.

In the latter half of the last century, Yorkshire Cricket Club played several games at the Holbeck 'Reckry' and two of them made the record books.

In 1868 they bowled out Lancashire in the Roses match for 30 and 34; then, 15 years later, England left-arm leg-break bowler Ted Peate, a native of Holbeck, took eight wickets for five runs as Surrey were skittled for 31.

In winter the ground was essentially a rugby ground, although occasionally soccer matches were played there.

Rugby seemed set for a long reign at Holbeck until, in 1897, the club were told that the lease would not be renewed.

Holbeck Rugby Club secretary Robert Walker soon thrashed out a deal with Bentley's Brewery to lease land opposite the Old Peacock at Elland Road the site of the current stadium.

Bentley's knew they were on to a good thing. They offered to sell at £1,100 on condition that the land was used as a football ground and that the brewery held the right to sell refreshments at the ground.

Not only could Bentley's sell inside the ground, they also owned two nearby pubs and could look forward to bumper takings behind the bars on match days.

However, Walker's plan was not all plain sailing. At a crowded meeting in Holbeck schoolroom in January 1897, some supporters said the new headquarters were too far away.

The opposition was led by Councillor Joseph Henry, but after several heated exchanges, the proposal to move Holbeck Rugby Club to Elland Road was backed by a large majority.

The club immediately set about creating the new ground but ran into a labour shortage because men were working on a big demolition scheme in the centre of Leeds which swept away Wood Street and established the Empire Theatre, County Arcade, Queen Victoria Street and King Edward Street.

But gradually the Elland Road ground took shape. The playing pitch was at right-angles to today's lay-out with the touchlines running parallel to Elland Road.

A new stand had not been included in the original scheme because Walker planned to buy one from the West Riding ground at Meanwood Road.

But that stand had been specially built over a beck that ran behind Meanwood Road and could not be moved to another site.

Despite that hiccup, Holbeck still had sufficient funds to build their own stand which was completed in time for the 1897-8 season.

The first soccer match at Elland Road was played on 23 April 1898, when Hunslet beat Harrogate 1-0 in the West Yorkshire Cup Final.

The first soccer club to use Elland Road as their home base was Leeds League club, Leeds Woodville, who played on alternate Saturdays, sharing with Holbeck Rugby Club. Woodville's opening game at Elland Road was a 3-0 victory over Hunslet Weslyan Mission on 13 September, 1902.

Elland Road was certainly well established by the time Holbeck Rugby Club surrendered their lease.

City Join the West Yorkshire League

Immediately the men behind the new Leeds City soccer club saw their opportunity. They were ambitious, with Football League status being the ultimate goal, and by securing such splendid facilities they knew it would help any future application to join the Football League.

Talks about taking over the Elland Road lease

were soon in full swing but the final details had not been ironed out in time for the start of the 1904-05 season.

Leeds City had joined the West Yorkshire League and opened their campaign with a 2-2 draw at Morley on 1 September 1904.

Two days later they played a 'home' game against Altofts at Wellington Ground, Low Road, Hunslet, because the Elland Road deal had not been quite finalised.

The club also entered the FA Cup, losing 3-1 in the qualifying round at Rockingham Colliery, near Barnsley, on 17 September.

Leeds City officials gave the go-ahead to sign the lease on 13 October, for an annual rent with an option to buy for not more than £5,000 the following March. When the lease was finally signed, in November, the purchase figure came down to £4,500.

Two days after the instructions to sign, the first-ever Leeds City team stepped out on to the Elland Road turf to meet Hull City in a friendly.

The 3,000 crowd were entertained by a local boys' match and a band before the main event which saw Leeds lose 2-0 to their visitors.

As the season went on, City staged a series of prestige friendlies against some of the top sides in the country like Sheffield United, Preston North End, Derby County and West Bromwich Albion.

These pulled in big crowds, who could see some of the game's most famous names in action. In the case of Steve Bloomer, Derby's England centre-

England international Fred Spiksley appeared in Leeds City's colours and helped convince the club's officials that League football was not just a dream.

Leeds City pictured in 1905-06, the club's first season in the Football League. Back row (left to right): R. Younger (director), R.S. Kirk (director), Charles Morgan, D. Whitaker (director), Parnell, Dooley, John McDonald, Austin, Fred Walker, Harry Singleton, R.M. Dow (director), George Swift (trainer). Middle row: Gilbert Gillies (secretary-manager), Fred Parnell, Bob Watson, Fred Hargraves, Dick Ray, John Morris, Bill Clay, Oliver. Tordoff (director). Front row: 'Roy, the City Dog', Harry Stringfellow, Tom Drain, James Henderson.

forward, they got within touching distance, as he ran the line when the Rams won 2-1 in March 1905.

Many of the friendlies clashed with West Yorkshire League fixtures which were fulfilled by a reserve team playing the same afternoon.

Not surprisingly, City failed to complete their full programme of 26 West Yorkshire League matches, something which was not uncommon among clubs in local leagues in those days.

City made a conscious effort to catch up and even played two West Yorkshire League games in one day at the end of the season – beating Huddersfield 1-0 and Upper Armley Christ Church 4-1. One home game against Dewsbury had to be cancelled because of an outbreak of smallpox in the Dewsbury area and the match was never rearranged.

Only five of the 14 clubs in the league managed to finish all their fixtures, including champions Bradford City Reserves, who collected 43 points, 22 more than Leeds City.

None of this bothered the Leeds City administrators, whose ploy to play high profile friendlies was an unprecedented success.

Not only did it bring in good crowds and gate receipts, but it educated the local sporting public and also helped Leeds City recruit some star names of their own.

England internationals Fred Spiksley (Sheffield Wednesday) and Tom Morren (Sheffield United) both played in the colours of Leeds City and although neither stayed for any length of time it convinced the club's officials that the dream of League football could be turned into reality.

City Join the Elite

After only one season in existence, Leeds City mounted their bid to join the elite of the Football League. In April 1905 the first Leeds City limited company was floated with capital of 10,000 £1 shares.

Three men held the majority of those shares, local clothier and businessman Norris Hepworth, who became City's first chairman, Ralph Younger, landlord of the Old Peacock, and A.W.Pullin, better known as 'Old Ebor', a *Yorkshire Evening Post* sports journalist.

Vice-chairman was Oliver Tordoff and the other directors were R.S.Kirk, Joseph Henry, D.Whitaker, John Furness, Frank Jarvis, W.Robinson, F.G.Dimery, W.Preston, W.G.Child, John Oliver, R.Younger and R.M.Dow, a former treasurer of Woolwich Arsenal.

Leeds City were now in a strong position to put their case to the Football League. They had an excellent ground, influential men behind the club, growing support and a new recruit to the Leeds City cause – secretary-manager Gilbert Gillies.

Gillies was chosen from 100 applications for the post. He had been officially appointed on 16 March 1905, on a three-year contract worth £156 a year.

As secretary-manager of Chesterfield he had played a key role in getting the Derbyshire club elected to the Football League in 1899 and the Leeds City officials reckoned he could do a similar job for their club.

City's confidence received a further boost when the Football League agreed to expand from 36 clubs to 40, and on 29 May 1905 Leeds City were duly elected, topping the poll with 25 votes.

Of the others, Port Vale and Burton United were both re-elected; Chelsea, who had neither team nor playing record, got in because they had cash and a ground; newcomers Clapton Orient and Stockport County were admitted, but Doncaster Rovers, the third club seeking re-election, failed following a disastrous season which saw them gain only eight points from 34 games.

Proud Leeds City was officially formed into a limited liability company on 5 June and the following month work began on a £1,050 stand for 5,000 people on the west side of the Elland Road ground, increasing the capacity to 22,000.

Whilst construction work went ahead around the field, Gillies began his building work on it.

Together with his trainer and right-hand man, George Swift, the former Loughborough left-back and Football League representative, Gillies began to assemble the Leeds City squad. City's first skipper was full-back Dick Ray, who had served under Gillies at Chesterfield and also had experience with Manchester City and Stockport County. Ray became one of the cornerstones around which professional soccer was built in Leeds, going on to manage Leeds United.

Other characters in City's first season included former Derby County and Burton United goalkeeper Harry Bromage and Welsh international forward Dickie Morris, from Liverpool.

Other new faces included full-backs John MacDonald (Ayr United and Blackburn Rovers), David Murray (Everton and Liverpool), halfbacks Charles Morgan (Tottenham Hotspur), Harry Stringfellow (Everton and Swindon), James Henderson (Bradford City), Fred Walker (Barrow) and forwards Fred Parnell (Derby County), Bob Watson (Woolwich Arsenal), Fred Hargraves (Burton United), Harry Singleton (Queen's Park Rangers) and Tom Drain (Bradford City).

Leeds City, clad in blue and old gold, had nailed their colours firmly to the Football League mast and were ready to set sail on a voyage of discovery.

Leeds City in the Football League

MANAGER Gilbert Gillies had worked quickly to put together a group of players of a standard good enough to cope with life in the Football League.

Interest was increasing in 'The Peacocks', nicknamed after the pub next door to Elland Road, and this was reflected in the increase in column-inches devoted to City's new venture in the local Press.

City kicked off their Football League career on 2 September 1905 with a derby match at Bradford City, whilst the Reserves entertained Nottingham Forest Reserves in a Midland League fixture at Elland Road.

The match at Valley Parade drew a 15,000 crowd which saw Bradford win 1-0 with a debut goal from Wallace Smith. The teams for this historic day were: **Bradford City:** James Garvey; Andrew Easton, John Halliday, George Robinson, Peter O'Rourke, James Millar, William Clarke, Andrew McGeachan, Wallace Smith, John McMillan, James Conlin. **Leeds City:** Harry Bromage; John McDonald, Dick Ray, Charles Morgan, Harry Stringfellow, James Henderson, Fred Parnell, Bob Watson, Fred Hargraves, Dickie Morris, Harry Singleton.

The following week, West Bromwich Albion were the visitors for the first Football League game at Elland Road and the Throstles went away with a comfortable 2-0 win through a couple of Freddie Haycock goals in front of a disappointing 6,802 crowd.

Two days later, on a Monday afternoon, only 3,000 turned up at Elland Road to see Tom Drain score both goals in City's 2-2 draw with Lincoln for a hard-earned first Football League point.

City's first win came the following Saturday, 16 September, when Harry Singleton scored the only goal at Leicester Fosse.

The Leeds public responded to the improvement in results and the next home game, a 3-1 win over Hull City, attracted a crowd of 13,654. Two goals from Dickie Morris and one from Fred Hargraves sealed City's first League victory at Elland Road where they only lost twice more that season.

However, the Tigers gained their revenge in the FA Cup the following month, winning 3-1 at Leeds after the Peacocks had forced a 1-1 draw at The Circle, Anlaby Road.

Morris was undoubtedly the star name in City's ranks and was already an established Welsh international before joining Leeds. He became City's first international player when he turned out at inside-right in Wales' 2-0 win over Scotland in March 1906 in Edinburgh, but three months later left Elland Road to join Grimsby Town.

Perhaps City's biggest achievement in their debut campaign was the inroads they made into the bedrock of support enjoyed by Rugby League. Across the city, the average attendance at Leeds RL slumped from 9,022 to 5,632 with many of the stay-away fans wooed by City and the dribbling code.

City's own attendances fluctuated enormously but Gillies was able to add more punch to his attack by signing David 'Soldier' Wilson, the former Dundee and Hearts player, from Hull City for £120 in December 1905.

Wilson had scored for the Tigers in that first-ever Leeds City victory at Elland Road and became an instant hit on his short move from the banks of the Humber to the West Riding.

He finished top scorer with 13 goals in only 15

League appearances, including four in a 6-1 demolition of Clapton Orient.

Matches in those days were physically rough, tough affairs full of shoulder-charges and hard tackling with heavy boots.

Injuries were part and parcel of the game but Leeds had more than their fair share during March 1906.

As they set off for a game at Grimsby on 17 March, City were already without Bob Watson, who had broken down at Burnley on his way to meet up with his colleagues.

In the first minute of the game, David Wilson went off with a torn ligament and the ten men were reduced to five fit men as goalkeeper Willis Walker, Fred Hargraves, Dick Ray, Charles Morgan and Dickie Morris all finished the match hobbling. Somehow Leeds scrambled a point from a 1-1 draw, courtesy of a David Murray goal.

On their return to Leeds, Morris and Wilson were practically carried off the train after it pulled into the Great Northern Station, were placed on a luggage wagon and trundled to a cab. That was not the end of City's injury troubles as a fortnight later they took on Chelsea in London with their trainer George Swift, who had represented the Football League in his playing days with Loughborough, forced to make the starting line-up.

Only nine fit players were able to reach London for the game, so a telegram was despatched to Elland Road for reserves to be sent to the capital. However, the reserve team had already gone to the North-East to fulfil a fixture, leaving only Harry Stringfellow available to catch the next train to London.

He arrived in time for the game, but Leeds still only had ten men. Fortunately, Swift, a classy full-back in his day, had retained his playing registration and turned out on the left wing.

However, one of City's defenders was injured during the match and Swift was pressed into service in his old role at full-back. Despite his brave efforts, City went down 4-0 to goals by Bob McRoberts (later to manage Birmingham), Frank Pearson, Jimmy Windridge and Tom McDermott.

Swift left City the following year to manage Chesterfield and later was in charge at Southampton. City were slowly building up a hardcore of supporters, but also attracted an unruly element to the club. Hooliganism blighted football, even in those days, with officials rather than opposing supporters coming in for plenty of stick.

This was not just confined to Leeds, where the worst incident occurred at the final home game of the 1905-06 season. City were beaten 3-1 by Manchester United, although some hot-headed Elland Roaders reckoned referee T.P.Campbell

(Blackburn) had cost City any chance of winning with some controversial decisions, including a Manchester penalty which England international Charles Sagar missed.

In a rough-and-tumble game Leeds also lost the services of centre-half John George with a dislocated elbow.

The unfortunate Mr Campbell received a hostile reception as he left the field and was hit on the nose by a flying lump of concrete and a sod of earth as he ran the gauntlet of furious fans.

The incident came only weeks after Campbell had been in charge of Manchester's game at Bradford City which had seen some ugly crowd scenes when Manchester player Robert Bonthron was attacked as he left the Valley Parade ground following United's 5-1 win there. Several Bradford spectators faced criminal charges and the FA closed Valley Parade for two weeks.

Campbell's appointment to the game at nearby Leeds a couple of months later was described by the *Leeds Mercury* as 'an unfortunate appointment – an embarrassment to the Leeds officials'.

The ill-feeling at Bradford towards Campbell clearly had not died down in the West Riding, but Leeds escaped any official censure.

'Soldier' Wilson's Demise and the Arrival of Billy McLeod

David Wilson's goals helped City to finish a highly respectable sixth in their maiden campaign but his talent never came to full fruition as he died at a home game against Burnley the following season.

City were just recovering from a poor start to the new campaign when the Wilson tragedy struck on 27 October 1906. The 23-year-old forward left the field against Burnley complaining of chest pains and was examined by a Dr Taylor, of New Wortley, who strongly advised Wilson not to go back on to the field.

However, as news came through that his City colleagues Harry Singleton and John Lavery, had been left hobbling with injuries in a bruising encounter, Wilson, showing typical courage, insisted on returning to the fray.

Despite advice from City officials Wilson, whose nickname 'Soldier' came from his service in the Boer War, jogged on to the pitch but within minutes came off again and collapsed in the tunnel leading to the dressing-rooms.

Wilson was carried to the treatment room but efforts to revive him proved fruitless and he lost his brief fight for life.

Wilson's sad demise cast a dark shadow over Elland Road but his loss opened the door for a man who was to become City's most famous son – Billy McLeod.

Gillies turned to the Lincoln City forward as his replacement for Wilson and the £500 paid to the Imps was to prove a masterly piece of business.

McLeod, like Wilson, was a native of Hebburn, near Newcastle upon Tyne, and finished 1905-06 with 15 goals to immediately make him a favourite with the fans.

In defence, goalkeeper Harry Bromage and Jimmy Kennedy, the former Brighton player, were rocks but City dipped to tenth place, winning only three away games.

But they did finish the season with the first piece of silverware to find its way to Elland Road – the West Riding Challenge Cup, won by the City Reserves.

They beat Kippax Parish Church, members of the West Riding League, with a couple of goals by Alf Harwood in the Final.

Harwood was a bit of a specialist when it came to collecting medals. An England amateur international, he had played for Crook Town when they beat King's Lynn in the 1901 Amateur Cup Final and later played for Bishop Auckland and Fulham before joining Leeds.

By the time he had arrived at Elland Road he had represented the Northern League, won two Durham Cup medals, Northern League and Southern League championship medals and two London League championship medals.

Despite this pedigree, Harwood made only one senior appearance for Leeds, scoring in a 2-1 win at Burnley in March 1907 before joining West Ham a few months later.

Anxious to build on the new public interest in soccer in Leeds, the FA decreed that Elland Road should host a North v South England trial on 22 January 1906. Elland Road was capable of holding 25,000 spectators by this time, but only 7,000 fans turned up to see the South win 2-0 with second-half goals by Vivian Woodward and Samuel Day.

The teams for this prestige occasion were: **North:** Robinson (Birmingham); Crompton (Blackburn Rovers), Rodway (Preston NE), Warren (Derby County), Veitch (Newcastle United), Bradley (Liverpool), Bond (Preston NE), Common (Middlesbrough), Brown (Sheffield United), Bache (Aston Villa), Gosnell (Newcastle United). **South:** Ashcroft (Woolwich Arsenal); Cross (Woolwich Arsenal), Riley (Brentford), Collins (Fulham), Bull (Tottenham Hotspur), Houlker (Southampton), Vassall (Old Carthusians), Day (Old Malvernians), Woodward (Tottenham Hotspur), Harris (Old Westminsters), Wright (Cambridge University).

Much attention was paid to improving the Elland Road arena and the month after the trial game, City paid £420 to the Monk's Bridge Iron Company for a parcel of land on the Churwell and Geldard Road side of the ground for future expansion.

The 1907-08 season saw Gillies reshape City's defence with goalkeeper Tom Naisby recruited from Sunderland to challenge Bromage's place between the posts. Harry Kay arrived from Bolton, Tom Hynds from Arsenal, Stan Cubberley from Cheshunt and William Bates, a right-back from Bolton.

The arrival of Bates was greeted with great

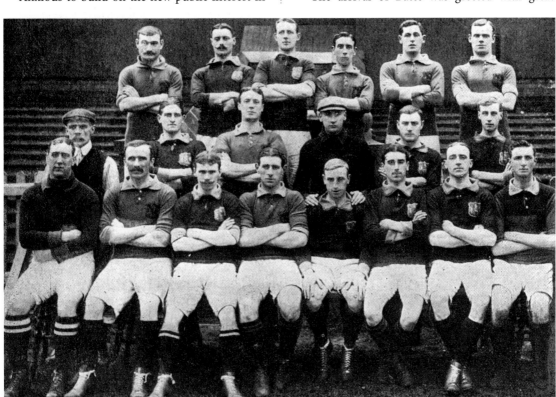

Leeds City, 1907-08. Back row (left to right): Bob Jefferson, Stan Cubberley, Fred Hargraves, John Lavery, Fred Croot, James Henderson. Middle row: Broad (trainer), J. Aldred, James Freebrough, Harry Bromage, Billy McLeod, Harry Kay. Front row: Jack Whitley, Tom Hynds, Fred Parnell, Tom Tompkins, Bill Thomas, James Thorpe, Jimmy Kennedy.

A crowd of 24,000 saw this 1-0 win over West Bromwich Albion at Elland Road in late September 1907.

enthusiasm because he was a Yorkshire cricketer, son of Billy Bates, the Yorkshire and England all-rounder.

Young William, it must be said, proved a far better cricketer than a footballer. He managed only 15 appearances for City in two seasons before disappearing from the scene.

He was a hard-hitting batsman with Yorkshire, but always seemed in the shadow of his father in his six years playing for the Broad Acres and moved on to Glamorgan after World War One to give the Welsh county ten years service.

To continue the sporting dynasty, William's son, Ted Bates, played for Norwich City and Southampton, before serving the latter for many years as manager.

Although Bates and several others made little early impact, the player of the season was undoubtedly Fred Croot, whose consistency saw him become the first City player to complete an ever-present season.

Croot, a former Sheffield United winger, had a magical left foot which provided a succession of accurate centres for the bustling McLeod. The ever-popular Croot clocked up 218 League games for City before heading north in 1919 to join Clydebank. Essentially a supplier, rather than a scorer of goals, Croot did net 38 League goals for the Peacocks. Secretary-manager Gillies had dipped into City's coffers to recruit his new men, but mediocre League performances and further failure in the FA Cup saw the club finish 1907-08 with a big deficit.

Tom Hynds, from Woolwich Arsenal, and Stan Cubberley, from Cheshunt, were part of a reshaped Leeds City defence for 1907-08. Cubberley went on to make 181 League appearances for the club.

One of the most hair-raising games of the season came at Lincoln on 22 February 1908, when gales ripped the roof off a stand at Sincil Bank, injuring five spectators.

Play was held up, but rather than call the game off, the match continued in farcical conditions in which players could hardly stand up and Leeds were eventually swept away in a 5-0 defeat.

The City directors reckoned Gillies had taken the club as far as he possibly could and so his contract was not renewed and he moved on to

manage Bradford Park Avenue, where he remained until February 1911.

Scott-Walford's Rough Diamonds from the Emerald Isle

City had already earmarked their new man for the job – Brighton boss Frank Scott-Walford, who had done much to establish the South Coast resort club as a force in the Southern League since he became their manager in March 1905.

Scott-Walford still had two years of his

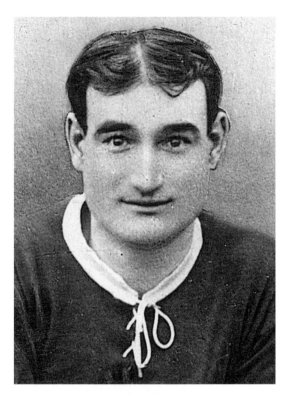

disappointment, then City officials and the FA were caught on the hop when Elland Road was deemed fit to stage the FA Cup semi-final between Barnsley and Everton in March 1910.

Elland Road was swamped as fans arrived from all directions. Neither the City administration nor the ground were geared up to cope with the 36,000-plus crowd. Those that got in could hardly see and thousands more were locked outside. Some of the turnstiles were closed even before some of the excursion trains and coaches from across the Pennines had arrived in Leeds.

Thousands of disgruntled locked out fans packed Beeston Hill and tottered gingerly on neighbouring rooftops, straining to get a glimpse of the action below.

Sunderland-born winger Bob Jefferson joined City from Bradford City in May 1906. In his first season he found the net a few times but in the 1908 close season moved on to Swindon Town, then in the Southern League, where he became quite a star.

Jimmy Burnett and Tom Rodger joined new manager Frank Scott-Walford from Brighton.

Brighton contract to run, but after lengthy talks with Leeds it was announced in March 1908 that he would be released by Brighton as soon as they could find a replacement to clear the way for Scott-Walford to take over at Elland Road.

With him he brought many of his Brighton players like Jimmy Burnett, Davie Dougal, Dickie Joynes, Tom Rodger, Willie McDonald and Tom Morris, but only the latter, who joined in February 1909, really established himself as a force in City's colours as a powerful centre-half.

John White and Tom McAllister, from Queen's Park Rangers and Brentford respectively, slotted in well with the improving Cubberley in defence but hopes of promotion nose-dived in mid-season following seven successive defeats and City finished 12th for the second year running.

Scott-Walford was working to a tight budget, but a 31,471 Elland Road crowd for an FA Cup second-round tie against West Ham helped improve the balance sheet, although City lost out on a money-spinning home game with Newcastle in the next round by losing the replay at West Ham. Cash was a constant source of difficulty for City, so Scott-Walford spent the 1909 close season in Ireland in an effort to pick up some bargains.

He returned with the Distillery forwards Billy Halligan and Tom Mulholland, with the former turning out to be a real find.

Perhaps the presence of the Irish contingent at Leeds prompted the FA to stage an amateur international against Ireland at Elland Road on 20 November 1909, the game ending 4-4 in front of 8,000 fans.

If the low crowd for that match was a

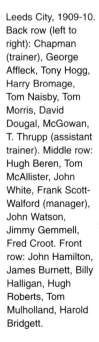

Leeds City, 1908-09. Back row (left to right): W. Preston (director), W. Robinson (director), Frank Scott-Walford (secretary-manager), R. Shotton, W. Child, H. Williams, H. Rickard, David Murray, James Burnett, C. Simpson, A. Eagle (director). Second row: T. Thrupp (assistant trainer), John White, Dickie Guy, William McDonald, Jimmy Gemmell, Sam McKeown, Harry Bromage, Tom Naisby, Jimmy Kennedy. Seated: David Dougal, Tom Rodger, Bob Watson, Adam Bowman, Tom McAllister, John Hamilton, Dickie Joynes. On ground: Stan Cubberley, Billy McLeod.

Leeds City, 1909-10. Back row (left to right): Chapman (trainer), George Affleck, Tony Hogg, Harry Bromage, Tom Naisby, Tom Morris, David Dougal, McGowan, T. Thrupp (assistant trainer). Middle row: Hugh Beren, Tom McAllister, John White, Frank Scott-Walford (manager), John Watson, Jimmy Gemmell, Fred Croot. Front row: John Hamilton, James Burnett, Billy Halligan, Hugh Roberts, Tom Mulholland, Harold Bridgett.

The match finished goalless, with Everton goalkeeper Billy Scott, later to join Leeds, having a fine game. But the lack of organisation was a bigger disappointment than the match.

The influential *Athletic News* reported: 'It is clear that the Association and the clubs concerned lost considerably by allotting the match to a small ground constructed for Second Division football and not for events of national importance.'

It had been a shambles and it was another 20 years before a new-look Elland Road was considered good enough to stage another FA Cup semi-final. That embarrassment was almost matched by City's performances on the pitch.

Of Scott-Walford's new men, only full-back George Affleck, signed from the Scottish junior club Penicuik, achieved lasting consistency, although Harry Bromage recaptured his goalkeeping slot from Tom Naisby and Halligan's eye for goal made him a hero on the terraces.

The rest of the signings were a disappointment, including Haydn Price, who had won five Welsh caps as an Aston Villa player, but failed to impress after joining City from Wrexham. Things began well enough with Halligan and Jimmy Gemmell, the former Stoke and Sunderland inside-forward, scoring twice each in a 5-0 opening day home win over Lincoln.

But it was a false dawn and a crushing 7-0 home defeat by Barnsley – the worst reverse in City's brief history – shattered morale at the club.

Attendances were poor and after only 24 appearances in which he scored a dozen goals in a struggling side, Halligan was sold to Derby County for £400. Athlone-born Halligan went on to enjoy a fine football League career which stretched beyond World War One.

He won his first Irish cap whilst with Derby, adding another after joining Wolves and later playing for Hull City, Preston North End, Oldham Athletic and Nelson before retiring in 1922.

City flitted around the bottom most of the season, conceding 80 goals in their 38 League games and just escaped having to apply for re-

Leeds City attack the Leicester Fosse goal during a Second Division match on the last day of the 1909-10 season. The game, watched by barely 2,000 spectators, ended in a 1-1 draw.

Billy Gillespie, an inside-forward signed from Irish club Derry City in May 1910. Gillespie went on to star with Sheffield United and won 25 Ireland caps.

election by a slender three-point margin. Beleaguered City were also struggling to keep their heads above financial waters throughout most of the season when they lost about £1,000.

In September 1910 shareholders were asked to take up debentures worth £4,000 which, together with £8,000 guaranteed by some directors, would secure the club's liabilities and provide working capital. A committee of shareholders was formed to work with the directors 'for the good of the club'. Desperate City even staged a couple of ladies days during the season in an effort to woo new supporters and additional much-needed cash as men were encouraged to take their wives or girlfriends to see City matches.

Scott-Walford was forced to cut City's wage bill to save a four-figure sum and, so encouraged by the Emerald Isle gem that he had found in Halligan, he returned to Ireland once again in summer 1911 in search of more bargains.

Back he came with the signatures of George Cunningham (Shelbourne), Mick Foley (Shelbourne), Joe Enright (Shelbourne), Billy Gillespie (Derry), Alec Creighton (Distillery), M. Curran (Portadown) and J.A.S.Hegan (Cliftonville). Of the new batch, Foley was the longest-serving at Leeds, clocking up 127 League games, but the pick of the crop, Gillespie, was released in the middle of the following season and allowed to join Sheffield United.

Gillespie went on to become a major star, winning 25 caps during a long and extremely productive stay with the Blades.

His thinning hair belied his speed and skill which marked him out as one of the outstanding inside-forwards of his generation. His departure to Bramall Lane was a big mistake on the part of Leeds City.

No less than five Irishmen played in the opening-day 2-1 home defeat against Blackpool, Enright scoring the City goal.

The first four League games were all lost but City edged their way unspectacularly to 11th place and made yet another early exit from the FA Cup, this time at the hands of Scott-Walford's old club, Brighton, and a further £1,000 was lost on the season's trading.

It was to prove the final season of Harry Bromage, the popular goalkeeper who moved on

Leeds City staff at the start of the 1911-12 season. Back row (left to right): S. Collins (trainer), John Clarkin, Albert Stead (groundsman), Sam Johnson, George Cunningham, Frank Heaney, Tony Hogg, Ted McDaniel, Les Murphy, Joe Moran, A. Roberts, Dick Roberts, William Briggs, Mick Foley, Jimmy Fortune, H. Harbourne. Front row: Hugh Roberts, Tom Mulholland, John Harkins, Stan Cubberley, Frank Scott-Walford (manager), Tom Morris, Chris Kelly, Joe Enright, Fred Croot. On ground: Alec Creighton, George Affleck, Billy Gillespie, Harold Bridgett.

to Doncaster Rovers after 143 League games in City's colours.

Although many of his Irish recruits had not been up to standard, Scott-Walford, still working under severe financial restraints, signed on more for the start of the 1911-12 season.

They included Leslie Murphy (Belfast Celtic), who was earmarked as Bromage's replacement, Joe Moran (Shelbourne), brothers Frank and John Heaney (St James' Gate), William Briggs (Belfast Celtic) and John Clarkin (Shelbourne).

Although both Enright and Moran played in Ireland's 4-1 defeat against Scotland in Belfast in March 1912, the new breed of Leeds players from across the Irish Sea were generally not up to scratch and the season gradually fell apart.

City's delight at having two internationals in their ranks temporarily helped lift the gloom at Elland Road. The week after Enright and Moran played for their country, City crashed 7-2 at Fulham to bring the spectre of re-election a step closer.

Three days after that humiliation, Elland Road was packed to the rafters by 45,000 fans – but none had come to see City.

They witnessed Barnsley and Bradford City slog out a 0-0 draw in the FA Cup fourth-round replay but the organisation was chaotic, with the referee having to stop play several times as the over-eager fans spilled on to the field.

The lessons of the 1910 FA Cup semi-final fiasco had not been learned – Elland Road was simply not geared up to cope with such large crowds.

Disgruntled supporters of both clubs forced their way through locked turnstiles and one poor gateman had his bagful of takings grabbed, although the thief was caught and taken to court.

The game went into extra-time, but the referee called an early halt to the proceedings because

mounted police were unable to stop the swarming masses from encroaching on to the field.

Predictably, the FA and the City club came in for some strong criticism in the Press for the lack of proper organisation.

The sniping undoubtedly hurt City, but not as much as the lack of cash which was really putting the squeeze on the club.

Cash Crisis, Receiver Called In

City had hit rock bottom financially and the bank announced that it was going to call in the club's £7,000 overdraft – a statement which sounded the death knell.

Poor City, after only seven years as a Football League club, it was on the brink of financial collapse.

To stave off immediate closure City's bene-factor, Norris Hepworth, poured more cash into the club's empty coffers and appointed a receiver, Tom Coombs, to run the club's affairs. Hepworth had been the saviour of the club, but the extent of his generosity did not become general knowledge until a public meeting at the Grand Central Hotel on 19 April 1912 revealed that Hepworth had spent a total of £15,000, fantastic riches in those times, in trying to keep City going over the years.

Later an extraordinary general meeting at the Salem Hall highlighted the depth of City's financial troubles. Their total liabilities stood at £15,782, total losses since the club's formation were £11,321 and assets at £7,084. Not surprisingly the meeting agreed that the company running City's finances should be wound up and that Coombs should take over running the club, something he did for the next three years.

On the field City only won one of their last 11 games against the financial backcloth of doom and gloom and were forced to apply for re-election.

They finished 19th with 28 points, the same as

Glossop, but the Derbyshire club scrambled away from the danger zone courtesy of a better goal-average.

New Broom Herbert Chapman Sweeps Clean

The pressure that had been building up over the months was beginning to tell on Scott-Walford.

He had fallen ill and decided to call it a day after over two years of working with virtually no cash to buy players. City were at their lowest ebb, they had no money, no manager and were forced to go cap-in-hand to the Football League to seek re-election.

Into the dreadful mess stepped new manager Herbert Chapman, a man destined to become one of the greatest managers of all time, reaching unprecedented success with Huddersfield Town and Arsenal after his days with Leeds. He arrived at Elland Road, having steered Northampton Town to the 1908-09 Southern League title, winning many plaudits for his canny tactics.

There was nothing in Chapman's early history to hint of the greatness to come. The son of a coalminer from Kiveton Park, near Sheffield, he was a mining engineer by trade, playing as a run-of-the-mill amateur inside-forward with Ashton North End, Stalybridge Rovers, Rochdale, Grimsby Town, Swindon Town, Sheppey United and Worksop between 1897 and 1901, when he turned professional with Northampton.

In May 1902 he reverted to his amateur status with Sheffield United, before turning professional again with Notts County in May 1903 in a £300 deal, joining Northampton again the following summer. In March 1905 he was signed by Tottenham Hotspur, then joined Northampton for a third spell in 1907, this time as player-manager.

From his first day in charge at Elland Road, Chapman threw himself into the club's affairs.

His first priority was to ensure that League football would be played in Leeds during 1912-13.

He campaigned long and hard on the club's behalf in the run up to the Football League annual meeting and it paid off. On 4 June 1912, City were re-elected with 33 votes, with Lincoln City (27 votes) replacing bottom club Gainsborough Trinity (9). The other applicants were Chesterfield Town (6), Darlington (1), Newcastle City (1), Cardiff City (1) and Doncaster Rovers (0).

Having ensured League football for at least another season, Chapman confidently predicted he would lead Leeds to promotion. That bold statement almost became reality in his first season, but City missed out by just two points.

The International Brigade

Chapman went about rebuilding the team in a business-like fashion. Many of the Irish players

Herbert Chapman, the Leeds City manager was about to be caught up in the infamous City scandal. Chapman survived the furore and went on to become one of the greatest managers in the history of the game.

returned home as Chapman abandoned the policy of picking up men from Ireland on the recommendation of others and opted for experience, although one of his recruits, Everton goalkeeper Billy Scott, was already an Irish international.

The elder brother of the legendary Liverpool goalkeeper Elisha Scott, Billy had already won 22 caps with Linfield and Everton before signing for Leeds in August 1912.

Scott's signing was one of four internationals Chapman managed to lure to Elland Road during his first season in charge.

His other pre-season star names were Evelyn Lintott, who had played for England seven times, and Scottish full-back George Law, who had played for his country when on the books of Rangers.

Centre-half Lintott, a schoolteacher, who also won amateur caps was joined at Elland Road midway through the season by Jimmy Speirs, his old Bradford City teammate, who had led the Paraders to their FA Cup Final win the previous year. The fact that Leeds were able to pay Bradford £1,400 for Speirs showed that tremendous savings had been made within the club, whilst gates had increased considerably, thanks to the improved standard of football the team were producing.

The calibre of such men showed Chapman meant business, but the season was barely a month old when Leeds found themselves in trouble with the FA over their new signings. Chapman had agreed to pay Scott, Lintott and Law each the full year's wage of £208 to the end of the following

April. But two months had already elapsed since the end of their previous contracts, so the players ended up getting more than the permitted £4 a week wage.

City realised the mistake when Aston Villa were taken to task by the League for the same offence. Rather than wait to be caught out, City reported themselves and the League dealt out a £125 fine plus expenses and ordered the players to return the extra payments.

Despite losing 4-0 to Fulham in the opening game of the 1912-13 campaign, Chapman's men played some fine attacking football throughout the season, particularly after the arrival of Speirs in December.

Speirs played at inside-left with another new face, Jimmy Robertson, signed from Barrow, at inside-right. The man to benefit from the presence of these two skilful performers was centre-forward Billy McLeod.

Bustling Billy banged in a City seasonal best of 27 goals out of a club record 70 as City finished in sixth place, their best position since their first-ever campaign in 1905-06.

Chapman's new men had revitalised the club and bigger crowds ensured that City finished the season £400 in profit.

Confident Chapman had pulled the club up by its boot laces and his enthusiasm even included the ordering of a club flag to be flown at Elland Road in an effort to spruce the place up.

Although he was a dominant figure he was anxious that his players should have their say, encouraging them to speak out at team talks and arranged a string of golfing sessions to relax his men and build up comradeship.

Chapman was not content to rest on his laurels and once again recruited heavily in time for the 1913-14 season. His prize capture was the brilliant amateur international winger Ivan Sharpe, the footballing journalist.

It was a question of 'have-pen-will-travel' for Sharpe as his football career with Watford, Glossop and Derby County dovetailed with his time on various local newspapers. When Sharpe started work at the *Evening Post*, he left Derby to play for Leeds. Regarded as one of the most accomplished wingers of his day, Sharpe possessed a gold medal from the 1912 Olympics, gained as a member of the victorious Great Britain football team in Stockholm.

Another new face was centre-half John Hampson, from Chapman's old club, Northampton, whilst Simpson Bainbridge, Arthur Price and Scottish inside-forward John Jackson, established themselves as first-team regulars after signing the previous season.

Elland Road, with some justification, was buzzing and there was a stampede for season tickets with £2,000 worth sold before a ball had been kicked in anger.

Sharpe and McLeod did not let the fans down as Leeds played some irresistible football throughout 1913-14, particularly at Elland Road, winning 15 of their 19 League games. The highlight came on 29 November 1913, when City thrashed Nottingham Forest 8-0, their record score. McLeod helped himself to four goals, Arthur Price two, John Hampson and Jimmy Speirs one apiece.

That win, in front of 14,000 fans, pushed City into third spot and promotion was on everyone's lips. But three successive defeats in January proved fatal as City finished in fourth place with 47 points. One of those defeats came at Park Avenue, where Bradford won 3-1 in front of a 32,184 crowd and finished runners-up to Notts County, two points ahead of Leeds.

Anxious to bolster his defence, Chapman signed right-back Fred Blackman from neighbouring Huddersfield Town in February. Blackman was a quality player, having played in an England trial and represented the Southern League when he was with Brighton. Blackman went straight into the team, replacing Charlie Copeland, a discovery from the North-East, who was to play a key role in City's ultimate closure.

An Unseasonal Argument and a Murky Row
The scandal triggered off by Copeland was still several years away, but City found themselves embroiled in controversy during 1913-14.

On Christmas Day, goals by McLeod and Hampson gave City a 2-1 win over Fulham, but Leeds were unable to pay the Cottagers their full share of the takings, so Fulham took immediate retribution by refusing to hand over City's share of the takings at Craven Cottage the following day after the inevitable McLeod goal had given City a festive double.

At an FA inquiry the following month, Leeds City said there had been a railway strike on Christmas Day. Many fans arrived late for the game and there were police present to stop them rushing the turnstiles, so the club had to take admission money 'on account'.

The inquiry accepted City's explanation and gave them a verbal warning for not taking money at the gate in the proper manner. Fulham were ordered to hand over the £20 4s 5d due to City from the Boxing Day attendance and also ordered to pay three guineas expenses.

The following month, City were involved in another bitter wrangle with a London club, this time Clapton Orient.

Orient had fixed their home game against City on 3 March with a 4.30pm kick-off, so late that the latter part of the game was played in near-darkness and City goalkeeper Billy Scott never saw the two late goals that came whistling out of the gloom into his net to give Orient a 3-1 win. Leeds appealed to the League, who let the result stand but fined Orient £25.

Meanwhile, McLeod continued to find the net in all conditions and finished the season with a club record 27 goals which pushed him to the fringe of an England international place. He was put on stand-by for England against Wales but never got the chance to pull on the white shirt of his country again.

Despite McLeod's goal haul, it was the mercurial Sharpe who had been the inspiration of the side. He was still an amateur and it was fitting that Elland Road should host the Amateur Cup Final on 4 April 1914, when Bishop Auckland beat Northern Nomads 1-0.

The following week, Leeds were held to a goalless draw by Woolwich Arsenal, who eventually finished third, in front of a 25,000 crowd with the veteran Fred Croot receiving the gate receipts. Left winger Croot was the third and final City beneficiary, following McLeod the previous season and goalkeeper Harry Bromage in 1911. Croot played only five more League games the following season to take his tally to 218 appearances before moving north of the border to join Clydebank.

Syndicate takes Over, War Clouds Gather

There was considerable debate as whether the 1914-15 season should go ahead after war had broken out during the late summer. By August, Britain had been sucked into the impending bloodbath and the first men from the British Expeditionary Forces had landed in France.

Football League president John McKenna and secretary Tom Charnley issued a statement on the eve of the new season declaring that, in the interests of morale in the country, football should continue. Clubs should do all they could to help war funds and players should train for National Service.

For Leeds, after going close to promotion, the following 1914-15 season was an anticlimax, opening with four successive defeats. Although City recovered from this poor start, inconsistency, particularly in defence, saw then slip to 15th place.

The overall performance was a particular disappointment to the syndicate of Leeds sportsmen who had bought the club in August

1914 and took over its running from Tom Coombs, the receiver.

The syndicate, led by Joseph Connor, president of the West Riding FA, guaranteed to put down £1,000 and pay an annual ground rent of £250.

Despite this security, City could not get their act together on the field, but when they did they were devastating.

McLeod added another scoring record to his collection by becoming the first City player to net five goals in a game, his nap hand being all the more remarkable as they were scored away from home.

McLeod's magical match came on 16 January, at Hull in a 6-2 triumph, Ivan Sharpe grabbing the other Leeds goal. The previous month they had hammered Leicester Fosse 7-2 at Elland Road, Arthur Price scoring a hat-trick.

But these were only individual successes in a disappointing season and manager Chapman looked as though he would have to start again to build a side good enough to achieve his dream of taking a side into the First Division. But for the war, Chapman may have fulfilled that dream.

The League was under continual pressure throughout the season to call a halt to their programme and several clubs, Leeds among them, discovered a dramatic drop in attendances.

League football was officially suspended on 3 July 1915 at a conference in Blackpool attended by representatives of the Football League, the Scottish League, the Irish League and the Southern League. Although League football in its present form would not continue, the game did not die altogether as war raged the length and breadth of Europe.

Mick Foley, Arthur Price, Jimmy Speirs and Billy McLeod training outside Elland Road before Leeds City's FA Cup first-round game at Gainsborough Trinity in January 1914. McLeod scored in City's 4-2 win but they lost at home to West Brom in the next round.

A City at War

THE Football League Management Committee agreed that some form of competition should be played to keep the game alive during what was to become known as the Great War.

The outcome was the setting up of regional competitions, followed by a two-month League competition. There would be no promotion or relegation and players would all play as amateurs, for expenses only – something that was to lead to the demise of Leeds City.

The game at home was still the national favourite and as early as December 1914 volunteers had collected leather footballs and sent them to the Front. They made a famous Christmas appearance that year as the warring armies came out of their trenches to play each other in a bizarre interlude during the fighting.

Later, footballs became 'army issue' and the game had become a compulsory activity by the end of 1917.

At home anti-German feeling was running high – former Leeds City goalkeeper Dr Cecil Reinhardt changed his name in the same way that the British Royal Family had bowed to public opinion and adopted the family name of Windsor in deference to their German ancestors.

Reinhardt, who was based in the chemistry department at Leeds University and made a dozen appearances for City, changed his name to Goodwin.

There was a big debate about whether the game should continue at home whilst men were falling in their thousands on the killing fields of Europe.

The Government did not actively encourage the game's continuation and clubs thought long and hard about whether they should play on. Derby County, pulled out of the competition after taking part in the 1915-16 season, whilst the North-East giants of Middlesbrough, Newcastle and Sunderland did not kick a ball until the cessation of hostilities.

One of the main beneficiaries of the closures on Teesside, Tyneside and Wearside was Leeds City, who provided a footballing outlet for players from those clubs, particularly Newcastle.

Wartime football on a regional basis cut down costs and some of the travelling difficulties encountered which clubs had experienced in the 1914-15 season. Southern clubs played in the London Combination and Lancashire clubs had a League of their own, whilst Leeds City played in the Midland Section which covered the area from Birmingham to Yorkshire.

With players volunteering or being conscripted for military service, playing strengths were severely stretched, so players were allowed to guest for other clubs, particularly when they were on leave or working locally.

The textile industry in West Yorkshire was in full swing producing uniforms, whilst local munitions firms were working around the clock to supply shells, bullets and vehicles.

These and other industries vital to the war effort provided the wartime spectator, but many of them could not get time off to see City in the company of off-duty personnel.

Regular faces missing from Elland Road when the 1915-16 season kicked-off included goalkeeper Tony Hogg, defenders Fred Blackman, Jack McQuillan and Harry Peart, and forwards Simpson Bainbridge, Jimmy Speirs and John Jackson.

McQuillan played for his old club, Hull City, as a guest until a grinding machine at the factory where he was working exploded, seriously injuring him, bringing his career as a footballer to a premature end.

Jackson returned to Scotland and appeared for both Rangers and Celtic during the war, whilst the others joined up.

Hogg and Blackman played for Fulham as guests, but only Bainbridge was to play for City again.

Evelyn Lintott had not made an appearance during 1914-15, despite re-signing in June 1914, and he opted to join up, even though he could have resumed his career at home as a teacher.

Ivan Sharpe pursued his journalistic career, making only one appearance, whilst scorer supreme Billy McLeod was called on by Bradford City because he was working in that city.

The Elland Road ranks had been decimated but they were lucky, however, to be able to call on a nucleus of old players in George Law, George Affleck, Tommy Lamph, John Hampson, Mick Foley, John Edmondson, Arthur Price and Fred Croot, at the start of 1915-16, whilst goalkeeper Willis Walker and full-back Charlie Copeland both made valuable contributions later in the season.

These men were supported by a posse of guest players, several of them, like Fred 'Fanny' Walden, being stars of the era.

The tiny Walden – he stood only 5ft 2½in tall and weighed 10st – was a real crowd-pleasing outside-right, who had sparkled for Tottenham before the war and earned full England honours.

His tremendous pace and slippery footwork always brought a great cheer as the little man wriggled past defenders who seemed twice his size.

The mini-marvel was also a talented cricketer, playing in 258 matches for Northamptonshire. He later became an umpire, standing in several Test matches.

Walden, Affleck and Foley were ever-presents in 1915-16, whilst future England international inside-forward Clem Stephenson (Aston Villa), the Newcastle trio of goalkeeper Bill Bradley, forwards Curtis Booth and Tom Bennett, Northampton forward Robert Hughes and Sunderland's Bob Hewison, who later helped run Leeds City during a critical period, all saw action in Leeds colours.

Despite the influx of all this new talent it was City regular Arthur Price who made the early headlines with a five-goal haul in a 7-1 home win over Barnsley.

Later in the season Barnsley were on the end of a 6-4 Leeds success in which Jack Peart, the Notts County centre-forward fired in four goals.

High scores were commonplace as teams often put out scratch sides with many players turning out in alien positions.

The standard of football varied but attendances rarely got above 10,000 as City finished tenth in the Midland Section Principal Tournament but won the Subsidiary Competition which was held at the end of the season when Willie Wilson from Hearts, on leave from the Royal Scots, was a prominent figure on the left wing.

By the time the 1916-17 season resumed, City regulars like George Affleck, Fred Croot, Tommy Lamph and John Edmondson had gone off to war, the last two guesting for Preston and Sheffield Wednesday respectively.

Also missing for pre-season training was the popular Mick Foley, who had remained in Ireland. The build-up to a new season was never one of Foley's favourite periods.

He usually reported back for duty a little bit overweight and had to endure hours in a Turkish bath to sweat off the excess poundage and his range of Irish expletives reverberating around Elland Road were sorely missed.

Burnley's Levi Thorpe filled the half-back vacancy left by Foley, whilst Grimsby's highly-rated forward Tommy Mayson occupied the left-wing slot vacated by Fred Croot.

At left-back was Newcastle's Billy Hampson, a player who was later to return to Leeds in the 1930s to have a five-year spell as manager.

His brother, Tommy, who went on to play for

'Fanny' Walden was one of several star guests to turn out for Leeds City during World War One.

Right-back Fred Blackman joined Leeds City in February 1914. A Londoner who had played for Woolwich Arsenal, Brighton and Huddersfield Town, he was a regular in City's 1914-15 line-up but when the Football League closed down for the duration, he returned to London and guested for Fulham He never played for City again and after the war joined QPR.

The Leeds City team which won the wartime Midlands Section Principal Tournament in 1916-17. Back row (left to right): Harry Sherwin, Charlie Copeland, Bob Hewison, Arthur Robinson, Billy Hampson, Levi Thorpe. Front row: George Cripps (secretary), Clem Stephenson, Billy Moore, Jack Peart, Arthur Price, Tommy Mayson and Dick Murrell (trainer).

West Ham, gave Willis Walker competition between the sticks, whilst Charlie Copeland, John Hampson and Arthur Price remained the only signed Leeds players left from the previous season.

But with Hewison, Sherwin, Peart and Clem Stephenson remaining as guests, Leeds could rely on a fairly settled side.

Their collective know-how certainly showed on the field as they won the Midland Section Principal Tournament, losing only two of their 30 games. Goals continued to pour in and hat-tricks were recorded by Price (twice), Peart, Stephenson and Billy Moore, a guest from Sunderland.

League Champions

Once again it was proving difficult to attract crowds in vast numbers and severe strain was being put on City's finances as they went into the 1917-18 season.

Some familiar names found their way back on the team-sheet with Tommy Lamph and Ernie Goodwin both returning after being discharged from service. Willis Walker, who had joined the Royal Navy, also came back for a stint in goal early in the season. But the most famous name to line-up in a Leeds shirt that season was Charles Buchan, Sunderland and England's subtle inside-forward who marked his only appearance for the Peacocks with a goal in a 2-0 win over Nottingham Forest.

Lesser lights also found their way into the team. Khaki trialists included Corporals Barrett, Chard and Grant, although Barrett was later listed as a private soldier.

Two schoolboy internationals called Arkle and Kettle, also got a game each, although English

Schools records do not list either player. Leeds did sign on a handful of young players they reckoned would make the grade, including Castleford-born Fred Baines, Harold Millership, later to win full Welsh honours, and Billy Kirton, another star in the making.

Despite having to draw upon more trialists and guests, the Midland Section Principal Tournament was won again with 23 wins, a draw and only four defeats, thanks to a free-scoring side which netted 75 goals.

In Jack Peart (20 goals) and Arthur Price (15 goals), City had a potent combination whilst the proliferation of Hampsons in the team must have confused opponents.

No less than five Hampsons turned out for City in 1917-18. Walker Hampson, of Burnley, and later, Charlton, briefly formed a full-back partnership with brother Billy.

Their brother Tommy was the first-choice goalkeeper, John Hampson, City's former peacetime centre-half also played, and on occasions his brother, recorded only as E.Hampson, turned out on the wings. The latter was the only home player to turn out against Leeds when he was loaned to Nottingham Forest to make up their complement when one of their eleven failed to reach the ground on time.

In the penultimate game of the season at Bramall Lane, Sheffield United loaned A. Spratt to Leeds after City turned up a man short because John Hampson had missed the train to Sheffield. Such instances were not particularly rare in the war years. Spratt also guested for Sheffield Wednesday and Rotherham County that season.

Billy Hampson, Bob Hewison, Jack Peart and Harry Sherwin, the Sunderland half-back, who later returned to Elland Road as a Leeds United player in 1921, played in every game in the Principal Tournament despite the uncertainties.

The conclusion of 1917-18 came with the introduction of a play-off over two legs with Midland Section champions, Leeds, taking on Stoke, champions of the Lancashire Section.

Leeds were unable to field their star man Clem Stephenson, who had just joined the Army, but they did play Newcastle's left-winger Billy Hibbert, and Ernie Goodwin, who appeared on the opposite flank, following a spell guesting for Rochdale.

The games against Stoke were regarded as 'unofficial championship' matches and both attracted attendances of 15,000 with the combined receipts of £913 going towards the National Footballers' War Fund.

The first leg at Elland Road saw Leeds win 2-0 with goals from Jack Peart and new man Hibbert. In the rematch at Stoke, Leeds had Bob Hewison carried off after half an hour but the ten men from Elland Road conceded only one goal – a Charlie Parker penalty – to win 2-1 on aggregate.

Leeds fielded the same side in both matches: Tommy Hampson; Harold Millership, Billy Hampson, Bob Hewison, Harry Sherwin, Tommy Lamph, Ernie Goodwin, Tom Cawley, Jack Peart, Arthur Price and Billy Hibbert.

Although never recognised in official records, it meant Leeds City were the League champions.

Jack Peart and Arthur Price had continued their fruitful attacking partnership and linked up for a third successive year when the 1918-19 season kicked-off.

Once again there was an enormous change in personnel with young Walter Cook holding down the goalkeeping job until Willis Walker returned after Armistice in November.

The defence remained basically intact, although a broken leg in the 2-1 home win over Rotherham County in October, ruled Hewison out for the rest of the season.

Hewison's loss was counterbalanced by the return of Clem Stephenson after his time in khaki, and Simpson Bainbridge, who was back in the team for the first time since 1916.

Leeds were unable to reproduce the consistent displays of the previous season and finished fourth behind Nottingham Forest, who went on to become League champions. Attendances were down, with 'Spanish flu' blamed. About 75 per cent of the population caught the virus which killed an estimated 150,000 civilians.

War guests also included Richard Barnshaw (Aberdare), James Cartwright (Manchester City), Tom Cawley (Rotherham), Fred Clipstone (Northampton), George Dawson (Preston NE), Harold Gough (Sheffield United), Tom Hall (Newcastle United), Edward Hudson (Manchester United), Frank Hudspeth (Newcastle United), James Hugall (Clapton Orient), F.James (Portsmouth), William Jennings (Notts County), Albert McLachlan (Aberdeen), Arthur Robinson (Blackburn), Stan Robinson (Bradford), Ally Trotter (Jarrow), Clem Voysey (Arsenal) and Andy Wilson (Hearts).

Of young City signings who appeared but moved on to other clubs during or just after the war, John Dunn (Luton), Fred Linfoot (Lincoln), Charles Sutcliffe (Bradford City) and Arthur Wainwright (Grimsby) were the most notable.

Clem Stephenson (above) and Charlie Buchan (below) were two more of City's wartime guests.

Frank Hudspeth, the Newcastle United star who appeared for Leeds City in wartime football.

The Ultimate Sacrifice

Millions lost their lives in the war, Leeds City players being among those who fell. They included two internationals, Jimmy Speirs and Evelyn Lintott.

Glasgow-born Speirs won his only Scottish cap with Rangers, where he excelled as an inside-forward and centre-forward. In 1909 he joined Bradford City and skippered them to their FA Cup Final success against Newcastle in 1911, when he scored the only goal in the replay at Old Trafford.

The following year he was signed by Herbert Chapman and proved a player of true quality, possessing an outstanding armoury of passes, both long and short, and a mean shot which brought him 32 League goals for Leeds.

At the end of the 1914-15 season, Speirs left Leeds and journeyed north to Inverness to enlist. He was killed in action around 20 August 1917, serving as a sergeant in the 7th Battalion, Cameron Highlanders. He had previously been awarded the Military Medal.

His sad loss came just over a year after another star of the age, Evelyn Lintott, died on the first day of the Somme, aged 33, whilst serving with the 15th Battalion, West Yorkshire Regiment.

The distinguished Lintott was a schoolteacher who built a reputation as an outstanding amateur left-half with St Luke's Training College, Exeter; Plymouth Argyle and Queen's Park Rangers, where he turned professional in May 1908.

The holder of seven full international caps and five amateur ones, he joined Bradford City in November 1908 and had a spell as secretary of the Players' Union until January 1911.

He arrived at Elland Road in June 1912 as Herbert Chapman sought to inject some more quality into his team.

The first City man known to lay down his life for King and Country was Lieutenant Gerald Kirk, of the 5th King's Own Royal Regiment, who was killed at Neuve Chapelle on 13 January 1915.

Kirk, a centre-half, who had two spells with Bradford City, made eight appearances for Leeds City in 1906-07. Eleven months after Kirk's ultimate sacrifice, Private David Bruce Murray, of the Argyll and Sutherland Highlanders, was killed in action at Loos, on 10 December 1915, aged 28.

Murray, a solid full-back with 83 League appearances for City to his credit between 1905 and 1909, had also been on the books at Rangers, Everton and Liverpool.

Three of the four Leeds men to die had Bradford City connections and it was another 'Bantam', Jack Peart, who finished as Leeds City's top scorer in wartime with a total of 71 goals in 107 appearances.

Peart, who spent 19 seasons in a nomadic scoring career covering every division of the Football League as well as the Southern Leagues, was Bradford City manager between 1930 and 1935.

He had gained a reputation as the 'most injured man in football' stemming from a broken leg in 1910 but always maintained a high goalscoring ratio at his many clubs.

Arthur Price clocked up the most wartime appearances, 120, scoring 59 times in the process. Price resumed his career with Leeds after the war and was bought by Sheffield Wednesday in the infamous City auction before finishing his playing days at Southend.

Clem Stephenson, an inside-left of exquisite skill from Aston Villa, was the most exciting of the guest players. Many Leeds fans had hoped Clem might join them on a full-time basis, particularly as his brother George was on City's books in 1919.

Instead, George joined his brother at Villa, before Clem was signed by Herbert Chapman for Huddersfield Town in 1921 in a £3,000 deal. Another brother Jimmy was at Villa Park and he also guested for City. A hero at Leeds Road, Clem collected three League Championship medals and an FA Cup winners' medal in 1922 to add to the two Cup medals he won with Villa.

Although Huddersfield ruled supreme in the Stephenson era of the 1920s, the men at Leeds City had been the dominant northern team during World War One.

Although a period of the game that has been largely ignored, particularly for record purposes, it had proved to be a successful one at Elland Road.

City's Scandalous Downfall

LEEDS City were already working against a backcloth of dissent when they resumed peacetime soccer in 1919.

Just weeks before the big kick-off the club found itself in serious trouble with the FA over allegations that illegal payments had been made to players during the war.

The charges were brought by former City full-back Charlie Copeland after a bitter row with the club over a pay rise.

The squabble snowballed over the months and ultimately led to City's downfall.

The public of Leeds were unaware of the scandal until shocked City were forced to disband and only then did the truth, or several versions of it, emerge through the columns of the local Press.

The problem took root when secretary-manager Herbert Chapman went to work in the manager's office at the Barnbow munitions factory in East Leeds to help with the war effort.

He recommended that his assistant at Elland Road, George Cripps, take over the paper work at City, whilst team selection was made by City chairman Joseph Connor and another director, J.C.Whiteman.

It was an uneasy alliance with Connor and Cripps, who was a schoolteacher by profession, often failing to see eye-to-eye. Connor, who was also president of the West Riding FA, reckoned that Cripps was incompetent and threatened to quit unless something was done about Cripps because City's books were in such a mess.

In 1917, Cripps, whose health was in decline, was relieved of the bookkeeping, which was now tackled by an accountant's clerk.

City were being run on a shoestring and with so little cash at their disposal the directors seriously considered closing down the club, but were persuaded to press on by Football League chairman John McKenna.

Rather than dispense with Cripps's services altogether, City had put him in charge of the team and correspondence. But the friction that had existed behind the scenes now spread to the playing staff – and almost led to a strike.

Cripps had become so unpopular with the players that before a Midland Section game at Nottingham Forest, skipper John Hampson sent a letter to the directors declaring that they would go on strike if Cripps travelled with the team.

Skipper John Hampson, who threatened to lead a players' strike if secretary George Cripps travelled with the team.

A strike would have almost certainly brought the club to its knees and Connor managed to persuade Hampson and his men to withdraw their threat.

This uneasy peace held until Chapman returned in 1918 to take over running the club once again. Cripps stepped down to his old position as assistant, but was unhappy at being forced out and contacted his solicitor, James Bromley, a former City director, claiming he would sue for wrongful dismissal.

Connor later revealed that Cripps had claimed £400 and had told Bromley that the board had paid improper expenses to players during the war. The Football League had decreed that during the war all registered professionals should play as amateurs, for expenses only.

Full details of Cripps' allegations have never emerged. Names have never been named in public, but it certainly made a big stir at Elland Road.

Cripps, via his solicitor, Bromley, thrashed out a deal with the Leeds board in January 1919.

The terms of the settlement included a clause that Cripps should hand over all paperwork relating to the, club – including his private cheque book, pass book and letters to and from various players – to Connor and Whiteman in the Leeds office of City's solicitor, Alderman William Clarke, in South Parade.

The papers were duly handed over, placed in a strongbox and locked safely away.

According to Connor's version of events, Cripps had given a written undertaking not to disclose any of the club's affairs and that Bromley gave his word that the evidence would remain confidential. Cripps was paid £55 in lieu of his claim – £345 less than his original claim.

Connor's story, given to the local Press after City's demise, did not tally with Bromley's version.

According to Bromley, he handed over a parcel of documents given to him by Cripps to be held in trust by Alderman Clarke and not to be opened without the consent of Connor and himself.

A condition of handing over the papers was that a £50 donation should be made to Leeds Infirmary by the City directors.

Bromley added that he later asked for a receipt for the donation but was told by Alderman Clarke that Connor did not wish to discuss City's affairs with him.

Whichever version is correct, it is clear the documents under lock and key must have contained some pretty explosive stuff. The fact that City were prepared to buy Cripps' silence when the club's finances were thin would point to incriminating evidence, but only those within the club really knew what was going on.

The evidence may have been out of sight, but it was not out of mind and within months the whole thorny issue of illegal payments rose its ugly head again.

Chapman was getting together his squad and putting his men through their pre-season paces ready for the new 1919-20 campaign when full-back Copeland's contract came up for renewal.

Copeland was regarded as a solid, if unspectacular right-back, having joined City from South Bank in August 1912.

Before the war he had made 45 League and FA Cup appearances in City's colours and a further 53 in wartime.

In the last pre-war season, Copeland had received £3 a week with a £1 weekly increase when he played in the first team. The board now offered him £3 10s (£3.50) for playing for the second team, and considerably more if he played for the first team, or they would let him go on a free transfer.

Copeland, who during the later wartime seasons had contested the right-back spot with former Blackpool defender Harry Millership, stunned the board by demanding £6 a week and threatening to report City to the FA and the League for making illegal payments to players during the war.

The board were furious and, although they ran the risk of Copeland going ahead with his threat, decided to give him a free transfer to Coventry City.

In July, Copeland, who either had got hold of some incriminating evidence or somehow knew the contents of the documents in the strongbox, spilled the beans to the FA.

A joint Football League and FA six-man committee was appointed to investigate the matter.

City's directors believed that Copeland's solicitor, Bromley, the man who had represented Cripps, may have given information about the documents to Copeland. Bromley was the link between Copeland and Cripps but he always denied passing on what knowledge he had of the documents to Copeland.

Bromley revealed that Copeland had played for City throughout the war years on the promise that his wages would be increased when the regulations were altered. In 1918, the League agreed to a general 50 per cent increase in wages, so, when Copeland asked for his increase, he was offered £3 10 shillings for a 39-week period and no summer wages. In short, Copeland was to get less cash.

Copeland said the board refused to meet him to talk things over, so he passed the matter on to his solicitor, Bromley.

The joint inquiry into the whole affair was chaired by FA chairman J.C.Clegg. The League was represented by their chairman John McKenna, Harry Keys and Arthur Dickinson.

The investigators ordered City to Manchester on 26 September 1919 to answer the allegations. City were duly represented by Alderman Clarke, who became Sir William Clarke in 1927.

He was asked to present the relevant documents to the commission but City stunned the investigating committee by saying they did not have the power to produce the club books.

City were ordered to produce them by 6 October or face the consequences.

It was generally recognised that several clubs had been guilty of illegal payments during the war years and had City handed over the books they may have got off relatively lightly. In previous similar cases, the League had been fairly sympathetic to clubs or individuals who had admitted to errors.

However, City's point-blank refusal to hand over evidence simply incurred the commission's wrath.

While this off-the-field drama was being played out, Chapman's men were going about their normal business on the pitch.

Two days before the documents deadline City set off to Wolverhampton, for what turned out to be their final League game.

A rail strike meant they travelled by charabanc to Molineux and won 4-2 with Billy McLeod getting a hat-trick and wing-half Tommy Lamph the other. Wolves' scorers were Wally Bate and Sammy Brooks. On the return journey the City coach gave several stranded people a lift back up north, among them was none other than Charlie Copeland, who had played in Coventry City's 2-1 home defeat against Leicester that day.

Two days later the inquiry's deadline arrived but City's documents did not, so the following Saturday's game against South Shields was postponed.

On 13 October 1913, the inquiry team emerged from the Russell Hotel in London to announce that Leeds City were to be expelled from the Football League, leaving the club to face extinction.

The bombshell came in an official statement from the inquiry: 'After the repeated warnings of the President and Committee they regard this violation of the financial regulations and the failure to produce documents vital to the full and complete inquiry so serious that expulsion from the League can be the only fitting punishment.

League chairman John McKenna, who had done much to keep City afloat during difficult financial waters in the recent past, added: "The authorities of the game intend to keep it absolutely clean. We will have no nonsense. The football stable must be cleansed and further breakages of the law regarding payments will be dealt with in such a severe manner that I now give warning that clubs and players must not expect the slightest leniency.

"Every member of the Commission was heartily sorry that Leeds had to be dealt with at all. We recognised that they had gone through troubled times before, they were a new club, that they had obtained a good holding in a rugby area, and that the club had bright prospects, but our case was clear – Leeds were defiant and could only be defiant through one cause – fear of the papers giving away certain secrets."

So City became the first club to be expelled by the Football League. An FA order formally closed down the club and Port Vale, who, ironically, would become the second League club to be expelled, took over City's fixtures with eight games of the 1919-20 League programme gone.

Even a personal plea by the Lord Mayor of Leeds, Alderman Joseph Henry, failed to budge the inquiry. A man with a great interest in sport, he offered to take over the club from the directors, but his offer fell on deaf ears.

The inquiry was in no mood for reconciliation. Five City officials were banned for life – Connor, Whiteman, fellow directors' S.Glover and G. Sykes, and secretary-manager Herbert Chapman, who was later exonerated after evidence was given that he was not at the club but working at a munitions factory when the illegal payments were allegedly made.

The City board had no option but to resign and Connor went down with one parting shot, claiming that the club had not had a fair hearing.

Connor's ban also meant that he had to step down from his post as president of the West Riding FA. His place was taken by Fred Waterhouse, a highly respected official in local soccer circles. As a boy, Waterhouse played for Rothwell School in 1878 and later became club secretary, referee and official, totalling 56 years service with the West Riding FA in his various capacities.

Alderman Henry complained that Port Vale, anxious for Football League membership, had put extra pressure on the inquiry to get Leeds thrown out, although no evidence was ever brought to support this claim.

All this belated squabbling did City little credit in the eyes of their shell-shocked supporters.

They had little inkling of the serious trouble City had landed themselves in and it was only after the club were punished that accusations and counter accusations were made by the parties involved did the fans get any real idea of what had gone on.

Exactly what happened may never be known, but the answer may still lie in a strongbox locked away in a dark vault buried under fading documents in some solicitor's office.

Players Under the Hammer

Apart from the supporters the other group to feel the sympathy of the footballing world were the players.

They now found themselves out of a job and went through the humiliating spectacle of being 'auctioned off' to the highest bidders.

The League promised the players that they would pay their wages until they were fixed up with new clubs and in their view the best way to do that was by auction.

The Commission into the whole affair asked former Newcastle United defender Bob Hewison, a guest player with City during the war, to act as secretary during the club's winding-up. It was a job he did whilst recovering from a broken leg he had sustained in 1918-19. Helping sort things out were Alderman Henry and Leeds accountant William H. Platts. Hewison was later player-manager at Northampton Town and manager at Queen's Park Rangers.

It does not say a lot for the inquiry team's judgement of character that Hewison was himself to become involved in an illegal payments scandal some years later!

He went on to become Bristol City's manager and on 15 October 1938 was suspended for the rest of that season by another joint League and FA inquiry for his part in payments made to amateur players.

The League, with Hewison's help, organised one of the most peculiar sights in soccer history – the auction of the City players.

Arrangements were made for the auctioneers, S.Whittam & Sons, to sell the goalposts, nets, boots, kit, physiotherapy equipment, billiard tables and even the shower baths – whilst the players went under the hammer at the Metropole Hotel in Leeds on 17 October.

Representatives from 30 League clubs turned up to submit bids in sealed envelopes for the players. The entire squad was sold off for £10,150, with individual fees set between £1,250 and £100 after prospective purchasers complained that the original prices were too high.

The auction was conducted by a special sub-committee set up by the Commission and comprised McKenna, Football League secretary

Harry Charnley, Charles Sutcliffe of Burnley, who later became the president of the Football League, John Lewis (Blackburn Rovers) and Harry Keys (West Bromwich Albion). No player was forced to join a club he did not want to, but the out-of-work players were keen to get back to business and none turned down the chance to be employed again.

The following players were auctioned off:
Billy McLeod to Notts County, £1,250.
George Affleck to Grimsby Town, £500.
William Ashurst to Lincoln City, £500.

Far left: Herbert Lounds and Harold Millership (right) were auctioned off to Rotherham County, who paid a total price of £1,250 for the pair, Millership being the most expensive at £1,000.

Far left: John Edmondson and Arthur Price, right, found themselves on the way to Sheffield Wednesday after going under the hammer at the Metropole Hotel, Leeds.

Billy Kirton to Aston Villa, £500.
George Stephenson to Aston Villa, £250.
John Hampson to Aston Villa, £1,000.
Simpson Bainbridge to Preston North End, £1,000.
Arthur Wainwright to Grimsby Town, £200.
Herbert Lounds to Rotherham County, £250.
Harold Millership to Rotherham County, £1,000.
Fred Linfoot to Lincoln City, £250.

Francis Chipperfield to Sheffield Wednesday, £100.
Willis Walker to South Shields, £800.
William Hopkins to South Shields, £800.
Arthur Price to Sheffield Wednesday, £750.
John Edmondson to Sheffield Wednesday, £800.
Ernest Goodwin to Manchester City, £250.
Tommy Lamph to Manchester City, £250.
Billy Pease to Northampton Town.
Walter Cook to Castleford Town.
Robert Wilkes to South Shields.
William Crowther to Lincoln City.

Had Chapman been able to keep his squad together, then he may have achieved his coveted goal of promotion to the First Division, for many of his men went on to become household names in the game, no less than five becoming internationals.

So how did the final City squad fare?

Hot-shot Billy McLeod, predictably the player who commanded the highest fee, left City with 171 League goals from 289 games to his credit. He failed to maintain that scoring ratio in the First Division with Notts County, netting only nine goals in 30 League games during the rest of the 1919-20 season as County were relegated. He moved to Doncaster in 1921.

Full-back George Affleck joined Grimsby Town – along with reserve Arthur Wainwright – after ten years and 182 League games in City's colours. Affleck had spent the summer completing his military service in Mesopotamia and after giving the Mariners stout service until his retirement in July 1925, he went to Holland to coach a team in Rotterdam.

Inside-left Wainwright marked his Grimsby debut with a goal but failed to make much impression at Blundell Park and later played for the Derbyshire side Gresley Rovers, Bristol Rovers and Barrow.

Aston Villa were among the biggest spenders at the auction and picked up two bargains in Billy Kirton and George Stephenson.

Kirton, whose only peacetime League game for City came in that final match at Molineux, had recently been converted from full-back to inside-forward. A nippy little player, he finished the season by scoring Villa's FA Cup Final winner against Huddersfield Town and collected a runners-up medal four years later. He scored on his England debut, against Ireland in October 1921, but surprisingly was never chosen again, despite consistently brilliant form at Villa where he clocked up 261 appearances and 59 goals before winding down his career with Coventry City, Kidderminster Harriers and Warwickshire side Leamington Town.

Stephenson, also an inside-forward, was an untried teenager when he joined Villa after the auction, but that club proved to be a shrewd judge of footballing flesh. Younger brother of England international Clem Stephenson, he went on to win three England caps between 1928 and 1931 after leaving Villa. His long and varied career saw him play for Derby County, Sheffield Wednesday, Preston North End and Charlton Athletic. After a spell as assistant manager to brother Clem at Huddersfield, George was appointed the Town boss in August 1947, leaving in March 1952 to become a blacksmith. A third Stephenson brother, Jimmy, also played League football – all three of them being on Villa's books.

City skipper John Hampson occupied no less than six different positions during his first season at Villa Park, but he was more settled after he joined Port Vale in September 1921 and later played for Hanley SC before retiring in 1930.

Another player to go on to make the big time was William Ashurst, who joined Second Division club Lincoln City along with centre-half Fred Linfoot and little-known reserve William Crowther.

Right-back Ashurst had joined Leeds in the summer, from Durham City, but had been confined to the reserves. A former miner from Willington in County Durham, he did well at Lincoln and, in June 1920, a £1,000 fee move took him to Notts County where he won five England caps and a Second Division championship medal in 1923. He joined West Brom for £3,100 in November 1926 before finishing his career with Newark Town.

Ashurst's brother, Eli, spent five seasons with Birmingham in the mid-1920s.

Linfoot was another who failed to appear in the Leeds senior ranks after previously playing for Smith's Dock and Newcastle Swifts.

Lincoln turned him into an outside-right and he later played for Chelsea, joining in July 1920, before going to Fulham in March 1924.

Keeping Ashurst out of the Leeds team was

Harry Millership, a pre-season signing from Blackpool.

He was snapped up at the auction by Rotherham County, who also bought Herbert Lounds, the former Gainsborough Trinity winger. Within four months of leaving Leeds, Millership won the first of his five Welsh caps, against Ireland.

Leeds-born right winger Billy Pease was another who went on to gain international honours before showing what he could do with Leeds.

He played rugby at school and only took up soccer during his wartime service with the Northumberland Fusiliers, where he was spotted by City and signed amateur forms in 1918-19.

At the auction he joined Herbert Chapman's old club, Northampton Town, but his career really took off when he joined Middlesbrough in May 1926, winning one England cap in 1927 and two Second Division championship medals. Extremely quick with an eye for goal, he toured South Africa with an FA party in 1929, but his career was ended by injury when he was with Luton Town whom he had joined in June 1933.

One of the few players to fetch four-figures at the auction was Simpson Bainbridge, who went across the Pennines to Preston for £1,000 after joining Leeds from Seaton Deleval in November 1912.

Bainbridge later left Preston for South Shields, who had signed several of his old teammates at the Metropole Hotel sale.

South Shields picked up Willis Walker, William Hopkins and reserve Robert Wilkes, with Walker being the prize catch.

Formerly with Sheffield United and Doncaster, Walker was among the best goalkeepers of his day. He held a place in the City side when the 1914-15 season drew to a close and regained his place between the sticks after coming out of the Royal Navy. After sterling service with South Shields, he joined Bradford Park Avenue in 1925.

Gosforth-born Walker was a sporting all-rounder, starring as a county cricketer with Nottinghamshire, during the summer, scoring 1,000 runs in a season ten times. He also played in the Bradford League with Keighley.

Hopkins, the former Sunderland centre-half had previously played for Stanley.

Half-back Tommy Lamph went to Manchester City with Ernest Goodwin. Both were from the North-East, Lamph joining Leeds from a local Gateshead club, whilst Goodwin had starred with Spennymoor.

Lamph actually returned to Elland Road as a Leeds United player in February 1921 via Derby County but the following year he was forced to quit the game, through illness.

Goodwin failed to make much headway at Hyde Road and went on to join Rochdale in May 1921.

Centre-forward John Edmondson and inside-forward Arthur Price both joined Yorkshire rivals Sheffield Wednesday. Edmondson, who had arrived at Elland Road from Preston, struggled to score goals with the Owls and had more success later in his career with Swansea Town and Exeter City.

Price was an established Leeds player, having netted 25 goals in 78 League games. He also turned out for Leeds 120 times during the war, more than any other player during the hostilities.

Price did fairly well with Wednesday before joining Southend United in 1922.

Had this squad of players stuck together, then Chapman may have moulded them into a side capable of winning the Second Division title – but we shall never know.

Although Leeds City died, the name lives on today. In 1988, Leeds Red Triangle League side, White Star, were given permission by the FA to change their name to Leeds City, who now play in the West Yorkshire League – exactly where the original City club kicked-off their competitive career.

Rising from the Ashes

THE city of Leeds was not going to take the destruction of their soccer team lying down. Within hours of the infamous auction at the Metropole Hotel, over 1,000 Leeds City supporters had crammed into the Salem Hall determined that their club would rise phoenix-like from the ashes. It was at this meeting that the seeds were sown for the birth of Leeds United.

Driving force behind the meeting was Leeds solicitor Alf Masser, an original shareholder of the City club who had a spell as its vice-chairman.

He was elected to chair the meeting which unanimously proposed that a professional club be formed and a supporters' club established.

A seven-man committee was set up comprising Masser, Joe Henry Junior, son of the Lord Mayor of Leeds who had pleaded unsuccessfully for City to be saved, Mark Barker, Charles Snape, R.E.H. Ramsden and two former City players, Dick Ray and Charles Morgan. Barker was to serve on the board for 23 years until his death in January 1943.

The following day, at Masser's home in Roundhay, it was agreed that Joe Henry junior would be United's chairman, Barker would be the treasurer and Harry Meek and N.D.Booth would act as joint secretaries.

Kaye Aspinall and Tom Coombs, the receiver who had done so much to get City's ailing finances back under control, were invited to join the committee, who dug deep into their pockets to get the new club up and running.

These men were all respected figures in the sporting life of Leeds, particularly Masser and Joe Henry junior, whose father ran a well-known Holbeck engineering firm, and the Henry family had been keen sponsors of Leeds City.

Masser's credentials were even more impressive. The son of a commercial traveller, he was educated at Churwell College, Yorkshire College and Leeds University.

He was a founder of Headingley Rugby Club, serving as both captain and secretary, and also was secretary to Leeds Springfield Cricket Club.

The committee appointed former City full-back Dick Ray as United's secretary-manager.

A native of Newcastle under Lyme, 46-year-old Ray had played for Burslem Port Vale, Manchester City, Macclesfield Town, Stockport County and Chesterfield before joining Leeds City in July 1905 for their maiden Football League season.

He retired in 1912 and served with the RASC during World War One. He was also a useful cricketer, playing for Laisterdyke in the powerful Bradford League.

Ray and the committee knew they had to act quickly while football fans in the city were still full of enthusiasm for the launch of the Leeds United venture. Any delay would not help the United cause so advertisements asking for local players were placed in the *Athletic News* and the local Press. There was undoubtedly a great deal of goodwill towards the new club and a significant breakthrough was made when they were invited by Mr J.Nicholson, the new secretary of the Midland League, to enter that competition.

Nicholson, the former Midland League president, had taken over his secretarial duties from Arthur Kingscott, who had just been appointed treasurer to the Football Association.

On 31 October, United were formally elected as members of the Midland League and effectively took the place of Leeds City Reserves.

As Ray was busy putting a side together, there was still the problem with what to do with Elland Road, which was regarded as one of the best sporting facilities in West Yorkshire.

An offer was even made to make good use of the rich clay deposits below the surface of the turf and turn it into a brickyard.

But the speed at which the newly-formed United made progress ensured a footballing future for Elland Road.

Whilst United was taking shape, local club Yorkshire Amateurs had been renting Elland Road and it was fitting that United's first official fixture, a friendly, should be against Yorkshire Amateurs at the ground.

The game was played on 15 November and United ran out 5-2 winners. The following week United opened their belated Midland League campaign with a goalless draw against Barnsley Reserves.

Huddersfield's bid to amalgamate

As all this frantic activity was taking place, West Riding neighbours Huddersfield Town were wrestling with major financial problems.

Huddersfield's wealthy chairman, J.Hilton Crowther, came up with a scheme for Town and the new United to merge to become Leeds Trinity – a plan which very nearly succeeded after getting approval from the Football League.

Town, like Leeds City in its early days, were struggling to compete with its local Rugby League club. Whilst the powerful rugby club played to big audiences at Fartown, Town were playing before meagre crowds at Leeds Road.

Town were kept going by the Crowther family, who made their fortune from the Crowther Brothers woollen mill in Milnsbridge. J.Hilton Crowther had a particular interest in soccer and in 1909 provided financial support for Town's bid for election to the Football League.

He joined the Huddersfield Town board along with his brothers Leonard, D.Stoner and Edgar, the latter a county golfer, and the four brothers pumped thousands of pounds into keeping Town ticking over.

J.Hilton Crowther was particularly generous to the club, but he never lost his sense of business acumen. He knew the time had come for Town club to stand on its own feet.

Matters came to a head when only 2,500 fans turned up to see a 3-0 victory over Fulham at Leeds Road on 1 November, realising receipts of just £90, whilst at Fartown, the rugby club coined in £1,600 from their Yorkshire Cup match against Hull. It was clear Town could not survive much longer on such paltry attendances.

Former Huddersfield Town chairman J. Hilton Crowther, who set about transforming Leeds United into a soccer power after his planned merger to form a club called Leeds Trinity fell through.

The Huddersfield directors had run out of patience and met to discuss the possibility of moving the club lock, stock and barrel to Leeds, which appeared to have a greater soccer support at grassroots level.

J.Hilton Crowther kept a close watch on the fight to rebuild senior soccer in Leeds after the demise of City and conjured up his audacious plan to move to Elland Road.

Despite not consulting his fellow directors, Crowther offered to amalgamate with the newly-formed Leeds United, a move which had the backing of some of the Huddersfield Town players.

Crowther and the Huddersfield secretary, Arthur Fairclough, spoke at a large, enthusiastic meeting of United supporters at the YMCA Hall, Albion Street, in Leeds, to outline the plan.

Both United committee member Mark Barker and the Lord Mayor, Alderman Joe Henry, backed the scheme to the hilt, although it was later revealed that the United committee had only agreed to amalgamation on a majority vote.

The meeting unanimously endorsed the amalgamation with the fine details of the move to be ironed out by Crowther and Leeds accountant William H.Platts, the sole lessee of the estate, who had been totally exonerated by the Commission investigating the Leeds City scandal.

Yorkshire Amateurs, the new tenants at Elland Road, said they were prepared to withdraw their tenancy at the ground to make way for the new club which would play under the banner of Leeds United, although at one stage the name Leeds Trinity had been considered.

All the players signed by Dick Ray for United, and the liabilities incurred, would be the responsibility of a team of nine directors made up of men from both clubs.

All that was needed was for the Football League

to approve the deal and it was felt they would give the go-ahead, particularly as Huddersfield objectors holding shares could have them paid back in full.

The Collapse of the Merger

Top-class soccer in Leeds appeared to be on the brink of an amazing recovery. It seemed too good to be true – and it was.

The day after the meeting in Leeds, at a Central League fixture, furious Huddersfield fans demonstrated on the Leeds Road pitch in front of the directors' box demanding an explanation. Town's fans felt they had been sold out but were given the opportunity to have their say at a public meeting at the Leeds Road ground the following day.

Amazingly the meeting attracted 3,000 people – more than the previous home League game – and a proposal was passed asking the Town directors to hold fire on the plan to move to neighbouring Leeds until the Huddersfield community had a chance to show it wanted first-class soccer.

A ten-man committee was set up to look into ways of paying off the substantial debentures held by the Crowther brothers.

Steps were taken to increase the capital of the company to £30,000 by an extra issue of 20,000 £1 shares. The race was now on to keep Huddersfield Town in Huddersfield.

Both pro and anti-amalgamation sides put their case to the Football League Management Committee at the Grand Hotel, Manchester, on 11 November.

The pro-lobby of J.Hilton Crowther, Arthur Fairclough and Alf Masser put their case first, followed by the men representing the group which wanted to stay in Huddersfield, William L.Hardcastle, the newly appointed Town chairman; Amos Brook Hirst, one of Town's original founders; and Huddersfield's chief constable, Captain Moore, a former soccer player and referee.

The meeting ruled that Town would be given a one-month deadline of 8 December 1919 – to raise £25,000, the sum calculated to be the debt owed to J.Hilton Crowther. He agreed to withdraw his interest in the Town club if the money was raised.

If Town failed to raise the cash, then the club would move to Elland Road to become part of the new Leeds United.

Over the next four weeks Huddersfield was gripped by fund-raising fever and the money slowly began to roll in, but with a week to go before the deadline date only £5,160 had been raised, although more pledges were still to come in.

When the deadline arrived, Town had collected sufficient letters and telegrams opposing the switch to Elland Road, many promising money, that the League Management Committee agreed to a stay of execution. The deadline was extended to New Year's Eve.

On the pitch, Town's playing performances had improved and the attendances were steadily beginning to increase.

For Town die-hards there finally appeared to be some light at the end of the tunnel, until the club was rocked by a further crisis.

Solicitors on behalf of J.Hilton Crowther and D.Stonor Crowther issued a writ on Town on 19 December, claiming £10,137 18s 6d for principal and interest due on promissory notes issued by Town between 16 April 1913 and 19 October 1919.

The debenture holders' trustees also gave notice of their intention to take over the Town premises. Days later it was announced that Arthur Fairclough, who was known to favour the move to Leeds, would be appointed Receiver.

An emergency board meeting on 23 December unanimously accepted Fairclough's resignation and proposed to appeal to the League Management Committee to allow the club to continue until the end of the season, by which time it was hoped its finances would be on an even keel. Town also took steps to answer the writ and gained vital breathing space after several High Court adjournments as the Crowthers' application became bogged down by complex legal arguments. Each delay held up the scheme to move to Leeds.

As all this hectic activity was taking place, Leeds United could merely watch and wait for the outcome.

United's first competitive match saw them held to a goalless draw at Elland Road by Barnsley Reserves on 22 November as they belatedly started their Midland League campaign.

United's enterprise and determination to regain their Football League status saw them rewarded with some useful attendances. Meanwhile, down the road at Huddersfield, fans and local industrialists continued to rally round their club.

'The Huddersfield Town Retention Fund' met on 11 January 1920 and were told that D.Stonor Crowther was reconsidering his position in the affair. The meeting also heard that £8,000 was instantly available.

The pendulum seemed to be swinging slowly towards the anti-amalgamation group and eventually they were in a position to buy out Hilton Crowther.

On 16 January 1920, the League Management Committee held an emergency meeting of all sides at the George Hotel, Huddersfield.

The two-hour meeting, chaired by John McKenna chairman of the Football League, declared that there was no further need of a Football League ruling – in short, the move to Elland Road had fallen through.

It was like a weight had been lifted from Town's players, who turned a season of near-disaster into one of great success. Not only did they clinch promotion to the First Division but also reached the 1920 FA Cup Final, losing 1-0 to Aston Villa at Stamford Bridge, former Leeds City player Billy Kirton netting the goal.

As Town achieved their remarkable transformation, Hilton Crowther set about building the new Leeds United into a soccer power.

Crowther, who had invested £2,400 in repairs to Elland Road after he took over the lease, put his considerable financial clout behind Leeds United.

He loaned United £35,000, to be repaid when Leeds gained promotion to Division One, and was welcomed with open arms by the United officials and he was appointed chairman in December 1920, taking over from Joe Henry junior. His fellow directors were Alf Maser, Mark Barker, Kaye Aspinall and William Platts.

The colourful Crowther, who married Wakefield-born Mona Vivian, a London revue star of the 1920s, was the financial platform on which United were built.

Crowther and Fairclough the dream ticket

Hilton Crowther carried an enormous amount of influence at United and got Arthur Fairclough to join Leeds as secretary-manager on 26 February, with Ray stepping down to be Fairclough's assistant. The Leeds-Huddersfield managerial link was continued at the start of the following season when Leeds City's former secretary-manager, Herbert Chapman, was appointed secretary at Huddersfield Town.

In March 1921, Chapman was appointed secretary-manager and went on to lead them to successive League titles in 1924 and 1925 after winning the FA Cup in 1922. Chapman was appointed manager at Arsenal in June 1925, steering them to FA Cup success in 1930 (with a convincing 2-0 victory over Huddersfield), then captured the League championship title the following season and again in 1933.

He was an extremely innovative manager who thought deeply about the game and its image. He even persuaded the London Transport Passenger Board to change the name of their Gillespie Road underground station to that of Arsenal.

Chapman died on 6 January 1934 after contracting pneumonia on a scouting mission, but the great man left the foundations of a great Arsenal side which equalled Huddersfield's feat of three successive titles by winning the Championship in 1933, 1934 and 1935.

Fairclough may not have achieved Chapman's fame, but was highly regarded in soccer circles after enjoying plenty of success with Barnsley, being born just outside that town, in the village of Redbrook in March 1873.

Ill-health cut short his own playing days at junior level, but in 1896 he joined the Barnsley committee, becoming secretary two years later when they entered the Football League.

After a spell out of the game, Fairclough, a Football League referee, worked for the Sheffield FA, then was appointed Barnsley's secretary-manager in 1904. He got Barnsley to the 1910 FA Cup Final, which they lost to Newcastle after a replay, but tasted success two years later when Barnsley beat West Brom 1-0 in a replayed Final following a goalless first match.

In April 1912 he joined Huddersfield and built a side that gained promotion and won the FA Cup, despite all the financial trauma of 1919-20.

He had formed a formidable working partnership with Hilton Crowther which the two men now re-established at Leeds.

Fairclough, Ray, together with trainer Dick Murrell and assistant trainer Albert Stead were continually on the look out for new talent as United sought to build a side good enough to hold its own in the Second Division.

United had already unearthed one gem – Ernie Hart, a future England international centre-half, who was signed in December 1919.

Young Hart was a miner from the Doncaster area who was playing for a local club, Woodlands Wesleyans when he was spotted by Leeds, who immediately recruited the precocious 18-year-old. Hart's talent was gradually nurtured alongside some experienced Midland League campaigners.

United slowly caught up their Midland League fixtures after their late start and finished in 12th place, collecting 31 points from 34 games.

Although it was an unspectacular record, it was something of a miracle considering that the Leeds City club had been killed off just over six months earlier.

United Join the Football League

NEW chairman J.Hilton Crowther spent much of the spring of 1920 travelling the country drumming up support for Leeds United's application to join the Football League.

He found there was quite a bit of sympathy from other clubs following the harsh punishment dealt out to Leeds City, so United went to the Football League's annual meeting full of optimism.

The strength of their playing staff may have been unknown, but United had an established ground, and, thanks to Crowther, financial backing.

On 31 May 1920, United's hopes were fulfilled as they topped the annual poll with 31 votes to gain election to the Football League. They were joined in Division Two by Cardiff City, who won 23 votes, and replaced Grimsby Town (20 votes) and Lincoln City (7).

However, all was not lost for Grimsby as they became founder members of Division Three that season, along with clubs from Division One of the Southern League (with the exception of Cardiff City). Having secured their election to the Second Division, Leeds now had to assemble a team good enough to compete in it.

The astute Fairclough quickly turned to a man around whom he could build a side – Jim Baker.

Baker had played under Fairclough at Huddersfield after joining them from Hartlepools in June 1914, having started his career at Portsmouth. A tough-as-teak centre-half, Baker was appointed United's first skipper and certainly had the pedigree for it – his brother Alf played for Arsenal and England, whilst a younger brother, Aaron, later played a couple of League games for United in 1927-8.

The full list of players on United's roster for that first season was:

Goalkeepers: Harold Jacklin, Billy Down, H.Jeffrey.

Full-backs: Bert Duffield, Jimmy Frew, Alf Smelt, Arthur Tillotson, Dick Coope.

Half-backs: Jim Baker, Ernie Hart, George Cooper, Jimmy Walton, Robert Musgrove, Jock McGee, George Stuart.

Forwards: Len Armitage, Ernie Goldthorpe, Merton Ellson, George Mason, Robert Thompson, John Lyon, Jerry Best, Fred Waterhouse, George Hill, John Brock, Walter Butler, Eugene O'Doherty, Billy Boardman, P. Reynolds, W. Fawcett, H.Spencer.

Centre-half Ernie Hart, who joined Leeds United from Doncaster junior football and went on to skipper the club and play for England.

Some of the players had only Midland League experience: men like Tillotson, who was recruited from Castleford Town, Smelt (Mexborough), brother of Len Smelt the well-known Burnley player; Ellson (Frickley), who was a schoolmaster by profession; and the Rotherham Town pair Mason and Hill.

Harold Jacklin, who had won a Central League championship medal with Blackpool, and Billy Down, a youngster from Ashington, were expected to contest the goalkeeping position.

Jimmy Frew provided more experience at left-back, forging an excellent combination with former Gainsborough Trinity man Duffield on the opposite flank.

Frew cost United £200 and was worth every penny. He had made his Scottish League debut with Hearts in 1914 and during the war played in a 'military international' for Scotland against England at Goodison Park in May 1916, during his service as a farrier with 1st Lowland Edinburgh Royal Garrison Artillery.

Other Scots in the squad were Stuart (Dundee), Brock from Edinburgh, and McGee, who was signed from Harrogate after trials. He was a worker on the Grantley estate at Harrogate.

The North-East provided United with several key men including former England Schools captain Musgrove (Durham City); Walton, who began with Cleator Moor before joining West Stanley in August 1919; Best, a former Newcastle United reserve who commanded a £100 fee; and centre-forward Robert Thompson, a former

Powderhall Sprint champion who joined Leeds with Musgrove from Durham.

Waterhouse, like skipper Baker, had played under Fairclough at Huddersfield as an amateur, whilst Armitage had gained experience with Sheffield Wednesday, Lyon had played for Hull City and Boardman arrived from Eccles with a reputation as a goalscorer.

Much was expected of Ernie Goldthorpe, son of well-known rugby player Walter Goldthorpe. Young Ernie was still only 22 and had won rave reviews from the London Press for his performances in Tottenham's London Combination side whilst he was stationed in the capital with the Guards during the war.

Injuries never allowed Goldthorpe to make a lasting impact at Leeds. O'Doherty (Blackpool), Butler (Leeds Steelworks), Coope (Laisterdyke) and Cooper (Kimberworth Old Boys), made fleeting appearances, whilst Fawcett (Bradford), Reynolds (Cudworth), Spencer and Jeffrey all failed to make United's first team.

Leeds City had wound up their career wearing blue and old gold striped shirts and white shorts, or knickers, as they were known in those days.

United opted to start their new campaign in blue and white striped shirts and white shorts.

Opener is a Vale of Tears

When the fixtures were announced it threw up a remarkable opening game, one which not even the Football League's current computer could have come up with.

Jimmy Walton, a wing-half from West Stanley who missed only one game in United's first season in the Football League.

Left-back Jimmy Frew joined Leeds United from Hearts in May 1920, for £200. In later years he ran a sports outfitters in Harehills and was, for many years, official supplier to United.

Inside-left Jack Lyon was signed from Hull City in July 1920, but despite holding down a regular place in City's first League season he moved into non-League football the following year.

United were to start the campaign at Port Vale, the club that had replaced Leeds City the previous season.

Vale had finished the 1919-20 season in 13th place with 40 points from 42 League games and were expected to fully extend United on their League debut at Bryan Street on 28 August.

So it proved as goals by Page and Blood, in front of a 15,000 crowd, gave Port Vale a 2-0 home win against this United side: Down; Duffield, Tillotson, Musgrove, Baker, Walton, Mason, Goldthorpe, Thompson, Lyon and Best.

Four days later, Jim Baker led his side out against South Shields at Elland Road for United's first Football League game on home soil.

An enthusiastic 16,958 crowd, paying £1,016 in receipts, turned up but South Shields spoiled the party by running out 2-1 winners with both goals by Woods, the former Norwich forward.

United had brought in Ellson and Armitage in that game for Goldthorpe and Thompson and it was Armitage who scored United's first-ever League goal.

Despite that disappointing result, a 15,000 crowd rolled up at Elland Road the following Saturday, 4 September, and witnessed United's first League victory. What made it all the sweeter was that it came against Port Vale, who were sent packing 3-1 with goals by Ellson (2) and Best.

United continued to blow hot and cold during the early weeks of the campaign and found goalscoring a problem until Thompson found some form in mid-season, including the first

Tommy Howarth joined United from Bristol City in March 1921, for the big fee of £1,750, and scored on his debut.

senior hat-trick by a United player, his treble coming in a 3-0 home win against Notts County on 11 December.

However, it could be argued that both Eugene O'Doherty and Walter Butler had claimed hat-tricks before Thompson.

Both came in the FA Cup when United fielded reserve sides in qualifying rounds against weak opposition, whilst the first team fulfilled Second Division fixtures. Because they were a new League side, United were obliged to enter the competition from the qualifying stages.

O'Doherty hit three in a 5-2 FA Cup win at Elland Road on 11 September, against Boothtown, a side from the Halifax district, whilst the Leeds first team were battling out a 1-1 draw at Leicester.

Boothtown reported United to the FA for failing to field their strongest side, pointing out that there should have been a bigger attendance, therefore more receipts, to which they were entitled to a share, had the United first team turned out.

Less than a year after Leeds City's demise, United found themselves in trouble with the FA – but this time the consequences were not so dire.

United were fined £50 and ordered to field their strongest side in future.

This immediately left United with a headache as they were due to play Leeds Steelworks in the next qualifying round a fortnight later, when they were scheduled to meet Blackpool at Bloomfield Road in a Second Division game on the same day.

United eventually came up with a compromise at a meeting with FA officials in Sheffield.

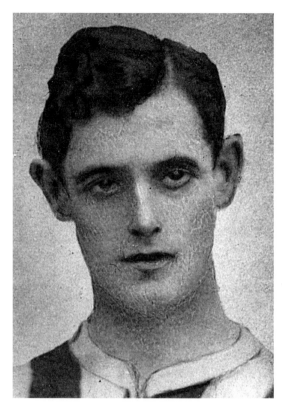

Leeds would have to battle through eight preliminary rounds before they eventually got to the first-round proper. That would mean having to switch a host of League games to midweek when attendances were generally lower, so the club would lose out financially as they tried to tackle their fixture pile-up.

United struck a bargain which was acceptable to all parties. They had been drawn against neighbours, Leeds Steelworks, who agreed to waive home advantage and move the tie from their small Hunslet Road enclosure to Elland Road.

United were allowed by the FA to field their second team without fear of further punishment, provided they pulled out of the competition after the game.

United's Reserves promptly beat Steelworks 7-0, Butler, a former Steelworks player, scoring a hat-trick against his old club in front of a 3,000 crowd, then withdrew from the tournament, safe in the knowledge that they would go straight in at the first round the following season.

Another small piece of history was made in United's 4-0 home win over Coventry on 1 December, when Ivan Sharpe became the first player to play for both Leeds City and Leeds United. Before the end of the season, Tommy Lamph became the only other player to achieve this feat.

Sharpe, who became editor of *Athletic News* a few years later, made only that one appearance for United in his customary left-wing berth, a position which United struggled to fill until the arrival of Basil Wood from Crook Town in November.

As Thompson's goals slowly dried up, Fairclough took drastic action to add some punch to his attack by forking out £1,750 for Bristol City centre-forward Tommy Howarth, with the player reputedly receiving £460, a staggering sum in those days.

Howarth's goals had been instrumental in Bristol City's exciting run to the FA Cup semi-final the previous season and he marked his Leeds debut on 12 March 1921 with United's goal in a 1-1 draw at Bury, Howarth's home-town club who had given him his first break in League football.

Howarth was the only player to score in United's last nine League games, when United only won one match, and finished the season with half a dozen goals from 11 League appearances.

Thompson, who had lost his place to Howarth, ended the campaign as top scorer with 11 goals from 23 League games as United finished 14th, thanks largely to a solid defence in which Baker, known to Leeds fans as 'T'Owd War 'Oss' had been inspirational, finishing as an ever present along with Billy Down and Bert Duffield.

United take Hart

Baker, who was to make 149 consecutive League and Cup appearances for United, was also able to help guide the highly regarded youngster Ernie Hart through his first few League games during the season.

Hart, a star in the making, took over Baker's number-five shirt the following season, with the United skipper moving to half-back.

Inside-forward Jim Moore won an FA Cup winners' medal with Barnsley in 1912, He joined Leeds from Southampton in May 1921 but was released a year later.

Jim Baker was United's first skipper and made 149 consecutive League and Cup appearances for the club. He was one of three brothers who all played League football, Aaron also being with Leeds and Alf with Arsenal.

Leeds United in
1920-21. Back row
(left to right): Jim
Baker, Dick Murrell
(trainer), Ernie Hart,
Billy Down, Mark
Barker (director),
Ralph Rodgerson, J.
Hilton Crowther
(president), Jimmy
Walton. Front row:
George Mason, Bert
Duffield, Tommy
Howarth, Merton
Ellson, Basil Wood,
Jimmy Frew.

The emergence of Hart was the biggest bonus for United during 1920-21 as Fairclough sought to strengthen his side.

In came experienced goalkeeper Fred Whalley from Grimsby, Sunderland half-back Harry Sherwin and veteran inside-forward Jim Moore, who had won an FA Cup winners' medal with Barnsley in 1912, when Fairclough was in charge at Oakwell.

Moore had spent the last two seasons at Southampton, after guesting for them during the war and was snapped up by Fairclough in May 1921.

Out went some of the North-East brigade – Robert Thompson to Ashington, Robert Musgrove went to Durham City, where he later became player-manager, Jerry Best went into non-League football before playing in the United States, and Jack Lyon joined his native Prescot.

With Ralph Rodgerson, who was signed from Huddersfield towards the end of the previous season, getting the verdict at left-back in place of Jimmy Frew, United's defence certainly had no lack of experience.

They began the 1921-2 season with a repeat of the previous season's opener, against Port Vale, except this time it was at Elland Road.

United made a flying start with a 2-1 win, courtesy of goals by Tommy Howarth and Jimmy Walton to send the 18,000 crowd home happy.

With Howarth looking particularly sharp,

George Mason was United's first-choice outside-right in their first season in the Football League. He joined from Frickley Colliery in July 1920 and moved to Swindon Town in June 1923.

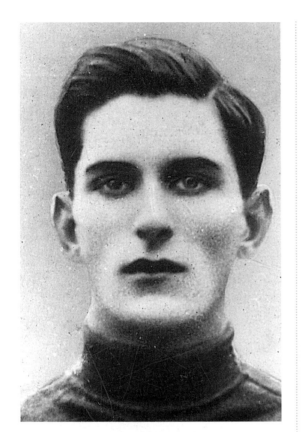 

Billy Down (left) and Bert Duffield (right) were models of consistency as Leeds United consolidated their place in the Football League.

United built on their good start to be unbeaten after seven games, by which time Ernie Hart was beginning to establish a regular place at centre-half.

But United could not maintain their form, so Fairclough turned to Huddersfield once again to pick up one of his former players – Jack Swan.

A forward noted for his powerful left-foot shooting, Swan had played in Huddersfield's 1920 FA Cup Final side which lost to Aston Villa, and was soon among the goals at Leeds, including a hat-trick in a 5-2 home win over Coventry.

One other treble was scored by a Leeds player during the season – Bill Poyntz, who had joined United from Llanelli in the close season as a reserve inside-forward. His hat-trick came in the 3-0 home win against Leicester City just hours after he had got married.

That great day in his career came exactly a week after one of his worst, when he became the first Leeds player to be sent off, in the 2-1 defeat at Bury.

Another bonus was the emergence of another player from the North-East, Walter Coates, from

Leeds United lost 3-0 at Upton Park in February 1921. Billy Down guards his goal as the United defence try to clear the ball.

North-Eastern League side Leadgate Park. He stepped out of the shadows to contest the right-wing spot with George Mason.

Fairclough had certainly assembled a squad with some strength in depth and they finished the season in eighth place, a significant improvement of six places on their debut campaign.

But the lack of genuine firepower, was still causing concern, Tommy Howarth finished with 13 League goals, but apart from Swan with ten, plus United's goal in their 2-1 first round FA Cup defeat at Swindon, no one else hit double figures.

The big signing in summer 1922 was left winger Joe Harris from Bristol City, where he had amassed over 200 appearances. He took over from Basil Wood, who had joined Sheffield Wednesday whilst Jim Moore left for Brighton.

United's early season lacked consistency although Ernie Hart and Jim Baker were forming a formidable defensive partnership.

But United still lacked pep up front, so they spent £750 on Sunderland's classy inside-forward Percy Whipp in November.

He made an immediate impact, scoring all three goals in the 3-1 win over West Ham the following day. Also making his debut in that game was Alan Noble, a right winger who had been picked up during the summer from Bournemouth.

Whipp became extremely popular with the Leeds supporters who dubbed him 'the Arch General' and he finished the season at the top of United's scoring charts with 15 goals.

United ended the season in seventh place and it

was clear that Fairclough was gradually moulding a side that could mount a promotion bid.

In Fred Whalley and Billy Down he had two reliable goalkeepers, Bert Duffield, Ernie Hart and captain Jim Baker were models of consistency in defence, whilst the arrival of Whipp had added a new dimension to the attack.

Some improvements continued to take place at Elland Road itself and the stadium was allocated an England trial game on 19 February 1923, although the game had to be called off because the pitch was covered by a blanket of snow.

The bitter weather may have disappointed United then, but sunnier times were ahead.

Promotion to
Division One

UNITED went into the 1923-4 season without assistant manager Dick Ray, who had done a great deal of work to help get United started after the demise of Leeds City. He had joined Doncaster Rovers as manager on their election to the Football League but Arthur Fairclough was able to fill the vacancy with another man of great calibre – Bill Norman, who arrived from Blackpool where he had been manager since 1919.

Norman had a reputation of being a colourful character and, after leaving Leeds to manage Hartlepools in 1927, astonished Hartlepools players by taking his clothes off in one winter training session and rolling in the snow to prove it was not as cold as some of them imagined.

Despite his 'iron-man' image, Norman was an excellent organiser and highly respected by the players who were put through their paces by trainer Dick Murrell.

Murrell, who was christened Aubrey, had also been trainer to Leeds City and was proud of the way he kept his men in tip-top condition. He would put them through gruelling runs around. the Elland Road pitch and right around the outside of the ground and sweat off any extra weight built up during the summer with a series of Turkish baths for the players.

Leeds may have been in good physical shape as they approached the 1923-4 season, but financially they were struggling.

Fairclough and Norman had to operate on a shoe-string budget, often raiding the North-East for good prospects from junior clubs or picking up reserves of bigger clubs who were on the look-out for regular first-team football.

They even took a leaf out of former Leeds City manager Frank Scott-Walford's book by recruiting a couple of players from Ireland, Shamrock Rovers pair Bob Fullam and John Joe Flood.

Neither made a lasting impact. Flood failed to make the first team at all, whilst Fullam had only seven outings, before they returned to Dublin at the end of the season.

Fullam created his own niche in Irish soccer history by scoring the Republic's first-ever goal in the 2-1 home defeat by Italy at Landsowne Road on 23 April 1927.

According to Irish legend, Fullam knocked out an Italian in that game with a free-kick and put him in hospital. When Fullam lined up to take another free-kick, the Italians appealed to the referee not to let him take it because his kick was so dangerous.

Fullam made United's opening line-up for the 1923-4 season, playing at inside-left alongside Joe Richmond, a centre-forward who had done well with the reserves the previous season after joining from Shildon. Richmond was quite a celebrity in the North-East after winning the French Medal Militaire in World War One, whilst serving as a flight-sergeant in the Royal Flying Corps.

Another Geordie, Bobby Mason, a centre-half from Whitburn, also started the season as first choice, whilst left-back George Speak joined from Preston for £250 – United's major signing of the summer.

A goal by former Bournemouth amateur winger Alan Noble gave United a point from a 1-1 draw from their opening game at Stoke. Noble was on target again in the next match as Crystal Palace were beaten 3-0 at Elland Road, Bob Fullam and Percy Whipp getting the others.

That, however, was United's only win in their opening six games and some pundits were already writing off United's chances of promotion.

Leeds United, champions of the Second Division, 1923-4. Back row (left to right): Harry Sherwin, Arthur Fairclough (manager), Bert Duffield, Dick Murrell (trainer), Billy Down, John Armand, Bill Menzies, Bill Norman (assistant manager). Front row: Walter Coates, Percy Whipp, Joe Richmond, Jim Baker, Jack Swan, Joe Harris, Ernie Hart.

Jack Swan ousted Bob Fullam and scored two goals on his return, ending the Second Division title-winning season as top scorer.

Fairclough decided to make changes, Billy Down took over in goal from Fred Whalley, Jack Swan ousted Fullam and Ernie Hart eventually regained his number-five shirt. Two goals from Swan gave United a 2-1 win at Hull City on 22 September and the following week Richmond scored a hat-trick in a 5-2 win against the same opposition.

That was the start of a great run which brought 19 points out of a possible 20 as United shot to the top of the table by the end of November, Down keeping six successive clean sheets in the process.

That run, the best to date by a United side, was: Hull City (won 2-1), Hull City (won 5-2), Clapton Orient (won 1-0), Clapton Orient (won 1-0), Port Vale (won 1-0), Port Vale (won 3-0), Bradford City (won 1-0), Bradford City (drew 0-0), Barnsley (won 3-1), Barnsley (won 3-1).

However, December proved disastrous with three successive defeats, two of them to title rivals, Bury. Once again doubts were raised about United's ability to last the promotion course.

But United recovered to regain their form and put together another hot streak of six wins on the bounce from the end of January to mid-March to make promotion a real prospect.

United were not only buzzing in the League, but in the FA Cup. Wins against Stoke and West Ham (after a replay) put them through to the third round at Aston Villa.

The game at Villa Park drew 51,600 fans, the biggest audience that a United side had played before at that time, and was reckoned to be a good

test of United's possible First Division credentials.

It proved an anticlimax as they were outclassed in a 3-0 romp for Villa, who included former Leeds City man Billy Kirton in their line-up.

But the Cup was only a diversion from the job in hand – chasing promotion.

United were able to field a fairly settled side and looked particularly lethal at Elland Road.

Jack Swan, Joe Richmond and Alan Noble were

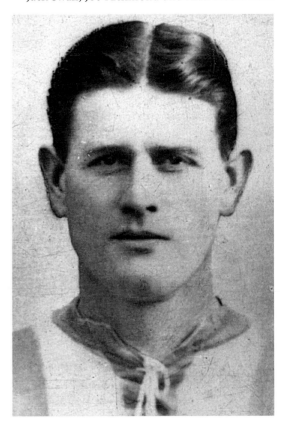

George Speak is in the back of the net, Billy Down can only look dismayed. West Ham's George Kay has just scored in the FA Cup game at Upton Park in February 1924. Leeds won the replay, though, before going out in the next round at Aston Villa.

all scoring regularly, Joe Harris looked as good a winger as any in the division, reserve left-back Bill Menzies was rock solid when he stepped in for George Speak, and Billy Down was so well entrenched in goal that Fred Whalley was allowed to join Fulham in March.

It was at Fulham the same month that United won 2-0 with goals by Percy Whipp and Bob Fullam, prompting the headline 'Fullam beats Fulham'. Indeed it was a significant victory as it put United in the driving seat at the top with only eight matches to play.

Then a bout of promotion nerves set in with one defeat and four draws in the next five matches.

That defeat and one of the draws were both against promotion rivals Derby County, who had put together a thrilling late-season run.

With three games to go, the promotion places were between United, Derby and Bury, with United holding pole position.

On Easter Monday, United hammered Stockport County 4-0 at Elland Road with goals by Swan (2), Richmond and Harris.

Meanwhile, a few miles down the road at Oakwell, Bury lost 2-0 to Barnsley – a result that sealed United's promotion.

Derby did not play until the following day, when they won 2-0 at Coventry to stay in the title hunt.

United had 52 points with two games left, whilst Derby and Bury both had 49 points with the Rams having two games remaining and Bury one.

United made sure of the championship on 26 April 1924 with a 1-0 home win over lowly Nelson, the winner coming just three minutes from the end, when Walter Coates netted from a Joe Harris corner to send the 20,000 crowd wild with delight.

Eventually news filtered through from Leicester, where Derby had lost 3-0, a result that confirmed United as Second Division champions – the first major award in the club's history.

Fans flooded on to the Elland Road pitch to salute their heroes and hear a series of speeches of congratulations and appeals for financial support to help United compete with the best teams in the land the following season.

For the record, Bury thrashed Coventry 5-0 that day to move into second place – a position they held on goal-average despite Derby's 4-0 home win over Leicester in their final game of the season.

Unfortunately, United could not end their campaign with a flourish, losing 3-1 to Nelson – a result which was still not good enough for the Lancashire club to stave off relegation.

It had been a memorable season for United in which their forwards had proved as sharp as any in the division. Swan finished as top scorer with 18 goals, whilst both Richmond and Whipp hit double figures the emergence of the little-known Richmond being a real bonus.

Down had been assured in between the posts, Duffield and Baker were their usual models of consistency, Scottish full-back Bill Menzies improved as the season went on, as did right winger Alan Noble, and Hart was regularly tipped for great things by the Press.

United's form at Elland Road had been particularly impressive, losing only twice – to Leicester and runners-up Bury.

Right-half Harry
Sherwin won a
Second Division
championship medal
with Leeds. He had
guested for Leeds
City and in 1917-18
had the rare
distinction, for
wartime soccer, of
not missing a game
all season.

Paying the debt to J.Arthur Crowther

It had been a remarkable achievement by Fairclough and Norman, who had little cash to play with, yet had moulded their men into a highly efficient unit.

However, promotion brought further financial problems as Crowther indicated he wanted to be bought out by the club and step down as chairman.

That left United the task of raising £35,000 to wipe out the debt to their benefactor, who had invested about £54,000 in United's affairs since United's election to the Football League.

Crowther remained on the board, but the role of chairman was taken over by Major Albert Braithwaite, who promptly promised £5,000 to the club if the Leeds public would raise £30,000.

The men running the club gave consent to the creation of 7,000 debentures of £5 each, payable either in cash or on calls, or on subscriptions of 10s down and 10s a month to carry interest at the rate of 7½ per cent. United urged the public to rally round and appealed to every shopkeeper and restaurant in the city to sell bonds so United could discharge their debt.

Crowther did not ditch United altogether, remaining on the board until his death in Blackpool on 23 March 1957. Crowther was not a man who became involved in football to make money – indeed, £15,000 of the United debt to Crowther was still unredeemed after World War Two.

He was genuinely interested in expanding soccer in the region and his service as a director at Huddersfield and Leeds totalled a staggering 49 years.

In addition, he was also instrumental in the foundation, in 1923, of the Yorkshire Midweek League, being its president until it was disbanded in 1949. The YML comprised the senior sides in the area and gave managers the chance to field reserve and experimental line-ups as part of their preparations for big games on Saturdays.

Crowther's replacement, Major Braithwaite, later to become Sir Albert, was a former pupil of Woodhouse Grange School, Bradford, a graduate of Leeds University and had a distinguished career with the West Yorkshire Regiment and Yorkshire Hussars.

An engineer, he was a director of Sir Lindsay Parkinson and Co and entered politics midway through his United chairmanship, being elected MP for the Buckrose division of the West Riding of Yorkshire in 1926.

But for the time being he was the figurehead at United and came up with several bright ideas, including asking a London composer to write a song for the club.

Major Braithwaite also announced that each person attending United's opening First Division game at Elland Road would receive a souvenir programme with an application for debentures enclosed.

Before United's First Division campaign began improvements to the Elland Road grandstand were made and the popular side extended to cater for the big crowds the club anticipated in their maiden season in the top flight.

During the 1923-4 season, Elland Road had hosted an England trial game, the North thrashing the South 5-1 with goals by Birmingham's Joe Bradford (2), Clem Stephenson (Huddersfield Town), David Jack (Bolton) and Stan Seymour (Newcastle). Bill Haines (Portsmouth) replied for the South. There was some great talent on show in that trial game, but, because of a lack of cash, Fairclough and Norman knew they could not afford to buy such stars as they prepared for the new campaign.

Unable to make any big signings, they added the following, mainly reserves, to their squad during the summer: Goalkeeper: Bill Moore (Seaham Colliery); Full-backs: Jim Kirkpatrick (Workington); Half-backs: Tom Duxbury (Preston), Josh Atkinson (Blackpool); Forwards: James Clark (Newcastle United), Jock Thom (Workington), Frank Mears (Stalybridge), Frank Watson (Blackpool), Fred Graver (West Stanley) and John Martin (Darlington).

They joined the following players retained from the previous season: Goalkeepers: Billy Down, Bill

On 20 December 1924, when Leeds United lost 6-1 at Highbury, the teams were skippered by brothers Jim Baker (left) of United and the Gunners' Alf Baker.

Johnson; Full-backs: Bert Duffield, George Speak, Bill Menzies, Albert Bell, Tom Bell; Half-backs: Harry Sherwin, Ernie Hart, Bobby Mason, Jim Baker, Aaron Baker, Len Baker, Len Smith; Forwards; Walter Coates, Alan Noble, Percy Whipp, Jack Lambert, Joe Richmond, Sam Powell, Jack Swan, Joe Harris and John Armand.

The only major departure of the summer was full-back Jimmy Frew, who joined Bradford City, playing on until December 1926 when injury terminated his career. He later became chief coach to the West Riding FA and ran a sports outfitters in Leeds, which became the official supplier to Leeds United for many years.

Life in the Top Flight

FINANCIAL circumstances forced United to rely on the same players who had won the Second Division championship to represent the club in the top flight.

Although no big signings had been made, the city was buzzing with expectancy as the new campaign approached.

The fixture list for 1924-5 had paired United at home on the opening day with Sunderland, who finished third the previous season.

A 33,722 crowd gathered at Elland Road for the historic match as veteran Jim Baker led the Peacocks out against the men from Roker Park.

The teams lined up as follows: **Leeds United:** Billy Down; Bert Duffield, Bill Menzies, Harry Sherwin, Ernie Hart, Jim Baker, Alan Noble, Percy Whipp, Joe Richmond, Jack Swan, Joe Harris. **Sunderland:** Albert McInroy; Warney Cresswell, Ernie England, Billy Clunas, Charlie Parker, Arthur Andrews, Billy Grimshaw, Charles Buchan, John Paterson, Arthur Hawes, Billy Ellis.

The spoils were shared, Jack Swan's goal earning United a point, Scottish international Paterson replying for Sunderland, whose goalkeeper, Albert McInroy, was to join United later in his career.

Defeats for United followed, at Notts County and Cardiff, before another 1-1 home draw, thanks to a Swan goal, in the return match against Notts County.

Victory did come in the fifth game and it proved a comprehensive one, Preston North End being hammered 4-0 at Elland Road by goals from Swan (2), Joe Harris and Jock Thom to give United their first-ever win in the First Division.

At the end of the month Swan scored United's goal in another 1-1 home draw, this time against his old club, Huddersfield, in a match which attracted a then record crowd of 41,800 to Elland Road. Huddersfield, guided to the League title by former Leeds boss Herbert Chapman in 1924, scored through Billy Smith.

Wins were hard to come by as the transition to First Division football was proving difficult, particularly away from home as United picked up only two wins on their travels.

Consistency was a big problem and was amply illustrated in December when United crashed 6-1 at Arsenal, then, five days later, bounced back to beat Aston Villa 6-0 at Elland Road on Christmas Day with all the goals coming in a spectacular first-half blitz from Whipp (3), Swan (2) and Hart.

That amazing success was followed by a dreadful run which brought only one win in 13 games and sent United spinning towards the relegation zone.

To prevent matters from getting worse United were forced to buy their way out of potential

Russell Wainscoat joined Leeds from Middlesbrough for £2,000 in March 1925. The following year he went on an FA tour to Canada and scored five goals in a game against Thunder Bay. He overcame a broken nose and a triple fracture of an arm with Leeds and in 1929 was capped for England.

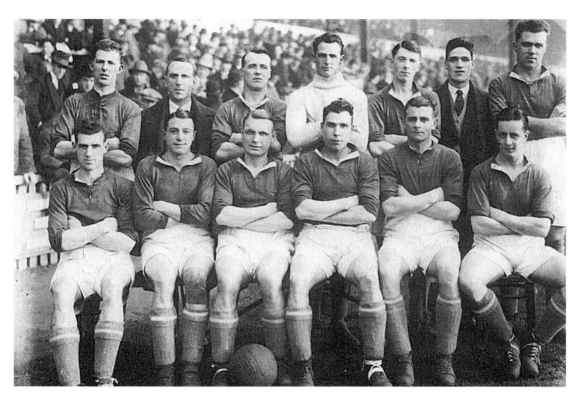

Leeds United, 1924-5. Back row (left to right): Josh Atkinson, Dick Murrell (trainer), George Speak, Dave Russell, Bill Menzies, Val Riley, Ernie Hart. Front row: Joe Harris, Sam Powell, Jim Baker, Fred Graver, Percy Whipp, Alan Noble.

trouble with three big signings in March – ace goalscorer Tom Jennings, inside-forward Russell Wainscoat and half-back Willis Edwards.

All three proved to be inspired purchases as United played their way to safety with three wins in the final five games seeing them finish 18th, well clear of bottom clubs Nottingham Forest and Preston. Jennings, a powerful Scot, was snapped up from Raith Rovers, where he was a member of their freescoring forward line which included Alex James and Jimmy McClelland, who was to blast United out of the 1926 FA Cup with a five-goal haul for Middlesbrough.

Tom Jennings the Goal Machine

Jennings, rejected by Spurs as a youngster, had featured in one of soccer's oddities, being a member of the Raith squad which was ship-wrecked on their way to play in the Canary Islands.

He first played for Leeds in a 1-1 home draw against Sheffield United on 14 March and the following week had been joined in the team by Wainscoat and Edwards for the trip to Newcastle.

The new boys did not get on too well at St James' Park, although the clever Wainscoat scored the Leeds goal in a 4-1 defeat. He had cost Leeds £2,000 from Middlesbrough after previously sparkling with Barnsley, for whom he scored a hat-trick on his Football League debut against Fulham on 6 March 1920.

Edwards was the least known of the new men – but Leeds nearly missed out on landing the talented half-back from Chesterfield for £1,500.

The deal was completed on 16 March, the transfer deadline day, and Edwards was quickly persuaded to sign for Leeds. The ink was barely dry on his new contract when representatives from Aston Villa arrived at his house, only to discover their quarry had been snatched from under their noses by Leeds.

Some years later, Edwards admitted that if the Villa men had arrived earlier, then he may well have gone to Villa Park rather than Elland Road.

Villa's loss was United's gain as Edwards quickly developed into a half-back of international class, making his England debut after less than a year in the First Division, when he was still only 22.

In fact, Edwards could have made an even quicker rise up soccer's ladder of success. He was still with his Derbyshire junior club, Newton Rangers, when Blackburn Rovers arranged for him to have a trial at Ewood Park and was literally on his way to Lancashire when Chesterfield intercepted him and signed him on for 30 shillings a week.

Edwards was a miner in those days and continued to work down the pit for several months when he was on Chesterfield's books.

The 1925-6 season saw United wave goodbye to several stalwarts including, skipper Jim Baker, full-back Bert Duffield, crackshot Jack Swan and winger Joe Harris as United's rebuilding pro-gramme gathered pace.

Baker played his final game against Everton at Elland Road on 6 March 1926 before joining Nelson for a season. He returned to Leeds to run the Smyths Arms in Geldard Road, a short stroll from the Elland Road ground where he had given such sterling service in his 200 League games. He later became a United director.

Tom Jennings charges towards Aston Villa goalkeeper Spiers in 1925-6. Villa won 3-1, Jennings scoring the Leeds goal.

The steady Duffield had amassed some 203 League games in United colours before moving to Bradford Park Avenue and later followed Baker into the licensed trade and had a spell working at the greyhound stadium in Elland Road.

New faces in the defence included two Scots, Jim Allan, a right-back from Airdrie, who replaced Duffield, and Tom Townsley, a Scottish international centre-half, who arrived at Elland Road on Christmas Day 1925 in a £5,000 deal with Falkirk.

Behind the defence, Bill Johnson forced his way out of the Central League side to take over from Billy Down, who had been transferred to Doncaster Rovers.

However, another goalkeeper, Jimmy Potts, snapped up from Blyth Spartans, came in for the last dozen games to earn high praise from the Press.

His rise to the goalkeeping job at Leeds was straight out of a *Boy's Own* magazine. After finishing his shift as a coal hewer at Ashington Colliery one Thursday, he signed for Leeds that night and made a brilliant First Division League debut against champions Huddersfield Town two days later.

There had also been changes in attack, with Swan moving on to Watford after netting exactly 50 League and Cup goals for United.

Swan had lost his place to the talented Wainscoat, who now formed a partnership on the left with winger Billy Jackson, whose arrival from Sunderland triggered the departure of Joe Harris to Fulham.

Turnbull – a Bobby Dazzler
But the major summer capture had been right winger Bobby Turnbull from Bradford Park Avenue. There was no doubt that Turnbull was a class act, albeit a moody one.

On his day there was no one to match him. Possessor of masterly footwork, his ability to dribble and cross the ball at speed made him a slippery customer – but, like many wingers, he lacked that vital ingredient, consistency.

A former steelworker from the South Bank area of Middlesbrough he was due to play for 'Boro in a friendly against Park Avenue at Ayresome Park in 1918. But Avenue were a man short, so Turnbull played for the West Yorkshire side and impressed them so much that he signed for them after the game.

The Avenue officials had made an inspired choice. Turnbull scored five times on his debut against Barnsley on New Year's Day 1918, was capped by England the following year and toured South Africa with an FA party in 1920.

Turnbull's arrival at Elland Road undoubtedly helped United take advantage of a change in the offside law which saw goals galore throughout the League in 1925. The law was altered so that a player could not be offside, if two (instead of three) opponents were nearer their own goal-line when the ball was last played.

The rule change had been prompted by full-backs who had pushed up towards the halfway line and perfected the offside trap, often killing a game stone dead.

In the first season of the new law; the total of Football League goals rose to 6,373 from 4,700 the previous season. It made matches more exciting and it took clubs a couple of years to revise their defensive tactics by introducing the 'stopper' centre-half – a player with a strictly defensive role 'invented' by Herbert Chapman.

No longer was the centre-half to have a roaming role which gave him license to link up with attack – but for a couple of years it was the forwards who ruled supreme. Turnbull's wing wizardry created openings for Tom Jennings, who took full advantage by setting a new seasonal scoring record for Leeds United with 26 goals.

Two of those goals came in the crucial final match of the season which saw United sink

Willis Edwards joined Leeds from Chesterfield for £1,500 in March 1925 and went on to make 417 League appearances for the Elland Road club.

Bobby Turnbull was the big signing of the 1925 close season and for the next six years he would delight Leeds fans with his dazzling footwork.

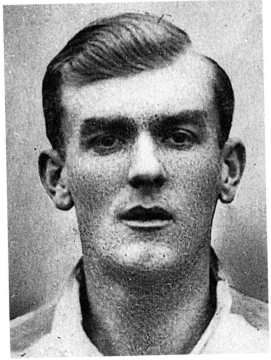

Tottenham 4-1 at Elland Road, with Turnbull and Whipp completing the scoring, to ensure United's First Division survival.

They had looked safe until a dreadful run in April brought only one point from five games to leave United in trouble.

There was a terrific late relegation scramble when United lost 2-1 at relegation rivals Manchester City in the penultimate game of the season.

City's win at Maine Road in midweek meant they only had to draw at Newcastle to stay up, even if United and fellow strugglers Burnley both won.

It all hinged on the final day of the season with either Leeds, Manchester City or Burnley going down with doomed Notts County.

Both United and Burnley won their games, but City lost 3-2 at Newcastle to a Hughie Gallagher hat-trick and slid into the Second Division.

But even Jennings' scoring heroics were overshadowed by his former Raith teammate Jock McClelland, who scored all five Middlesbrough goals as they sent United crashing out of the FA Cup at the first hurdle.

England Call on Edwards

It was also a memorable season for new boy Edwards, who made the step up in class from Chesterfield with the greatest of ease.

Bill Johnson, much of whose time at Leeds was spent in the shadows due to injury, saves a shot against Arsenal at Highbury in September 1925, but United still went down 4-1.

His ball control, crisp passing and incisive tackling quickly established him as one of the best wing-halves in the country and he hugely deserved the honour of becoming the first United man and the 500th player, to be capped by England when he lined up in the shock 3-1 defeat by Wales at Selhurst Park in March 1926 – the first of his 16 international appearances.

That haul of caps could well have been more, but it was always suspected that the Football League took a dim view of his contract to give newspaper forecasts of the following Saturday's games, even though Leeds games were never included in his tips.

United gained further prestige when Wainscoat was picked at the end of season to tour Canada with an FA party, hitting five goals in one game against Thunder Bay at Fort William.

Jennings proved irresistible in 1926-7, improving the club League scoring record to 35, yet it was still not good enough to prevent United sliding back into Division Two.

As he hammered in goals at one end, a leaky defence struggled to come to terms with the new offside law and let in 89 goals.

But for the bravery of goalkeeper Jimmy Potts it could have gone beyond the 100 mark. The former miner used every part of his 6ft and 12st frame to dominate the penalty area, earning a reputation as one of the safest and most daring goalkeepers in the business.

But he got precious little protection, despite the likes of Willis Edwards, Tom Townsley and Bill Menzies in front of him.

Menzies was regarded as a thin, almost frail, left-back but his slimline features proved deceptive as he put bite into his tackles and plenty of meat into his shoulder-charges.

Jennings Goes Goal Crazy

But the balance of power had tilted towards the forwards. Scoring revels were the order of the day and Jennings responded in spectacular fashion, including a remarkable run of 19 goals in only nine games.

That included a scoring sequence of three successive hat-tricks, a feat equalled only by Liverpool's Jack Balmer in 1947.

Jennings' record-breaking heroics began with three in the 4-1 win over Arsenal at Elland Road on 25 September, all four in the 4-2 win at Liverpool the following week and another four-timer seven days later in the 4-1 home win over Blackburn. As the goals poured in, so did the fans, with the holiday game against Newcastle on 27 December establishing a new Elland Road crowd record of 48,590.

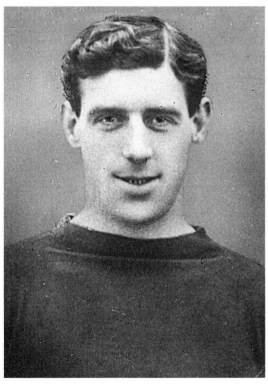

The fourth-round FA Cup tie against Bolton also pulled in 42,694 a month later, but United found no solace in the Cup competition and went out after a replay at Burnden Park.

They also suffered a wretched League run from November to April, collecting only one win from 18 games, despite the introduction of some new men.

Two boys from the Wakefield area had burst on the scene after cutting their teeth in the Central League, Harry Roberts and George Reed.

Roberts, from Crofton, provided the stability at right-back which United had not enjoyed since Bert Duffield's departure.

Altofts-born Reed was sharp in the tackle and occupied the left-half spot as United chopped and changed their defence to find their best combination.

Even the arrival in November of Newcastle's lithe winger Tom Mitchell, for £785, could not turn the tide as United's slide down the table continued.

Mitchell had not kicked a football in an organised game until he was 18, but after only a handful of games with Prudhoe United in his native Durham, was enrolled by Newcastle United.

Largely a reserve at Newcastle, he was also a shrewd businessman, running a sports outfitters in Whitley Bay and later took his organisational skills into soccer management at York City, also setting up a sports shop in that city.

In a major gamble to stave off the drop, United took the football world by surprise by lashing out a record £5,600 on Hearts inside-forward John White.

The transfer fee was one of the biggest of its day and White was one of the star names of Scottish football.

He began at Albion Rovers in 1920, after leaving the Navy, and within two years had been capped by Scotland and signed by Hearts for £2,700. In five seasons at Hearts he netted 102 goals, including four in successive games in 1925-6.

One of four brothers who played professionally, White had also been the leading scorer in Scotland in 1922-3.

United saw White as the man to team up with fellow Scot Tom Jennings and steer United away from the bottom reaches of the table.

It was a high risk policy and one which failed as White's early displays did not live up to expectations and United finished second-to-bottom above West Brom whom they accompanied into the Second Division.

Fairclough and Norman accepted responsibility and quit at the end of the season.

Fairclough left soccer to run a pub, but emerged as secretary-manager of Barnsley in May 1929, whilst Norman was appointed manager at Hartlepool in August 1927.

The duo had done a fine job at Elland Road, but believed they had taken United as far as they could.

Whoever would take over the managerial reins would inherit a side packed with potential and in the likes of Jennings, White, Turnbull, Edwards and Hart possessed some of the finest footballers in the country.

In 1925, Leeds saw the departure of two members of the 1923-4 Second Division title-winning team, left-back George Speak (left) and outside-right Joe Harris. Speak came from Preston for £250 in August 1923 and retired in the summer of 1925. Harris came from Bristol City in July 1922 and moved to Fulham in October 1925.

The Yo-Yo Years

UNITED'S directors turned to former player Dick Ray to guide them back to the First Division.

In his four years at Doncaster, Ray had done a solid if unspectacular job and his knowledge of the Elland Road set-up made him first choice for the post.

He was an outspoken character, who liked to do things his own way and wielded plenty of power at Leeds, where he had responsibility for both team selection and playing policy.

There was some pressure on Ray to sell his star men, but he kept hold of them all to underline his determination to get Leeds back up at the first attempt.

Clearly, things at Elland Road had come a long way since Ray had run the Leeds City's Midland League side on a weekly wage bill of £11.

One of his first jobs was to release 30-year-old Percy Whipp – who had given four and a half years' excellent service to Leeds – to Clapton Orient.

Another United forward, winger Billy Jackson, also headed for London, linking up with West Ham United, whilst Jock Thom moved to Bristol Rovers for £175, and reserve centre-half Bobby Mason and second-string full-back Jim Kirkpatrick went to Watford.

Ray used his contacts in the Doncaster area to snap up a powerful young tank-like forward called Charlie Keetley, a former Rolls-Royce worker, who had been driving in the goals in the Derby and District League with regularity, hitting 80 for local club, Alvaston and Boulton.

The Keetley Clan

Ray would certainly have had little difficulty in locating the burly 21-year-old, as no less than four of his brothers, Frank, Harold, Joe and Tom, were on the books of Ray's former club, Doncaster.

The Keetley dynasty also saw Charlie's other brothers on the payroll of League clubs, Arthur

with Spurs, Jack with Hull City and Albert at Burton United.

Charlie arrived at Leeds as back-up for the prolific scoring duo of Tom Jennings and John White and was to have a vital role to play as United's promotion push reached its climax.

United's quality squad meant they were among the favourites for promotion and a spectacular 5-1 first-day win at South Shields with goals from White (2), Wainscoat, Mitchell and Jennings, confirmed United's power.

It soon became clear that United and Manchester City were the teams to beat in the division, City handing out Leeds' first reverse of the campaign in September when they won 2-1.

But United played some irresistible stuff at times with goals flying in from all angles. Not

Skipper Tom Townsley was an ever-present in a season which saw a remarkable run-in to the Second Division title. A Scottish international defender, Townsley joined Leeds from Falkirk in December 1925, for £5,000, and missed only four games in the next three and half seasons.

surprisingly, scouts began to flock to Elland Road in the hope of some rich pickings.

Their chief target was the revitalised White, who had overcome his nervy start to football south of Hadrian's Wall and was the subject of a sensational £6,000 bid by Sheffield United in November.

United could have banked a quick profit had they sold White, but he had a crucial role to play in the promotion stakes, the bid was rejected and the message became loud and clear to other clubs: 'Hands off our stars.'

United peaked with seven successive wins, starting in December, and did not even miss leading marksman Tom Jennings when he was ruled out for a spell midway through the season.

Jennings suffered from periodic bouts of blood poisoning and just as it seemed as though United's goal power would wane through his absence, young Keetley took over the centre-forward's jersey and took domestic soccer by storm.

Even Leeds supporters knew little about him until he scored seven times in a 10-1 Central League thrashing of Bolton Wanderers on 10 November 1927.

The following month the dark-haired youngster with a power-packed shot made his debut and went on to blast an amazing 18 goals in 16 League games. Keetley scored in each of his first three games, then netted a hat-trick in the next, a 3-2 home win over Bristol City in January.

It was a fairy-tale stuff with rampant United finishing the season with a club record 98 goals with the two centre-forwards scoring 39 of them. Keetley had 18 and Jennings 21 in 26 games to end as joint topscorer with fellow Scot, White.

With Russell Wainscoat chipping in with another 18, it all added up to goals galore for United, who failed to score in only three matches.

Although the forwards hogged the headlines, the defence played their part too.

In a remarkable run-in to the title the defence kept nine successive clean sheets, the outstanding Jimmy Potts playing in eight of those games.

Skipper Tom Townsley and George Reed were ever-presents, whilst Willis Edwards was still considered the best half-back in the country by the England selectors, even though he was playing Second Division football.

Leeds picked up 18 points out of a possible 20, thanks largely to that proud defensive record to set up the showdown of the season at Elland Road against arch rivals Manchester City.

Two goals by Keetley and one by White gave United a promotion-clinching 3-2 win at Chelsea on 21 April in front of 47,562 fans at Stamford Bridge.

That meant the title would be between United and City with just three hours of United's season remaining to settle a few old scores with the men from Maine Road.

City had not only been the first club to beat United that season but also ensured United's poor FA Cup record continued by beating them 1-0 in the third round at Maine Road.

Title Decider

Leeds went into what was billed as the 'title decider' with both ground advantage and an edge in points, but City held the upper hand when it came to goal-average.

United had 57 points and two games, against City and at Stoke, remaining. City had 55 points with three to play, at United, at home to Southampton and at Notts County.

The Second Division was on a knife-edge with United knowing victory would leave them with one hand on the championship.

It was a game everyone wanted to see and a huge crowd of 48,470 squeezed into every nook and cranny of Elland Road for the 25 April blockbuster.

The match proved something of an anticlimax and a bit one-sided with City richly deserving their 1-0 win to take over the leadership.

City received a great ovation from a sporting crowd as they left the field and United were able to console themselves with club record receipts of £3,083.

It was City's third win over United that season, so few would deny them the title which they sewed up three days later with a crushing 6-1 home win over Southampton.

United's season ended in anticlimax as they were thrashed 5-1 at Stoke, but it could not take the gloss off a memorable campaign in which their brand of attacking soccer had not only won them promotion, but also an army of admirers.

United had struggled in their only previous experience in the First Division, but this time around had much more in-depth quality in their squad.

Ray was convinced the men who had produced such stirring soccer in the titanic race for the Second Division title race were as good as any in the country.

There were no big name departures in the summer, only a handful of reserves, and the policy certainly paid early dividends.

The prolific Charlie Keetley carried on where he left off by smashing a 1928-9 opening day hat-trick on his First Division debut as United stormed to a 4-1 win over Aston Villa in front of 26,588 fans at Elland Road.

Keetley was now firmly in possession of the centre-forward position, with the more experienced Tom Jennings having to bide his time in the Reserves.

United made a sizzling start, winning eight and drawing two of their first dozen matches.

All of a sudden the name Leeds United was on everyone's lips, including the England selectors.

Willis Edwards, still only 25 despite his prematurely thinning hair, achieved every school-boy's dream by captaining England for the first time on his 12th international appearance, in the 2-1 win over Ireland at Goodison Park.

That came shortly after Edwards led United to a sweet 4-1 home win over Manchester City, the side that had pipped them to the Division Two title the previous season.

John White netted a hat-trick on a day which saw Tom Cochrane, a young winger from North-East junior side, St Peter's Albion, make his Football League bow.

Ray had earmarked Cochrane as one for the future and had worked long and hard to get his man.

Cochrane had previously had trials with Hull City and Sheffield Wednesday in the days when Ray was manager at Doncaster. Ray kept a note of Cochrane's name and after taking over at Leeds he persuaded the young Tynesider to turn professional at Elland Road.

As Cochrane was trying to establish himself in the Leeds side, Edwards went from strength to strength, leading England in each of his last five internationals.

Playing proudly alongside him in the 3-2 win over Wales at Swansea on 17 November was beefy centre-half Ernie Hart, making his England debut.

It was the first time that two United players were in the same England line-up.

Although it was a great double honour for the club, it was long before the days when League games were postponed because of international calls and United went into their match at home to Sheffield Wednesday the same afternoon without their two England stars.

Milburns Make their Mark

Not surprisingly an understrength United went down 2-0 in a match which marked the debut of George Milburn, a name which was to become part of Elland Road folklore.

Milburn had arrived at Leeds earlier that year as a centre-half from Ashington and was joined at the club six months later by his elder brother, Jack, from Spen Black and White.

They were brothers-in-law of United goalkeeper Jimmy Potts and the number of Milburns on United's books swelled to three in 1935, when they were joined by younger brother, Jim.

A fourth brother, Stan, also played for Chesterfield, Leicester and Rochdale; cousin Jackie was a goalscoring legend at Newcastle, whilst the famous 1966 World Cup-winning duo, Bobby and Jack Charlton, were cousins of the Milburn brothers.

Cochrane and the Milburns were to have a part to play in United's future, but the present-day Leeds stars continued to shine with the excellent Wainscoat becoming the third United player to be capped by England that season when he played against Scotland at Hampden Park; Edwards was also in the side.

Unfortunately, all the euphoria over United's super start started to fade and any slight hope of a serious title challenge evaporated in spring 1929.

Only one win was achieved in the last ten games and they finished in 13th place with 41 points, 11 behind champions Sheffield Wednesday.

Any semblance of good form over the last leg of the season would surely have lifted them into the top five, but some days United just seemed to switch off.

Big wins were mixed in with some hefty defeats, the heaviest being the 8-2 defeat at West Ham, where centre-forward Vic Watson hammered six goals, a record for any player against United, past reserve goalkeeper James Wilson. It was only Wilson's third senior United outing, and not surprisingly, his last.

United had a team of which they could be proud but like previous Leeds sides failed to make any impression in the FA Cup.

At Exeter, of the Third Division South, only a rare fluke goal from just outside his own half by Bill Menzies earned United a late replay.

Although United won 5-1 when the teams met again, Huddersfield crushed United 3-0 in the fourth round to snuff out United's hopes for another year.

Ray's Faith is Rewarded

As Ernie Hart and Bobby Turnbull joined the FA tour of South Africa during the summer, manager Dick Ray was left to ponder what to do with his squad.

They had done brilliantly at times, yet had finished the season dismally. Should he make changes?

Ray eventually stood by his men, although John Armand, a capable inside-forward deputy, was sold to Swansea Town for £500.

The manager's faith was justified as 1929-30 turned out to be United's best of the pre-Revie era.

like inside-forward Eric Longden, centre-half Ben Underwood, winger Johnny Mahon and forward George McNestry, all signed from Ray's former club, Doncaster, waiting for their chance.

Ray had maintained a fine network of scouts in the Doncaster area and appeared to have picked up another gem in former miner Dave Mangnall, from Maltby Colliery.

The centre-forward had been scratching about in United's reserve sides for several months before he went goal crazy on 25 September 1929, four days after his 22nd birthday.

He blasted in no less than ten goals in a sensational 13-0 Northern Midweek League game over Stockport County at Elland Road.

It was marksmanship which Ray could not ignore and four days later the rookie forward was given his League debut, United whipping Burnley 3-0 with goals from Wainscoat, Hart and White.

Although he did not score, Mangnall did well enough to keep Tom Jennings out of the team and scored six times in nine consecutive appearances before being transferred to Huddersfield Town for £3,000.

It was to prove a rare miscalculation by Ray, particularly as Jennings appeared to be losing some of his early sharpness and Keetley was ruled out for much of the season with illness.

Mangnall went on to score 141 League goals in 218 League appearances up to World War Two, including a record 42 League and Cup goals for Huddersfield in 1931-2.

Mangnall's mini-run and some dazzling form from Bobby Turnbull got Leeds off to a flying start, which included a sequence of seven successive wins. The final victory, 1-0, in that run came against Birmingham on 19 October and was achieved without Willis Edwards and Ernie Hart, who were helping England to a 3-0 win against Ireland at Belfast.

The man at outside-right for Ireland that day was certainly no stranger to the Leeds duo; it was their club mate Harry Duggan, who was playing his first game as a Northern Ireland player, although had represented the Republic of Ireland as a youngster against Italy.

The former stonemason from Dublin had been plugging quietly away in Leeds Reserves after signing from his local club, Richmond United in May 1925 as a 19-year-old.

He had not played in the United first team since January 1927, but the inexperienced winger was still considered good enough for international football by the Irish selectors.

Duggan was being kept in the shadows at Leeds by the sparkling Bobby Turnbull, who may have lost a good deal of his hair but none of his skill.

George Milburn made his debut at Hillsborough and embarked upon a career which saw him make 157 League appearances for Leeds.

They finished fifth, clocked up their record score and, into the bargain, netted a £5,395 profit on the season.

Once again the mainstays of the side were the likes of Willis Edwards, Ernie Hart, Russell Wainscoat, Tom Mitchell, George Reed and Harry Roberts, but the new breed were also forcing their way through from the Reserves.

Competition for places was healthy with men

Leeds United in 1929-30. Back row (left to right): Dick Ray (manager), George Reed, Ernie Hart, Jimmy Potts, George Milburn, George Wilson, Tom Jennings, Arthur Campey (trainer). Front row: Bobby Turnbull, John White, Willis Edwards, Harry Roberts, Russell Wainscoat, Tom Mitchell.

Both Turnbull and Russell Wainscoat were playing some of the best football of their careers, Wainscoat finishing as top scorer with 15 League goals.

He also scored a hat-trick as United swamped Crystal Palace 8-1 in the FA Cup third round to establish a club record score which stood until Spora Luxembourg were beaten 9-0 in the Inter-Cities Fairs Cup in October 1967.

But if Leeds fans thought the long-awaited Cup run had arrived, then they had to think again as United were beaten 4-1 at West Ham in the next round.

Vic Watson, the man who shot six past United in the League the previous season, scored all the Hammers' goals. In fact, Watson scored an astonishing 16 goals in only four games against Leeds – four in the FA Cup, a double hat-trick and two hat-tricks in League games!

The only Cup glory Leeds sampled in 1929-30 came when Elland Road staged the FA Cup semi-final between Arsenal and Hull City, the first semi-final at the ground for 20 years. The Tigers shared four goals with Arsenal, whose centre-forward was Jack Lambert, a former Leeds reserve.

Another player who turned out for both Leeds and Arsenal, 'Iron Man' Wilf Copping, was signed the same month as that semi-final. Tough guy Wilf was just 20 when he signed for Leeds from Yorkshire junior side, Middlecliffe Rovers, and was to make his mark, sometimes literally, on the top-class soccer scene in years to come.

In other years, United had spluttered as the season drew to a close, but this time round they finished on a high, thanks largely to the return from illness of Charlie Keetley.

The fans' favourite kept up his remarkable strike rate by scoring ten times in the last eight games to lift Leeds into fifth place.

Pundits were already talking about United as possible League Championship contenders for 1930-31, but everyone at Elland Road was going to be in for a shock.

Relegation Blues

Inside-forward John White, now 33, returned to Hearts for £2,500, but Dick Ray found the money could not be used for team-building.

Leeds United goalkeeper Jimmy Potts handles cleanly at Highbury on the opening day of the 1929-30 season. Leeds, though, lost 4-0 but still managed to finish the season in fifth place.

to the reputation of United's half-back line.'

That half-back line now read Edwards-Hart-Copping, and went on to be the most feared of its day with each of the mighty trio winning England honours. Only the Bremner-Charlton-Hunter combination of the 1960s and 70s has surpassed it at Leeds. Copping certainly showed the *Yorkshire Post* he was a quick learner, being the only ever-present that season.

The luckless Reed, unable to recapture his place, moved on to Plymouth with his great friend, Harry Roberts, who had been displaced at full-back by Jack Milburn.

Another man to make his breakthrough was the energetic inside-right Billy Furness, a £50 bargain from non-League Usworth Colliery a couple of years earlier.

In his fifth game of the season, Furness scored twice in the 7-3 rout of Blackpool at Bloomfield Road, the only time United have scored seven goals away from home in a League game.

Inside a minute, Blackpool were reduced to ten men because of injury and United took full advantage with Keetley (2), Cochrane (2) and Turnbull adding to Furness' double blast.

But apart from a spectacular 7-0 home win over Middlesbrough the following month, and a 5-0 thumping of struggling Manchester United, Leeds fans had little to cheer.

There was no doubt that Dick Ray had some outstanding individuals on the books; the problem was that a succession of injuries prevented him from fielding a settled side.

Although the Edwards-Hart-Copping backbone did its best and Charlie Keetley maintained his outstanding scoring ratio, United suffered through the constant chopping and changing.

Confidence began to eat away after the New Year and although Ray made desperate efforts to sign a much-needed inside-forward, he failed in successive bids to land Harry Davies (Huddersfield Town), Bobby Bruce (Middlesbrough) and John Allen (Sheffield Wednesday), the latter a former Leeds reserve who had been allowed to leave.

Dave Mangnall, who kept Tom Jennings out of the team. Mangnall had a whirlwind career at Leeds. Signed from Maltby Colliery, he scored ten goals in a 13-0 win over Stockport in a Northern Midweek League game. Four days later, on 28 September 1929, he was given his first-team debut, at home to Burnley, but after scoring six times in nine consecutive appearances, he was transferred to Huddersfield that December. He had a useful career with Huddersfield, West Ham and Millwall.

The club had slipped into the red and were still trying to redeem £30,000-worth of debentures upon which interest was being paid at the rate of 7 per cent – double the Bank Rate of the day.

In a pre-season game, George Reed picked up a bad knee injury and failed to make the starting line-up for the opener against Portsmouth at Elland Road. His place went to young Copping, whose debut saw United held 2-2, Turnbull and Keetley, the United marksmen.

The *Yorkshire Post* report of the match said: 'Copping, whilst displaying latent talent, has something to learn before he will be able to live up

West Ham goalkeeper Ted Hufton makes a fine one-handed save from Tom Jennings in the fourth-round FA Cup game at Upton Park in January 1930. Leeds lost 4-1, yet again dogged by the Hammers' Vic Watson.

United's First Division life hung by a thread for weeks, yet they could still have stayed up if results went their way on the final Saturday.

Manchester United were already down and either Leeds or Blackpool would join them.

Leeds needed to win and hope Blackpool would lose against Manchester City. The Elland Road club did their bit, beating Derby 3-1, but Blackpool grabbed an equaliser 11 minutes from the end of their home game to snatch a priceless point from a 2-2 draw.

Remarkably, Blackpool had conceded 125 League goals and still stayed up!

Ray remained optimistic: "I am sorry for the boys and sorry for the directors, but we are not going to mope about it. We are going to put our backs into the task that lies ahead of us."

United were not as bad as their record suggested and had been extremely unlucky with a catalogue of injuries.

They even raised hopes of a good FA Cup run with wins over Huddersfield and Newcastle, only to lose 3-1 at lowly Exeter when a place in the sixth round seemed to be there for the taking.

The Huddersfield tie saw the arrival of another young player – and the departure of one of the old guard.

With Charlie Keetley out through injury, Tom Jennings fully expected a recall, but in a major shock, Ray handed the centre-forward shirt to a

Jimmy Potts, arguably Leeds' best goalkeeper of the inter-war period, cannot stop this shot by Arsenal's Jack Lambert at Highbury in September 1930. Lambert had spent a brief time with Leeds earlier in his career.

crew-cut teenager from the Barnsley area, Arthur Hydes.

Young Hydes, a former sweet-factory worker, responded with one of the goals in United's 2-0 win over their lofty neighbours. It was the first time United had beaten Town in 13 outings since joining the League. But Jennings was not celebrating.

He realised it was the end of his distinguished career at Elland Road and immediately slapped in a transfer request.

He played only one more game for Leeds before moving to Chester with goalkeeper Willie Johnson, taking with him a stack of Elland Road memories.

In 167 League games for United, Jennings netted 112 goals, a club record that was to stand until the incomparable John Charles arrived on the scene.

Jennings, who later managed Bangor City and Third Lanark, was remarkably overlooked by the Scottish selectors, despite scoring for the Anglo Scots in a 1-1 draw with the Home Scots in a 1928 trial game.

Two other old United favourites on the move shortly afterwards were Russell Wainscoat and Tom Mitchell.

At the age of 33, Wainscoat, having netted 85 goals in 215 League games, went to Hull City to weave his inside-forward magic at Analby Road and was rewarded with a Third Division North championship medal in 1933.

Tom Mitchell, who was approaching his 32nd birthday, made the short journey east to join York City, where he had a spell as manager after World War Two.

There was also a change at boardroom level during 1931, Major Braithwaite, having less and less time to devote to United because of his political affairs, stepped down as chairman.

Twenty years later, as Sir Albert Braithwaite, he was elected MP for West Harrow, but committed suicide on 20 October 1959 in London, aged 66.

Leeds City alderman and solicitor Eric Clarke was elected chairman in August 1931 in Braithwaite's place. He had joined the board in 1925 and had spent three years as chairman of the finance committee.

United had made a loss of £1,286 during the relegation season, so once again Ray had to be prudent with his spending, his only signing of note being reserve goalkeeper Stan Moore, who joined Leeds after starring for Worksop Town against United in a pre-season friendly.

Perversely, United won their opening two fixtures of 1931-2, at Swansea and Port Vale, then lost the next two, both at Elland Road, to Barnsley and Millwall.

But they soon got into their stride and reeled off a superb club record of nine successive wins to shoot to the top of the table.

This remarkable run brought victories over Bristol City (away) 2-0, Oldham (home) 5-0, Bury (away) 4-1, Wolves (home) 2-1, Charlton (away) 1-0, Stoke (home) 2-0, Manchester United (away) 5-2, Preston (home) 4-1, Burnley (away) 5-0.

The Edwards-Hart-Copping combination was a class above anything else in the division. Keetley maintained his eye for goal and there were useful scoring contributions from inside-forwards Billy Furness and Glashoughton-born Joe Firth, yet another young man plucked from the coalfields.

On wing patrol were Harry Duggan, now established on the Irish international scene, and Tom Cochrane, who had finally won over his terrace critics. Cochrane had a difficult job in filling Tom Mitchell's boots and took plenty of stick from the crowd in his early days, but his hard running displays eventually earned the respect of the fans.

Cochrane missed only one game in 1931-2, full-back Jack Milburn being the only ever-present.

United and Wolves pulled away from the rest of the pack with free-scoring Wolves hitting a purple patch in March to reach the finishing tape as champions.

United were runners-up, two points behind, after collecting only two wins in their final ten games, a sticky patch which cost them the title.

None the less, United had bounced back into Division One at the first attempt, for the second time in their history.

First Division – Second Time Around

PROMOTION came at a price for United, whose loss of £3,500 was double that of the previous season.

Yet again manager Dick Ray had little financial room to manoeuvre but his team shaped up well on their return to the First Division.

The biggest bonus came with the form of inside-left Billy Furness and 'Iron Man' Wilf Copping, who both earned their England international spurs at the end of the season.

Centre-forward Charlie Keetley came close to adding his name to the international role of honour by being selected as reserve for the Football League against the Irish League at Belfast in October 1932. At centre-forward that day was George Brown, who scored a hat-trick in a 5-2 win. Brown later had a spell at Leeds after joining them from Burnley in 1935.

Keetley was considered for the match in Belfast after a stirring reintroduction to the First Division in which he scored five goals in his first five appearances.

Defensively, United looked as good as any side in the country with Copping lining up against the experienced Ernie Hart, another who was still being picked for England.

The Milburns had also forged a formidable full-back partnership – George on the right and Jack on the left – which was unbroken throughout the season. With both men ever-present, Bill Menzies felt it was time to move on, joining Goole Town after 11½ years outstanding service at Elland Road.

United made a fine start to the season after losing their opening two fixtures. They lost only twice more in 1932, establishing a new record attendance for Elland Road in the process.

United's good form had been eclipsed by the brilliance of a rampant Arsenal side, now under the leadership of former Leeds City boss Herbert Chapman.

The Gunners were fresh from a 9-2 thrashing of Sheffield United, in which former Leeds reserve centre-forward Jack Lambert scored five times, when confident Leeds arrived at Highbury on Boxing Day.

In-form Arsenal were favourites to win, but Leeds grabbed a famous 2-1 victory with Keetley netting both United goals.

Elland Road Bursts at the Seams

That remarkable result immediately had Leeds pencilled-in as dark horses for the Championship and 24 hours later a massive crowd turned up to see the pre-match with Arsenal at Elland Road.

The 56,796 spectators smashed the previous best at Elland Road, setting record receipts of £3,508 in the process. It was an attendance record that was to stand for 35 years.

Victory would have strengthened United's claims that they could still go for the title, but they were held to a goalless draw by the star-studded Gunners and then began to fall away over the second half of the season.

There was some compensation for United in the FA Cup, when they equalled their best performance by reaching the fifth round, before losing 2-0 at Everton.

On the way they eliminated holders Newcastle 3-0 in the third round on Tyneside, Arthur Hydes bagging a fine hat-trick.

Hydes, instantly recognisable with his closely-cropped hair, was proving a handful for First Division defences, even though his partner, Keetley, missed several games through injury.

Hydes, quick and aggressive, revelled in the extra responsibility and finished the campaign as the leading scorer with 20 League and Cup goals, whilst Keetley had a return of 14 from 24 League games with United finishing a creditable eighth.

United duo Copping and Furness won England caps in the 1-1 draw against Italy in Rome. Furness turned out to be a 'one-cap wonder' but for tough-tackling Copping it was the first of 20 appearances for his country.

About the same time, Dick Ray was getting another potential England star to put pen to an Elland Road contract, Bert Sproston.

Ray always had an eye for classy talent and snapped up the cultured 17-year-old wing-half from Sandbach Ramblers after he had been rejected by Huddersfield Town.

It was to prove a smart piece of business for United as Sproston became one of the club's prized assets after converting to right-back.

Masser Takes the Chair

There were also developments behind the scenes during the summer at Elland Road with Eric Clarke stepping down as chairman.

He was replaced by another alderman and solicitor, Alf Masser, one of the best-known figures in the city.

Masser had been an original shareholder of the Leeds City club and at one time its vice-chairman. During World War One he severed his association with Leeds City, but immediately after its demise was one of the driving forces which helped launch the new Leeds United.

It was Masser, a noted advocate, who successfully put the case for United's entry to the Football League to the League's administrators in May 1920.

He later stood down from the board, largely to concentrate on his legal business and his work for Leeds City Council, whom he gave 40 years' unbroken service as an alderman.

As chairman of the Council's Parks Committee he was instrumental in establishing municipal golf courses in the city and the introduction of Sunday games on Council-owned parks.

The energetic Masser's influence went beyond Elland Road during the 1930s, being a key figure in the Football League negotiations which obtained money for the game from the football pools.

He also narrowly missed becoming the first United chairman to serve on the Football League management committee, just failing in elections in 1937 and 1939.

Half-back Heroes – Edwards, Hart and Copping

If a vote had been taken at Elland Road for the most popular player at the club in 1933-4, it would

Bert Sproston, who joined Leeds United as a 17-year-old and went on to play for England.

Leeds United in
1933-4. Back row
(left to right): Cyril
Hornby, George
Milburn, Stan
Moore, Fred Jones,
Jack Milburn, Wilf
Copping. Front row:
Johnny Mahon,
Harry Roper, Ernie
Hart, Charlie
Keetley, Billy
Furness, Tom
Cochrane.

have been won hands down by the powerful Copping, who cemented his status as the new star of the side with a series of stirring displays.

Copping was utterly fearless, a one-man tackling machine who hit unsuspecting forwards with shoulder charges like a bull. He never shaved on match days, his five o'clock shadow adding to his hard-man image.

Behind him Stan Moore had replaced Jimmy Potts in goal and enjoyed a splendid season, playing in all United's matches.

Up front, Hydes plundered 16 goals in 19 games, including four in a 5-2 home win over Middlesbrough, before an injury at Newcastle in January put him out for the rest of the season.

With Charlie Keetley also suffering from injury and loss of form, Ray had to reshape his forward line in the second half of the season.

Irish international winger Harry Duggan took on the centre-forward role whilst reserves John Mahon and Joe Firth were pressed into action.

Ray also had to cover the loss of ace defender Willis Edwards for three months after the England star picked up an injury.

Edwards' return to the United line-up against Leicester at Elland Road on 7 April 1934 restored the famous Edwards-Hart-Copping line-up.

The veteran Edwards had always been an inspirational figure and it was perhaps his presence that worked United into such a frenzy that they slaughtered Leicester 8-0.

It was United's biggest-ever League victory and, ironically, was achieved without the club's leading marksmen, Keetley and Hydes.

Billy Furness was in prime form while Mahon led the Filberts a merry dance on the right wing with his speed and deadly centres. Four men scored two goals apiece, Mahon, Furness, Firth and Duggan in a one-sided encounter against a poor Leicester side.

It was a one-off result in a frustrating season for Ray, who did well to paper over the cracks of an injury-hit squad as Leeds finished comfortably in mid-table.

Ray's skilful management had not gone unnoticed at the highest level and he was appointed the first-ever team manager of a Football League XI, receiving a gold medal for the honour. The representative side, which included Copping, drew 2-2 at Ibrox with the Scottish League.

But Copping was to part company with Ray and United in June 1934 when he joined Arsenal in a sensational £6,000 deal.

When Copping-less United crashed to a record 8-1 defeat at Stoke in the second match of the 1934-5 season, there were murmurings of discontent among the fans.

Stanley Matthews scored four goals in that game which threw up an amazing piece of soccer trivia: United's record League win and defeat came in the space of seven matches.

A month after that sorry Stoke show, United switched their colours from blue and white stripes to blue and gold halved shirts, white shorts and blue stockings with gold tops. It made little difference as the new kit was 'christened' with an emphatic 3-0 home defeat against Liverpool.

Apart from Copping, veteran goalkeeper Jimmy Potts had moved on in the summer to Port Vale after clocking up 247 League appearances between the posts for United.

Those two popular United stars were followed by another in October 1934, when Charlie Keetley left for Bradford City, having netted a remarkable 108 League goals in 160 games.

However, United were boosted by the return of Arthur Hydes after injury in the same month and he marked his comeback with a goal in a 2-0 home win over Everton.

Hydes held the centre-forward position for virtually the rest of the season to finish top scorer with 22 League goals and was helped by the brilliance of Furness, who was having another magnificent season.

Furness broke his collar-bone against Norwich when United were sent spinning out of the FA Cup by the Third Division South side in a replay at Elland Road. Ironically, Furness went on to join Norwich a couple of seasons later.

Ray of Light is Eclipsed
Injuries had not helped Ray's planning and the successes were largely individual ones, although United did manage to beat Huddersfield in a League game for the first time since joining the Football League, Harry Duggan scoring both goals in a 2-0 success at Elland Road to end an unwanted 17-match sequence against their West Riding neighbours.

Ray did recruit experienced campaigners in Scottish international centre-half Jock McDougall and centre-forward Jack Kelly but both were soon laid low by injuries.

McDougall had been capped once by Scotland as an Airdrie player before joining Sunderland for £5,000, from where he joined Leeds in November 1934.

McDougall was already out of the side when Kelly was signed from Newcastle United for £1,150 three months later.

Leeds still continued to hover around the relegation zone and Ray decided he had done as much as he could with United and quit his £1,000-a-year job in March.

About a month later he took over as boss at Bradford City, where Jack Peart, the man who had scored so many goals as a guest for Leeds City in wartime, had just left.

Dick Ray resigned his £1,000-a-year job as Leeds manager in March 1935. He had served the club as player, captain, committeeman and manager. A month after leaving Leeds, Ray was appointed manager of Bradford City.

United kept scrambling a few points and eventually finished 18th after a season of frustration.

Ray, who had made an enormous contribution to United's cause, stayed at Valley Parade until February 1938 and later did some scouting for Millwall.

During World War Two he was running a garage business in Leeds and also had an interest in billiard saloons in the city. It was a sad day for United when he died in St James' Hospital, Leeds, on 28 December 1952, aged 75. When he moved from Elland Road he left a legacy which included two highly polished gems – Bert Sproston and a young inside-forward, Eric Stephenson.

Sproston was already shaping into a cultured right-back, whilst Stephenson, who was being groomed as a possible successor to Billy Furness, was given his League debut during 1934-5 after training with United as an amateur.

They were just two of the jewels new manager Billy Hampson inherited when he slipped into the Elland Road hot seat vacated by Ray.

Jack Milburn and Willis Edwards were still shoring up the defence, Billy Furness continued to sparkle and Tom Cochrane was proving a slippery customer on the left wing.

Ray had left something to build on and Hampson quickly got to work, recruiting men with vast experience.

Hampson, like Ray, was a Leeds City old boy, having turned out for the Peacocks as a guest during World War One when he was a Newcastle player.

Hampson remained loyal with Newcastle for many years, despite having a long spell of reserve-team football. His patience eventually paid off as he won a regular first-team place and became one of the oldest FA Cup Finalists when he played right-back in the Magpies' 2-0 win over Aston Villa in 1924, when he was 41 years and eight months old.

Burly Billy moved to South Shields and gave up playing in March 1930, when he was appointed manager of Carlisle United, where he discovered the legendary Bill Shankly.

After a spell running Ashington, he took on the Leeds job with a reputation as being a hard, but extremely fair man.

Perhaps it was Hampson's long playing career which prompted him to favour experience as he signed on two former England veterans raised in his native North-East.

In came former England international goalkeeper Albert McInroy, aged 34, from Sunderland, and George Brown, the 32-year-old Burnley centre-forward, who had rattled in 142 League goals for Huddersfield in the 1920s before joining Aston Villa for £5,000.

Brown arrived in September after United failed to win any of their opening five games and soon struck up a productive scoring partnership with Jack Kelly.

Brown's skill and eye for goal made him the pick of the forwards, yet surprisingly he failed to score in the biggest win of the season when United thrashed Sheffield Wednesday 7-2 after leading 6-1 at half-time!

Harry Duggan, still doing a good job on the right wing, scored a hat-trick that day and had found himself a new Irish international for company in the shape of Bobby Browne.

Left-half Browne had already played for the Irish League against the Football League twice when at Derry City before a £1,500 transfer to Leeds in October 1935, where he replaced Cyril Hornby, who moved on to Sunderland four months later.

Ten days after signing for Leeds, Browne won the first of his eight Northern Ireland caps when he played in the side which lost 3-1 to England in Belfast.

With Jock MacDougall taking over the stopper role from Ernie Hart to play alongside Willis Edwards, United certainly had their fair share of 'old 'un's' in the team but gave as good as they got to finish 11th.

They also enjoyed a brief flirtation with FA Cup success, knocking out Wolves and Bury before losing in the fifth round at Sheffield United, where the crowd of 68,287 was a record for Bramall Lane.

Ernie Hart managed only four outings in Hampson's first season and before the start of 1936-7 had joined Mansfield Town after 17 seasons at Elland Road.

He had made a total of 472 appearances for United, a pre-World War Two record for the club, and had deservedly earned two benefit cheques for his solid service.

The ultimate in consistency, Hart had carved his own niche in Leeds United's history and Elland Road did not seem the same without him.

He later had a spell as manager of non-League Tunbridge Wells, did a bit of scouting for Leeds and Coventry and went into the haulage and bus-service business until his untimely death in 1954, aged 52.

It was another of the old guard, Willis Edwards, who proved to be United's star performer of the 1936-7 season and even at the age of 33 there were some observers who reckoned he was still worth an England place.

The influence of Edwards undoubtedly rubbed off on Bert Sproston, who gained his first cap in October 1936 when England went down to a surprise 2-1 defeat at Cardiff.

United fans also had some surprises that month as Hampson got cracking in the transfer market.

In the space of a fortnight, George Brown joined Darlington as player-manager, Tom Cochrane moved to Middlesbrough and fellow winger Harry Duggan headed for Newport County.

The left-wing position which Cochrane had held unchallenged for nearly six years went to Arthur Buckley, a £2,500 signing from Oldham, while Sammy Armes came out of the Reserves to fill the opposite flank.

Indeed, in a season of chopping and changing, United predictably struggled, particularly away from home where they could muster only three points, a win at Sheffield Wednesday and a draw at Manchester United.

Arthur Hydes returned temporarily to first-team action, playing alongside George Ainsley, an inside-forward who joined from Sunderland before Christmas.

Despite all the comings and goings, United were in a precarious position with only a good home record keeping their heads above water.

Gordon a Tonic

The man who turned out to be the club's saviour was a strapping 6ft-tall South African, Gordon Hodgson, whom many thought was past his sell-by date when he joined United from Aston Villa for £1,500 in March 1937, a month short of his 34th birthday.

But the veteran Johannesburg-born leader proved to be an inspired purchase, despite a torrid introduction to life with Leeds in a 7-1 debut defeat against Everton at Goodison, although he scored United's consolation.

That was a traumatic return to Merseyside where Hodgson had been idolised during his days at Liverpool.

He arrived in England with the South African touring team in 1925. A boiler-maker by trade, he was signed by Liverpool, for whom he scored a stunning 233 goals in 258 League games.

Such fire power earned him three England caps before his £3,000 move to Villa, where he stayed for only four months before United engaged his services.

His vim and vigour was invaluable in the closing weeks as United preserved their First Division status by winning both their final home games, 3-0 and 3-1, against Sunderland and Portsmouth respectively, to finish 19th.

It had been an uncomfortable season for the first team, but for the Reserves it proved a memorable campaign as George Milburn led them to United's first Central League title in the club's history.

Manager Billy Hampson had brought on several promising youngsters in the 'stiffs', including 17-year-old Welshman Aubrey Powell, and Ken Gadsby, a 20-year-old full-back who, like Hodgson, made his senior Leeds debut in the Everton débâcle.

Powell, snapped up as an amateur from Swansea, broke his leg at Preston shortly after his first-team debut, whilst Gadsby, signed from Wilf Copping's old club, Middlecliffe Rovers, certainly had the pedigree to reach the top; his father was a member of Barnsley's 1910 FA Cup Final side.

Another famous son at Elland Road was 6ft 2in centre-half Tom Holley, whose father George played for Sunderland, Wolves and England. Young Tom had joined United as a wing-half for £3,500 from Barnsley, where his dad was trainer.

With these up-and-coming young men in reserve, right-back Bert Sproston winning his first England cap in the 5-1 win over Ireland in Belfast and Eric Stephenson shaping into a cultured inside-left, United could look to the future with a fair degree of optimism.

Hampson also had an eye on the future and at the end of the season swept out several senior members of the club.

Centre-half Jock McDougall retired, goalkeeper Albert McInroy moved to Gateshead, Billy Furness went to Norwich City and George Milburn joined Chesterfield. Furness commanded a £2,700 fee and went on to become trainer-coach at Carrow Road, whilst Milburn left one brother, Jack, to join up with another, Stan, at Chesterfield and later became that club's assistant manager.

There was also a change of chairman in July as former Football League referee Ernest Pullan was elected in succession to Masser.

Pullan had been one of United's most active directors on the playing front and even acted as team manager for a few weeks when Dick Ray resigned in March 1935.

Although he had a pretty big summer clear-out, manager Hampson stayed out of the transfer market and opted to give some of his young successful reserves more opportunities.

It was a policy which paid off with Jim Makinson, a signing from non-League Clitheroe, doing a fine job at right-half – a position which had been occupied for so many years by Willis Edwards – having a fine season.

Edwards was now in semi-retirement and taking a leading role in the coaching of the players.

Right winger Sammy Armes, who had played under Hampson at Carlisle, blossomed on one flank, whilst Arthur Buckley shone on the other.

Bert Sproston developed into England's first-choice right-back and Eric Stephenson crowned a marvellous season by winning his first England cap against Scotland at Wembley, a game which saw Sproston make his fifth appearance for his country.

Although the younger players caught the eye, it was the old campaigner Gordon Hodgson who was the star of 1937-8.

Hodgson was a powerful all-round athlete who had been a fast bowler for Lancashire CCC in the early 1930s.

With Hydes laid low by injury once more, Hodgson was unchallenged for the centre-forward

South African Gordon Hodgson was in the veteran stage when he joined Leeds in March 1937, but he led their attack with gusto in the years leading up to World War Two.

Leeds United at the start of the 1937-8 season. Back row (left to right): Billy Hampson (manager), Bert Sproston, Jim Makinson, Reg Savage, Jack Milburn, Bobby Browne, Tom Holley. Front row: Sammy Armes, George Ainsley, Gordon Hodgson, Eric Stephenson, Arthur Buckley.

Eric Stephenson, crowned a great first season with his first international cap.

slot and powered in 25 goals in 36 League games, including all Leeds' goals in a 4-4 draw against Everton at Elland Road.

With Hodgson in full cry it was clear why Hampson decided to let Hydes go to Newport at the end of the season and Jack Kelly, midway through it, to Birmingham.

Hydes had continued to suffer from a series of injuries and had really been out of the first-team picture for a couple of seasons, but he left behind a fine strike record of 82 goals from 137 appearances.

United finished the Christmas programme in second place behind Brentford and were very much in the 1937-8 title race.

But the rot set in between mid-February and April when they failed to win a game in nine outings, picking up only four draws, starting with their eight-goal extravaganza against the men from Goodison Park.

United were saved from total anticlimax by the arrival of two Irish stars, goalkeeper Jim Twomey and teenage winger David Cochrane.

Twomey's career took off like a rocket and he won his first Irish cap when he was still a reserve at Elland Road.

A woodworking machinist by trade, he was a

three days later made his full Leeds debut at Blackpool – exactly a week after turning out for the Reserves on the same ground.

David Cochrane, no relation to that other famous Leeds winger, Tom Cochrane, was still only 17 when Hampson gambled £2,000 on his ability. His amazing pace and ball skills earmarked him as a player for the future and

Tom Holley, gave Leeds great service either side of World War Two.

part-timer with Newry Town when he gave a magnificent display for the Irish League against the Football League in October 1937.

League clubs were quickly in pursuit of the Irishman and Leeds boss Hampson beat his rivals to Twomey's signature two months later.

Twomey was blooded in the Central League, then sprang to prominence in March, making his Ireland debut on the 16th against Wales, kept a clean sheet in an impressive performance and

Sammy Armes, now blossoming on the right wing.

Hampson had no hesitation in asking the directors to shell out such a big fee to get the young Portadown starlet.

Cochrane, whose father had played for Linfield, made his Leeds debut towards the end of March and won his first cap for Ireland eight months later.

Rugby returned to Elland Road on 30 April 1938, when Hunslet and Leeds clashed in the Rugby League Championship Final. A huge crowd of 54,112 packed into the ground to see Hunslet win 8-2.

There were certainly a lot less than that to see the Combined Universities take on an Amateur XI at Elland Road two months before that big Rugby League showdown. But those who did bother to attend would have seen a curious sight, players wearing numbered shirts for the first time at Elland Road.

John Thomson seems to have got the back of his head to the ball in the 1-1 draw against Bolton Wanderers at Elland Road in November 1937. Bolton's goalkeeper is Fred Swift, brother of the legendary Manchester City and England goalkeeper, Frank, who perished in the 1958 Munich air disaster.

It was one of several experiments with shirt-numbers sanctioned by the FA during the 1930s before it was officially introduced at the start of the curtailed 1939-40 season.

United had finished the 1937-8 campaign in ninth place, disappointing considering their position halfway through the season, and with a tidy profit of £3,872.

But the predictions were for harder financial times ahead and when Spurs came in with a £9,500 bid for Bert Sproston, very close to a Football League record, in June 1938, the United directors decided to sell their prized asset.

Sproston stayed at Tottenham only a matter of months because he could not settle in the capital, but Spurs quickly recouped their cash by selling him for the same price to Manchester City.

He travelled north with the Spurs team on a Friday, the deal was completed that night and the following afternoon he turned out for City against his old Tottenham teammates.

Hardly any of the Sproston cash which Leeds had obtained was available to Hampson for team building, so he switched Jack Milburn to right-back and gave Ken Gadsby an extended run at left-back.

Up front, Hodgson, now 34, went into his 14th League season and showed he had lost none of his appetite for goals, setting a United record by bagging five in the 8-2 thrashing of Leicester City on 1 October 1938, when visiting goalkeeper Sandy McClaren tore the tendons in an instep and was taken off.

Hampson had gambled that day on the selection of Jack Hargreaves, a reserve winger from Sheffield junior football, and the precocious new-comer, Cochrane.

Both were an instant hit and occupied the wing positions for most of the rest of the season in preference to Sammy Armes and Arthur Buckley.

There was also a welcome return to action for inside-forward Aubrey Powell, who defied medical advice and battled back from his broken leg after missing the entire 1937-8 season.

Jack Milburn eventually lost his place to Leeds-

born England Schoolboy international Les Goldberg and moved on to join Billy Furness at Norwich in March 1939.

But that transfer news was overshadowed by the return of Wilf Copping from Arsenal the same month, to add more backbone to an over-generous defence.

In the end it was a patchy, disappointing season, in which United had begun well once again, then fizzled out into mid-table mediocrity. However, Ken Gadsby and inside-forward George Ainsley earned some reward for their efforts by being selected for the FA tour of South Africa, in which both played in the Third Test Match, as they were called, in Johannesburg, although neither qualified as full internationals.

The only new face in United's 1939-40 line-up was Norman Wharton, a goalkeeper already in his mid-30s, who had shone during York City's thrilling FA Cup runs of the 1930s.

But Wharton had little time to get to know his new colleagues as the season was abandoned after only three games – Leeds lost two and drew one – because of the outbreak of World War Two. It would be six years before League football resumed.

Jack Milburn cannot prevent Charlton's George Tadman scoring his second goal in the FA Cup fourth-round game at The Valley in January 1938.

Norman Wharton, 36, was the only new face for United at the start of the 1939-40 season. The goalkeeper had played for Barrow, Preston, Sheffield United, Norwich (where he won a Third Division South championship medal), Doncaster and York. He made two appearances in the aborted season and retired during the war.

Leeds in World War Two

DURING the 1938-9 season, events in Europe – Germany's invasion of Czecho-slovakia and the Munich crisis – geared spectators towards believing that they were witnessing the last pre-war season.

Indeed, when the summer of 1939 arrived, it was widely accepted that conflict was inevitable. Military reservists had been called-up and plans to shut down entertainments had been discussed.

Against this background, Leeds United manager Billy Hampson pressed on with his plans for the new season and had the following players at his disposal before the kick-off against Preston on 26 August:

George Ainsley (signed from Bolton Wanderers in December 1936); John Brown (Third Lanark, May 1939); Bobby Browne (Derry City, October 1935); Arthur Buckley (Oldham Athletic, October 1936); David Cochrane (Portadown, November 1937); Wilf Copping (Arsenal, March 1939); Len Dunderdale (Watford, March 1939); Ken Gadsby (Middlecliffe Rovers, October 1934); Les Goldberg (local juniors, 1935); Jack Hargreaves (Sheffield juniors, August 1934); Billy Heaton (Whitkirk, December 1937); Gerry Henry (Outwood Stormcocks, 1937); Gordon Hodgson (Aston Villa, March 1937); Tom Holley (Barnsley, July 1936); Bob Kane (St Roch's, September 1935); Jim Makinson (Clitheroe, October 1935); James McGraw (Benburb, May 1938); Jim Milburn (Ashington, November 1935); Robert Montgomery (Portadown, September 1938); Aubrey Powell (Swansea Town, November 1935); George Scaife (local amateurs, May 1937); John Short (St Hilda's, February 1937); Alf Stephens (East Cramlington BW, September 1938); Bill Stephens (East Cramlington BW, September 1938); Eric Stephenson (Harrogate, September 1934); Harry Sutherland (Sedgeley Park, June 1938); Leslie Thompson (Middlecliffe Rovers, cs 1937); Jim Twomey (Newry Town, December 1937); Harry Vickers (local juniors 1937); Norman Wharton (York City, August 1939).

Jim Twomey strained a tendon in the opener against Preston with George Ainsley taking over between the posts for two-thirds of the game, but thanks to Ainsley, United hung on for a point in a goalless draw.

Hero Ainsley turned villain in midweek when he missed two clear-cut chances against Charlton, who snatched the points with the only goal 12 minutes from time, from George Tadman.

The Germans had already invaded Poland when Sheffield United ran out to play at Elland Road on 2 September. The atmosphere was tense with war possibly only hours away.

Even though the season was only three games old, United already had 14 men on the injured list and it was no surprise when the Blades won 1-0 in a game which saw Jim Milburn make his Leeds debut.

It hardly mattered that Leeds were bottom of the First Division when Neville Chamberlain announced that Britain was at war the following morning.

Football was suspended as a ban on the assembly of crowds was imposed and the contracts of all players were suspended. Many players were liable for conscription under the National Service Bill which enabled the call up of men aged between 18 and 41.

On 11 September, the Players Union gave permission for players to participate in games should the FA decide to reintroduce them and within days United lost 3-2 against Halifax Town in a friendly at The Shay.

The following week saw an honourable 2-2 draw at Newcastle and on the last day of the month, a 1,805 crowd saw manager Billy Hampson play as an emergency goalkeeper in a 3-1 win at Derby. Bradford City reversed that scoreline the next Saturday at Valley Parade, and on 14 October the first wartime friendly at Elland Road was played.

Cars were not allowed in streets in close proximity to the ground and the club's own car park was closed. The ground capacity had been halved, but that proved more than ample as United and Grimsby fought out a 2-2 draw.

Barnsley beat United 5-4 in a thriller at Oakwell before competitive football returned to Elland Road in the shape of Bradford City in the Regional League North-East Division, the first competition administered in wartime by the Football League.

By now many players were in receipt of a maximum 30 shillings £1.50) a week in wages and it was only by permission of the Army that United were able to play at Elland Road. Military requisition of premises led to administrative work being done in the Elland Road boardroom, visiting dressing-room and the tearooms. The War Office allowed United the use of the offices for only two hours a week on a Saturday.

Regular sentries were posted around the ground and on many occasions, directors and administration staff were challenged during the blackout.

A 3,000 crowd, complete with boxed gas masks,

saw United start their campaign in fine style with a 3-0 win, courtesy of Gordon Hodgson (2) and John Brown. George Swindin of Arsenal had become a policeman in Bradford and became United's first guest player as regular goalkeepers Jim Twomey and Norman Wharton were on war duty.

Severe weather saw only one game played from Christmas to 9 March as freezing fog and sub-zero temperatures in the harshest winter in 45 years claimed hundreds of lives.

With the banning of radio and newspaper weather forecasts it became difficult to arrange League games so a series of friendlies were arranged, but they attracted only sparse crowds.

Rationing had been introduced in January, but football continued to struggle on – and what a struggle it proved to be. The last home game of the 1939-40 season brought the only defeat at Elland Road, where Newcastle drew a paltry crowd of 200. Leeds had finished fifth out of 11 clubs competing in their division from the West Riding, Northumberland and Durham.

A knock-out competition called the League War Cup, run on a home and away basis, paired United with Sheffield Wednesday.

An Alf Stephens hat-trick steered Leeds to a 6-3 win over the Owls and despite going down 3-2 in the second leg, Leeds went through 8-5 on aggregate. However, Sunderland won the next round with the only goal over two games to eliminate United.

High-scoring matches were commonplace, nevertheless, as settled defences were hard to find because players were continually required or released by the Services.

For the second half of the season manager Billy Hampson secured goalkeeper Alex Lee from the RAF and by the end of the campaign several other United players were in uniform. Bobby Browne, Wilf Copping and Eric Stephenson became Sergeant PT instructors in the Army, whilst other recruits to khaki uniforms included Arthur Buckley, Billy Heaton, Tom Holley, Jim Milburn, Robert Montgomery, Bob Kane, Harry Sutherland, and twins Alf and Bill Stephens, whilst George Ainsley and Jack Hargreaves donned RAF blue.

Many of the players turned out for clubs nearest their training bases, notably for Aldershot who boasted one of the strongest sides in the country.

The summer of 1940 was one of the worst periods of the war with France falling on 22 June, three weeks after the BEF evacuation from the Dunkirk beaches.

When the new season, such as it was, kicked-off on 31 August, the Battle of Britain was under way and the terrifying Blitz had begun.

Arsenal goalkeeper George Swindin, by now a wartime policeman in Bradford, became Leeds United's first guest player of World War Two.

Throughout the country, tens of thousands of people were to lose their homes during the bombing by the Luftwaffe and the wail of air-raid sirens became familiar to the people of Leeds as bombs rained down on Kirkstall Forge and other centres of industry. Happily, though, Leeds suffered less than many industrial centres.

Somehow football continued in its makeshift form with Leeds United taking part in the North Regional League which involved teams as far north as Newcastle, south to Chesterfield, east to Hull City and west to Everton.

Chesterfield won both their games at Elland Road and when they triumphed 3-2 in the second match, goalkeeper Alex Lee played in an outfield position for Leeds because of injury and scored both goals.

United secured 15th place from 36 clubs at an average of 1.148 in a season where goal-average determined League positions.

Jim Makinson was the only ever-present, including appearances in the League War Cup, in a season in which 38 players were fielded.

Many were guests, Len Townsend (Brentford) finishing as top scorer with 11 goals. Other well-known players of the day who turned out for Leeds included Horace Baird (Huddersfield), Harold Baker (Bradford), George Burditt (Wrexham), Tom Farrage (Birmingham), Harry Goslin (Bolton), John Daniels (Tranmere), Hugh McTavish (Watford), Harold Meens (Hull City), Septimus Spike (Newcastle), United old boy Jack Milburn (Norwich) and Johnny Mahon (Huddersfield), a winger who had played for Leeds well before the war.

In the summer of 1941, Britain stood alone in the war against Hitler but the unquenchable spirit of the nation was even reflected among the United supporters who donated their clothes ration coupons so the club could have a new strip.

The 1941-2 season saw the Northern Section split into two championships with the first ending at Christmas – a time when hopes were raised on the Allies front by the entry of the USA into the conflict following Japan's attack on Pearl Harbor.

Leeds struggled on their travels with only one win, but centre-forward Gerry Henry played in all 18 games, scoring 15 goals, including four in a game against Newcastle.

In the second championship, United did not qualify for a League position as their 17 games was one short of inclusion in the table.

All but two games played were double-headers, with results counting to either the Combined Counties Cup or the League War Cup qualifying competition as well as the League.

Henry added 13 more goals in the second half of the season, including four against Doncaster, to collect a seasonal tally of 28.

A staggering 53 players were used, of which 21 were registered Leeds United players and included a newcomer, Colin Adam.

Among the guests were Beaumont Asquith (Barnsley), Reg Attwell (West Ham), George Bratley (Hull City), Stan Burton (Wolves), Tom Bush (Liverpool), Reg Clarke (Aldershot), Harry Eastham (Brentford), Peter Harvey (West Ham), Alex Keeping (Fulham), Willie Kidd (Chesterfield), Eric Lichfield (Newcastle), Archie Livingston (Newcastle), Duncan McClure (Hearts), Ralph Maddison (Doncaster Rovers), Bernard Ramsden (Liverpool), Johnny Shafto (Liverpool), Robert Shanks (Crystal Palace), John Turner (Bristol City), George Warburton (Chester) and John Wesley (Bradford).

The 1942-3 season took the same format as its predecessor with two titles available. In the first championship, United struggled to 43rd out of 48 clubs, and did little better in the second championship, finishing 47th out of 54 teams.

There were some terrible beatings, including a 9-0 hammering at Newcastle on 23 January 1943 – the heaviest defeat at any level by a Leeds United first team.

But such were the uncertainties of wartime football that United slammed Newcastle 7-2 at Elland Road the following week, with nine of the side that had lost so heavily at St James' Park seven days earlier. Aubrey Powell, hotly tipped as a future Welsh international, scored four times for Leeds.

Leeds were involved in another curious game with Newcastle before the end of the season when they fought back from 4-0 down with 20 minutes to go to win 5-4.

Leeds fulfilled a 34-game programme, using a remarkable 70 players and included new signings Albert Wakefield, a forward from Stanningley Works, defender Frank Butterworth, brothers Harry and Rex Houldershaw and Dennis Kirby, a wing-half who continued to work in his reserved occupation as a miner.

Once again the club leant heavily on guest players which included the following roll-call of talent: Jimmy Argue (Birmingham), Cliff Binns (Barnsley), Frank Bokas (Barnsley), Walter Boyes (Everton), Tom Bush (Liverpool), Robson Campbell (Charlton), Albert Dainty (Preston), John Daniels (Tranmere), Harry Eastham (Brentford), Reg Fallaize (Halifax), Norman Fowler (Middlesbrough), Bernard Harper (Barnsley), Billy Harris (Watford), John Harston (Wolves), Jack Hick (Bristol City), Bill Jones (Barnsley), Bill 'W.H.' Jones (Liverpool), Bill Kinghorn (Liverpool), Reg Lambert (Liverpool),

John MacInnes (Liverpool), Amos Moss (Aston Villa), George Patterson (Liverpool), Arthur Rhodes (Cardiff), Eddie Rutherford (Rangers), Phil Taylor (Liverpool), Walter Taylor (Grimsby), Ray Warren (Bristol Rovers), George Wilcox (Derby), Ken Wilkinson (Huddersfield), Tom Williams (Cardiff) and Richard Woffinden (Barnsley).

Guest List Guessing Game

With more players than ever in uniform, further emphasis was placed on the guest system as players in the Services required a commanding officer's approval for leave.

When Service duties allowed, players were released and they arrived from all directions on the morning of the match, or travelling independently from the main party to away games.

It proved an administrative nightmare. Rarely did teams turn out 'as selected' and on one match day at 12.30pm, United secretary Arthur Crowther had received notification of five late withdrawals, but a side was fielded that afternoon.

Away games regularly saw trainer Bob Roxburgh, the former Newcastle player, drag men off station platforms and through the carriage window of a locked door into corridors already crowded with suffocating travellers.

Availability of guests was generally by word of mouth recommendation from players, officials and even supporters.

Often this led to farce. The selection of Sid Anson for a home game against York City proved that point.

Leeds had been informed that Stan Hanson, the Bolton Wanderers player, had been posted to a nearby military camp.

Needless to say Leeds got the wrong man and fielded the unheard of Sid Anson, whose performance was not quite what United fans had expected.

It was only after the game, which United won 2-1, that the real story emerged. Stan Hanson was abroad at the time and Sid Anson had been only too pleased at the honour of playing for Leeds United.

There was a great air of optimism on the war front as the 1943-4 campaign commenced but United's aspirations were soon dashed. A 7-1 hammering at Sunderland was followed by a couple of 5-1 home defeats against the Rokermen and neighbours Bradford City.

The first championship finished with United 27th out of 50 clubs, Gerry Henry again finishing as top scorer with a dozen goals.

Seven straight wins at Elland Road brought hopes of success in the second championship, but

away form was poor, including an 8-1 humiliation at York, so United managed 35th place.

Of the class of 1939, only United men Ken Gadsby, Gerry Henry, Jim McGraw, Jim Makinson and Aubrey Powell, soon to earn wartime honours for Wales, were appearing with any regularity. Both Willis Edwards and Gordon Hodgson had taken up coaching and secretarial duties to ensure United were able to field a team each Saturday.

Stoke City's George Antonio guested for Leeds in 1943-4.

Once again the club were dependent on guests and among those who played under United's banner in the 1943-4 season were George Antonio (Stoke), Reg Attwell (West Ham), Walter Boyes (Everton), Jack Challinor (Stoke), Norman Corbett (West Ham), Robert Curry (Sheffield Wednesday), John Daniels (Tranmere), John Davie (Brighton), Cecil Davies (Charlton), George Dewis (Leicester), George Darling (Tottenham), John Dowen (Hull), Reg Fallaize (Halifax), Arthur Farrell (Bradford), Tom Galley (Wolves), Arthur Glover (Barnsley), Sid Jones (Arsenal), Clarrie Jordan (Doncaster), John Kirton (Stoke), Walter McKellar (Huddersfield), Johnny Mahon (Huddersfield), George Milburn (Chesterfield), Jack Milburn (Norwich), Tom O'Neill (New-castle), Herbert Padgett (Sheffield Wednesday), Tom Paton (Bournemouth), George Poland (Liverpool), Arthur Rhodes (Cardiff), Alf Rozier (Fulham), Norman Sharp (Everton), Freddie Steel (Stoke), Tim Ward (Derby), George Wilcox (Derby), Cyril Williams (Bristol City) and Horace Wright (Wolves).

Another to be added to the list above was Everton centre-half Maurice Lindley, who became a crucial part of the successful back-room staff of the Revie era.

United also continued to sign on players,

Leeds United with guest players in 1944-5. Back row (left to right): Bob Roxburgh (trainer), Frank Butterworth, Bob Shotton (Barnsley), Jim Twomey, Jack Milburn, Robson Campbell (Chelsea), Sam Weaver (Chelsea). Front row: Eddie Burbanks (Sunderland), Cyril Coyne, Gerry Henry, Tom Hindle, John Paton (Celtic).

including John Dutchman, Tom Hindle, John Hodgson, Maurice Lawn, Jackie Moule, Billy Tatton and Jack Yeomanson.

The Allied invasion of Normandy in June 1944 gave everybody a great boost and when the 1944-5 season kicked-off, attendances shot up throughout the country.

Attendances at Elland Road hit five-figures for the first time since 1939, but on the field United failed to find any consistency, finishing 22nd out of 54 teams in the first championship and 32nd out of 60 in the second championship.

Hindle, a former Keighley Town player, finished as top scorer with 26 goals.

The mystery of the season came as the team bus was returning from a game in Hartlepools on 25 November 1944, when a projectile shot through the coach and narrowly missed Jack Milburn and his brother Jimmy, who was accompanying the team while recovering from wounds received on active service in Belgium.

The bus was stopped and small holes were found in windows on either side of the vehicle. They were similar to bullet holes but no gun shot had been heard and nothing seen as the bus had meandered down a dark and deserted country lane.

One wag reckoned that the Germans were trying to finish Jimmy Milburn off, but no explanation was ever discovered as to what exactly had happened.

Among those guesting for United in 1944-5 were Walter Birch (Rochdale), Frank Bokas (Barnsley), Sammy Booth (Cardiff), Eddie Burbanks (Sunderland), who later joined Leeds for a brief spell under Raich Carter, Tom Byrom (Tranmere), Alf Calverley (Huddersfield), Robson Campbell (Chelsea), John Daniels (Tranmere), Steve Forde (West Ham), Colin Gleave (Stockport), Arthur Glover (Barnsley), Ken Harper (Walsall), John James (Bradford), Johnny Mahon (Huddersfield), Jack Milburn (Norwich), Norman Morton (Sunderland), Sid 'Skinner' Normanton (Barnsley), John Paton (Celtic), Bill Pickering (Sheffield Wednesday), Jacob Ruecroft (Halifax), Bob Shotton (Barnsley), Tom Ward (Sheffield Wednesday) and Sam Weaver (Chelsea).

Fallen Heroes

The season ended for United at the end of April and within a fortnight there was peace in Europe.

The final wartime season had proved a tragedy to United as three players lost their lives in the war.

England international Eric Stephenson, a stylish inside-forward, had gone on from being a PTI to receive a commission from the Brigade of Gurkhas and had achieved the rank of major when he was killed in action in Burma on 8 September 1944 at the age of 30.

The following year, on 28 July 1945, Leslie Thompson (24), who had won three England Schoolboy caps in 1936, also lost his life, whilst serving in Burma with the 2nd Battalion, The Welch Regiment. The young man from the Dearne Valley area arrived at Leeds from Middlecliffe Rovers, the club which had produced Wilf Copping and Ken Gadsby.

Irishman Robert Montgomery, one of the first Leeds players to enlist, shortly after joining the club from Portadown, was the first Leeds player to be reported dead in 1944. He was killed over Germany on 30 January, whilst serving as a sergeant with 514 Squadron, RAFVR.

Former United forward Alan Fowler, who had joined Swindon Town, was a sergeant in the Dorset Regiment when he was killed in France on 10 July 1944, aged 37. A plaque dedicated to his memory can be found at Swindon's County Ground.

Guest players Tom Farrage and Harry Goslin also died. Private Farrage was killed whilst fighting with the Parachute Regiment at Arnhem on 23 September 1944. He was 26. Lieutenant Goslin was killed in Italy on 18 December 1943.

Several Leeds players were involved in the Services, some seeing action abroad and others being restricted to British camps.

Billy Heaton, Tom Holley, and Jim Milburn saw active service in India, the latter being later wounded in Belgium where Aubrey Powell was also stationed.

Bob Kane was with the Royal Artillery in Gibraltar, whilst Albert Wakefield saw service in Italy where he played so well in Services football that several Italian clubs were keen to sign him.

Wilf Copping was involved in the North African campaign whilst the Stephens twins, Alf and Bill, were both Royal Engineers and were taken prisoner, ending up in the same POW camp.

Another captive was the Earl of Harewood, president of Leeds United since 1961. An Old Etonian, he was held in Colditz from November 1944 following direct orders from Adolf Hitler that he became one of a small group of VIP hostages.

A captain in the Grenadier Guards, he had been wounded and captured shortly after D-Day.

Goalkeeper Alex Lee, who left Leeds for Northampton Town during the war, was awarded the Air Force Medal.

Two well-known United personalities also disappeared from the Elland Road scene – Albert Stead and Mark Barker.

Stead retired in 1945 after over 40 years' service as trainer and groundsman, being at the club when the change over from rugby to soccer took place.

WARTIME REPRESENTATIVE GAMES AT ELLAND ROAD

13 December 1941
FA XI 2   RAF 2
Rowley, Compton   Smith, Dodds
FA XI: Hesford (Huddersfield T); Goldberg (Leeds U), Beattie (Preston NE), Willingham (Huddersfield T), Vose (Manchester U), Mercer (Everton), Birkett (Newcastle U), Mannion (Middlesbrough), Rowley (Manchester U), Hagan (Sheffield U), D.Compton (Arsenal).
RAF: Marks (Arsenal); A.Turner (Charlton A), Hapgood (Arsenal), Soo (Stoke C), Jones (Everton), Paterson (Celtic), Kirchen (Arsenal), Smith (Crystal Palace), Dodds (Blackpool), Jones (Arsenal), Wrigglesworth (Manchester U).
Attendance: 13,000

21 February 1942
Northern Command 1   Scottish Command 1
Robinson   Hamilton
Northern Command: Harkness (Hearts); Westwood (Manchester C), Beattie (Preston NE), Kirton (Stoke C), Holley (Leeds U), McInnes (Liverpool), Powell (Leeds U), Balmer (Liverpool), Steele (Stoke C), Robinson (Sheffield), Boyes (Everton).
Scottish Command: Lynch (Dundee); Carabine (Third Lanark), Winning (Rangers), Busby (Liverpool), Betmead (Grimsby T), Collier (Third Lanark), Campbell (Falkirk), Walker (Hearts), Hamilton (Aberdeen), McCall (Aberdeen), Johnson (Motherwell).
Attendance: 8,500

26 December 1942
The Army 3   The RAF 1
Hagan, Westcott 2   Dodds
The Army: Swift (Manchester C); Carabine (Third Lanark), L.Compton (Arsenal), Britton (Everton), Cullis (Wolves), Mercer (Everton), Birkett (Newcastle U), Hagan (Sheffield U), Westcott (Wolves), Bremner (Arsenal), D.Compton (Arsenal).
RAF: Marks (Arsenal); Hardwick (Middlesbrough), Hughes (Birmingham), Shankly (Preston NE), Joy (Arsenal), Paterson (Celtic), Matthews (Stoke C), Carter (Sunderland), Dodds (Blackpool), Soo (Stoke C), Kirchen (Arsenal).
Attendance: 20,000 (Receipts of £1,056 went to the RAF Benevolent Fund and Army charities).

George Laking of Middlesbrough, another of United's many wartime guest players.

Barker, who was on United's first board of directors, died in January 1943 after 23 years' continual service, leaving J.Hilton Crowther as the only survivor from the original directors.

It was not an easy task keeping the club going during the war years, but chairman Ernest Pullan did a marvellous job. A director since 1926, he had become chairman in 1937 and continued until 1948.

With the war gradually coming to an end, the Football League decided not to return to normal until 1946-7 because so many players were still in the Services and clubs needed time to repair scarred grounds and playing surfaces.

One last 'wartime' season was played in 1945-6, with United featuring as one of 22 clubs in the Football League Northern Section.

Just the one championship of 42 games was played with the players receiving £4 a week.

United opened up with five successive defeats and eventually finished bottom with only 25 points, George Ainsley finishing as top scorer with 20 goals.

The defence had a torrid time, leaking 118 goals, including nine at Bradford and eight at Preston.

Among the new men United signed up were Bill Alberry, Bob Batey, Jack Duthoit, Harry Fearnley, Dennis Grainger, Donald Pogson and Arthur Price.

On the guest list were the likes of Doug Blair (Blackpool), Eddie Burbanks (Sunderland), Jackie Chew (Burnley), Austin Collier (York), Robert Duffy (Blackpool), George Hudson (Portsmouth), Lloyd Iceton (Preston), Eric Jones (Brentford), Sid Jones (Arsenal), Fred Laidman (Sunderland), George Laking (Middlesbrough), Harry Oliver (Hartlepools), Willie Parker (Wolves), Alf Pope (Halifax), Willie Skidmore (Wolves), Jack Smith (Chelsea) and Fred Westlake (Sheffield Wednesday).

In 1945-6, however, the FA Cup was staged after a seven-year lay-off and it was decided for the first, and only, time that games would be played over two legs on a home and away basis.

Leeds were paired with Middlesbrough and, in common with a stack of other games, the tie produced an avalanche of goals.

The first leg at Elland Road finished 4-4 and although they scored first at Ayresome Park, United crashed 7-2 – all Middlesbrough's goals coming in a remarkable first half.

Elland Road also hosted several representative games during the war.

Post-war Depression

PICKING up the pieces after World War Two was never going to be easy but no one could have foreseen the horrendous season United were going to suffer.

They finished bottom of Division One, well detached from the rest of the pack, after winning only six games.

Astonishingly only one point was obtained in away matches and a run of defeats at home, which started at Christmas, made the position irretrievable.

Both the number of points (18) and defeats (30) were an unwanted record as morale collapsed over the last four months of the season when only two points were obtained from the last 17 matches.

On paper Billy Hampson seemed to have a decent side at his disposal, sticking loyally by many of the men who played under him in the late 1930s but it soon became apparent that too many had lost their best playing years to the war.

Pre-war survivors included George Ainsley, Les Goldberg, Bobby Browne, Aubrey Powell, Tom Holley, Jim Twomey, Ken Gadsby and David Cochrane.

Technically, Jim Milburn could be added to that list. He had made his debut in the final game of the aborted 1939-40 season and had to wait seven years before making his proper League debut in the opening game of the 1946-7 season at Preston.

Lining up with them were an assortment of rookie players who had made a good impression in wartime games, young men like Gerry Henry and John Short.

Ainsley was selected to lead the attack and veteran Gordon Hodgson, who had done an excellent coaching job for United during the hostilities, joined Port Vale as manager.

Hodgson had struck just over half a century of

Veteran centre-half Ken Willingham joined Leeds United in March 1947, after 14 years with Huddersfield and a short spell with Sunderland.

goals in 82 League games for United and certainly saved them from relegation in 1936-7.

Tragically he died only five years after leaving Elland Road when he was still in office at Port Vale.

Hampson knew he had to strengthen the team but United were hard-up so he was fairly limited in what he could do, making only modest signings.

His biggest gamble was made by signing versatile Eire international Con Martin for £8,000 from Glentoran in the hope that he could be used in a variety of roles.

A couple of months later, Harry Clarke, the Darlington centre-forward was added to the squad, but he suffered a nightmare time at Elland Road, scoring only once in 14 games and never featuring on a winning side.

By the time former England international defender Ken Willingham joined Leeds from Sunderland, United were already as good as relegated.

Right-half Willingham, 34, had been one of

Leeds United delegate Mr S.L. Blenkinsop addresses the 1947 annual meeting of the Football League in London. The game was just getting back on its feet and attendances were booming in direct contrast to the austerity of early post-war Britain.

Huddersfield Town's pre-war all-time greats, winning a dozen England caps, but not even his vast experience could stem the depression at Elland Road.

Troubles were not just confined to the pitch. The directors were still wrestling with the problem of debentures which was hanging like a millstone around the club's neck.

At the annual meeting in the Griffin Hotel in Leeds, several holders of large shares agreed to take ordinary shares in lieu of their debentures, while others surrendered their holding entirely.

The value of the debenture was reduced by about £15,000 and shareholders voted the directors power to borrow up to £25,000 to help keep the club afloat.

There was also a shake-up on the board with three new directors elected – Percy Woodward, Harold Marjason and Robert Wilkinson.

Inevitably there was a change on the playing front after such a disastrous season with Hampson stepping down as team manager and taking on the role of chief scout, a position he held for only eight months before he went freelance.

Edwards Takes Charge for a Year

The new man in the manager's chair was Willis Edwards, who had been assistant trainer to Bob Roxburgh since hanging up his boots.

Edwards had old gold and blue blood running through his veins but the United stalwart was unable to reverse the losing trend and there were genuine fears that United would slide straight

through the Second Division into the Third Division North for the first time in the club's history.

Edwards began by clearing out a big batch of reserves and transferring Irish international Bobby Browne to York City and opted to stand by the men who were on call at the end of the 1946-7 season.

United tuned up for their first spell in the Second Division in 16 years with a three-match tour to the Republic of Ireland, where the emphasis was placed on attack, something which had been blunted in the previous dreadful season.

The responsibility of goalscoring was heaped upon the shoulders of Albert Wakefield, a 25-year-old Pudsey-born player who had excelled in services football and could have earned a living in the Italian League at the end of the war. He had played for Leeds in wartime and while serving in Italy turned down offers from clubs in that country.

Wakefield certainly added more punch to United's attack with 21 League goals but the team struggled for consistency and more changes were made throughout the season.

George Ainsley and Gerry Henry both went to Bradford in November 1947 and Edwards replaced them in attack and defence respectively with Ken Chisholm and Jim Bullions.

A fighter pilot during the war, Chisholm looked set for a high-flying soccer career which began in his native Scotland at Partick Thistle, joining Leeds from the latter where his probings at inside-

forward saw several English clubs run the rule over his progress.

Bullions, another Scot, the youngest member of Derby County's 1946 FA Cup winning side, was a ball-winner who had turned down an offer to play for Blackpool in his earlier days to start work as a miner in Derbyshire.

A third newcomer arrived towards the end of the season in the shape of Jim McCabe in a swap deal with Middlesbrough.

United paid £10,000 and threw in goalkeeper John Hodgson into the bargain for the versatile Derry man McCabe, who was knocking on the door for full Irish honours.

The Irish selectors answered within months of his move to Leeds by picking him to play against Scotland.

United's final 1947-8 position of 18th in Division Two was the club's lowest since it joined the League and apart from the goals of Wakefield, the strength of Holley at the back and the craft of Welsh international inside-forward Aubrey Powell, there was little for United's fans to cheer about.

Holley was now starting to forge a new career as a journalist with the *Yorkshire Evening Post*, keeping the fans in touch with events behind the scenes at the club as well as on the pitch.

Despite two poor seasons in succession, the Elland Road faithful continued to turn up in their thousands. They had been starved of competitive soccer throughout the war and football enjoyed a boom in attendances in the immediate post-war years, with struggling Leeds being no exception.

Haulier Sam Bolton Moves up a Gear
The rigours of wartime had left their mark on Elland Road and there was not a lot of cash about to improve and tidy the ground. Plans to concrete the terracing behind the Geldard Road End had to be postponed because the club were denied a licence by the Ministry of Works, which did not deem it essential work in these post-war days of austerity.

Building work was still required on the team too but Willis Edwards decided he was not the man to do it.

After only a year in charge, he resigned in April 1948, and returned to his old job as assistant trainer.

The stalwart Edwards remained on the backroom staff a further ten years to take his total service with the club to 35 – an outstanding record. He later worked in a jam factory in Leeds and by the time he died, aged 85, in 1988, he had lived long enough to witness the club's golden era under Don Revie. But those halcyon days could never have been imagined as United, struggling for cash and managerless, finished the 1947-8 season at a low ebb.

But one man who was determined to look on the bright side was chairman Sam Bolton, who had been elected earlier in the year following the resignation of Eric Clarke, who had done so much to keep the club running during wartime.

Bolton, a wealthy motor-haulage contractor, had gone a long way down the road to success in business and was determined to get United along the same track.

Born and bred in Leeds, he was educated at Hunslet School and joined Thomas Spence Ltd, a haulage company, and went on to become its managing director.

During World War One he served with the Coldstream Guards before joining the Royal Flying Corps. During World War Two he served as a captain in the RAF, winning the DFC.

A soccer fanatic, he played for Rothwell White Rose in the Leeds League, watched Leeds City play as a 'bob-side' youngster a reference to the days when it cost a shilling to watch a game – and was good enough to have trials with Leeds City.

Although he was not taken on by City, he followed their fortunes, and that of United, closely and in 1945 had completed the rise from United fan to United director.

A large man of immense drive, Bolton thrived on hard work and lifted the profile of his post as chairman even though he was also serving the people of Leeds in his capacity as a Tory city councillor.

He was a typical Tyke, bluff and straight to the point – a trait which no doubt helped persuade one of the biggest names in soccer management to come to ailing United's aid, the legendary Major Frank Buckley.

Jimmy Bullions had just won an FA Cup winners' medal with Derby County before signing for Leeds in November 1947.

A Major Coup

THE capture of the redoubtable Major Frank Buckley got the football world buzzing. Buckley was regarded as one of the most free-thinking managers in the game, a man whose reign at Wolves won much acclaim.

He had turned the Molineux club from a debt-ridden side struggling near the bottom of Division Two into one of the most entertaining teams in the First Division.

Now Leeds wanted him to do the same kind of job at Elland Road, even though the Major had reached the age of 64.

Some considered him to be an eccentric maverick but his knowledge of the game was unsurpassed and his arrival at Leeds immediately got the city talking.

Major Frank Buckley, pictured at the Co-op Arcade, Leeds, just after taking over as manager at Elland Road.

One thing was certain, life was certainly not going to be dull with the Major around.

His managerial skills have tended to overshadow the fact that he was also an outstanding centre-half before the war, winning an England cap against Ireland in 1914.

After spells with Aston Villa, Brighton, Manchester United and Manchester City, Buckley enjoyed two fine seasons with Birmingham before joining Derby in May 1911 where he won his England honour – albeit in a shock defeat by Ireland. During his playing days he also helped run a pig farm with his brother, Chris, the former Aston Villa and Arsenal defender.

But it was within the soccer world where he was to cultivate a reputation as being a strict disciplinarian full of innovative ideas.

He retired from his last club, Bradford City, in 1918 and served as a major in the Footballers' Battalion – a rank which was to stick with him throughout his managerial days. He was first appointed boss of Norwich City, staying for a year, before becoming a commercial traveller in London until July 1923, when he became Blackpool's manager.

Four years later he went to struggling Wolves and transformed the club, guiding them to the Division Two title in 1932 and making them a power during the war years. He introduced new training methods at Molineux and Wolves were undoubtedly one of the fittest sides in the land.

The Major was also no mug when it came to the financial aspect of running a club.

By boldly selling off star players and bringing on youngsters, he was able to wipe out Wolves' debts and in a four-year period leading up to World War Two he netted Wolves an estimated £110,658 in transfer fees.

At first it was not always a popular policy and furious Wolves fans demonstrated loudly against the sale of their best players, but the Major stuck by his guns, rode out the criticism and turned

Wolves into one of the most powerful clubs in the land.

One of the most publicised stunts he pulled at Molineux, and one which he was to repeat at Leeds, was treating some of his players with monkey gland extract.

The idea was to sharpen players' thinking, but whether it worked could not be discovered and many thought it was just a psychological ploy by the crafty Major to get the players to believe in themselves.

Such managerial skills earned him a life contract with Wolves, but in March 1944 he moved on to Notts County, who were reported to be paying him a record salary of £4,000.

Money, though, is not always everything and after two years at Meadow Lane he joined Hull City where he stayed two further seasons before being persuaded by Sam Bolton to join Leeds United.

Selling Stars to Lower Debts

Anyone who thought the strict Buckley had mellowed over the years was wrong as he swept through Elland Road like a tornado, taking charge of virtually every aspect of the club.

Always a man to speak his mind and a clever publicist, Buckley told the board he could bring success to the club, but first they had to get their finances in order and said United would not get anywhere until the £30,000 debentures weighing the club down were wiped out.

Cost-cutting became the Major's battle orders. Admission prices on the Lowfields Road terraces were raised and some of United's top talent was sold off.

The first to go was slender Welsh international inside-forward Aubrey Powell, who went to Everton for £10,000. United banked a similar sum when another international, the versatile Irish star Con Martin, departed to Aston Villa shortly afterwards.

The Major, a constant advocate of youth, was not afraid to give some of the younger players an extended run in the side.

He would spend hours scouring the parks of Leeds looking for potential stars and was determined to get the club more involved in the community by organising and refereeing games himself for younger players invited for trials.

It was not long before some of the youngsters started to come through, although some only played a handful of senior games.

Half-back David McAdam was plucked from Derbyshire non-League club Stapenhill WMC and thrust into Division Two action within months.

Leeds-born Len Browning, a 6ft 2in slimline 20-year-old centre-forward, who was excellent in the air, led the line alongside the experienced Ken Chisholm, after Albert Wakefield was kept out of action with a cartilage problem.

Jimmy Dunn, signed from Scottish junior club Rutherglen Glencairn, cemented his place alongside Jim Milburn at right-back after breaking through the previous season.

Although the Major was a born leader off the pitch, he still required a man to lead his men on the field, so he turned back the clock to his Wolves days to sign half-back Tommy Burden.

Buckley had given Burden his first break at Wolves as a 16-year-old and after the war, Burden had studied physical education at Loughborough College and was on Chester's books, when he linked up with the Major for a second time.

Taking Unusual Steps in Training

Buckley's preparations for the new season were meticulous. Players were put through long, gruelling training sessions while the Major emphasised the need for tip-top fitness by demonstrating high-kicking routines and press-ups to players who were over 40 years younger than him.

His training methods were revolutionary, sometimes bizarre. Players would pair up with each other and dance on the pitch while popular music blared out over the public address system – the idea being to give them more balance and dexterity.

For accurate shooting practice, house bricks were piled up and a football placed on top with the result that any inaccurate kick would lead to a bruised foot!

Buckley also pioneered a mechanical 'kicking machine'. Built like a tubular steel rocket, it was able to release footballs, one at a time, at varying heights. It was used to test goalkeepers, sharpen up players' heading ability and their first-time trapping and kicking skills.

Yet, despite all these new-fangled ideas, United crashed 6-2 on the opening day of the 1948-9 season at Leicester, goals by Ken Chisholm and John Short, one of United's wartime discoveries, saving United from total humiliation.

By October, United were in mid-table, but Buckley was convinced that his men were not playing to their full potential because they could not quickly recognise their teammates in old gold and blue halved shirts.

So he organised a practice match with one team in plain shirts and the other in the club colours while chairman Sam Bolton and director Percy Woodward watched from the touchlines.

The persuasive Buckley got the board to change the strip to old gold shirts, blue sleeves and collars, white shorts and black, blue and old gold hooped socks.

But the change of club colours did not bring a real revival in the team's fortunes.

It took United's players some time to become accustomed to the Major's methods and this was reflected on the pitch as they laboured to put together cohesive football.

Buckley and his team faced a mounting barrage of criticism in those early months which came to a head when Newport County, bottom of the Third Division South, outplayed United in the third round of the FA Cup at Elland Road to win more easily than the 3-1 scoreline suggests.

Boo-boys barracked the players and were already calling for the Major to go, but he remained defiant.

"In 12 months time the people of Leeds will be acclaiming Leeds United and me," he boldly predicted.

The prophecy was to prove correct, but in the meantime the battling Major had to resolve the crisis of confidence that was sweeping through Elland Road.

He dived into the transfer market to stem the flow of bad results, exchanging Ken Chisholm for Leicester City's Ray Iggleden, and swapping inside-forward Tom Hindle, another product of wartime football, for Billy Rudd of York City.

Centre-forward Eddie McMorran, a former Irish blacksmith, was signed from Manchester City, and £2,000 was spent on Mansfield goalkeeper Harry Searson.

To balance the books, inside-forward John Short had been transferred to Millwall for £4,000 and winger Billy Heaton fetched £7,000 when he was sold to Southampton.

To make such wholesale changes during a season was a pretty drastic step, but it worked as United managed to pick up enough points in the final few months to creep into 15th place, just two points clear of relegation.

Browning showed plenty of promise in his first season, finishing as top scorer with 13 goals from 24 League games, Jim Milburn was the only ever-present, while skipper Tommy Burden, the experienced Jim McCabe, and his fellow Irish international David Cochrane, could also look back on their performance with a degree of pride.

Journalist centre-half Tom Holley was coming to the end of his career but the astute Major Buckley had already found a ready-made replacement in the shape of a man-mountain of a teenager from Wales, John Charles, who was first spotted by United's scout in Wales, Jack Pickard.

Buckley signed Charles on his 16th birthday from under Swansea's noses and within three months the strapping Welsh lad made his first-team debut as Holley's replacement in a friendly against Queen of the South, when he marked Scottish international centre-forward Billy Houliston out of the game.

A fortnight later, on 23 April 1949, the teenage newcomer made his Football League debut in a goalless draw at Blackburn.

Those among the 18,873 crowd at Ewood Park that day probably did not realise it, but they had witnessed the birth of a football legend.

The Reign of King John

JOHN Charles had done enough in the final few games of the 1948-9 season to convince Major Buckley that he would have to look no further for a replacement for Tom Holley. Holley had decided to quit to concentrate on a full-time journalistic career, first with the *Yorkshire Evening Post*, then the *Sunday People*.

Having a ready-made replacement in young Charles saved United a small fortune and Buckley spent much of the summer wheeling and dealing to reshape his squad.

Out went goalkeeper Jim Twomey to Halifax, whilst centre-forward Albert Wakefield departed in a swap deal with Southend United for Frank Dudley, a versatile forward with a reputation for his powerful shooting.

One of the few good things to come out of the previous season's shock FA Cup defeat against Newport County was the capture of two of the Welsh club's heroes.

Little winger Harold Williams had tormented Leeds that afternoon, despite completing his early morning milk-round on the day of the big game.

The diminutive Williams, who wore size 5½ boots, already had a couple of Welsh caps to his name when he joined United in the summer with goalkeeper Alick Grant in exchange for £12,000 plus reserve centre-half Roly Depear, who was valued at £4,000.

Although Grant, a schoolteacher never made United's first team, little Williams did a grand job. Two-footed, he could play on either flank and it was fitting that the man who had been United's FA Cup torturer turned into one of their stars in a long overdue run in the competition.

Both United and their predecessors Leeds City had an appalling record in the FA Cup, neither ever managing to get past three rounds.

FA Cup Fever

That was to change in 1949-50 as Major Buckley worked some of his footballing magic.

United were just starting to show signs of clicking together when they were handed a third-round tie at Carlisle United, then managed by a young Bill Shankly. In past seasons it was the sort of game United would have lost, but in a devastating display United won 5-2 with goals from Frank Dudley (2), Len Browning, Harold Williams and David Cochrane.

That result lit the blue touch-paper on United's season and they began to burn off their opponents with some brilliant football – both in the FA Cup and in the Second Division.

Williams netted United's goal in the 1-1 fourth-round meeting with First Division Bolton.

Not even the most optimistic of United fans gave their team much hope in the replay but on a Burnden Park pitch ankle-deep in slush, battling United skated through to the fifth round with a giantkilling 3-2 win.

Goals by Frank Dudley and Len Browning put United in command, but the Trotters hit back to take the game into extra-time with goals by Harry McShane and Nat Lofthouse.

On a strength-sapping pitch it was United who grabbed the winner through Dudley after Browning had headed on a John Charles free-kick.

The result triggered an epidemic of FA Cup fever in Leeds. Everyone wanted to get in on the act and there was a massive demand for tickets to see the fifth-round tie against Cardiff at Elland Road.

To make sure die-hard fans did not miss out, the board decided to sell tickets for the tie at a Central League game against Bolton Reserves at Elland Road the Saturday before the Cardiff game.

John Charles, the greatest Leeds United player outside the Revie era. Charles signed for Leeds just after his 16th birthday and within three months had made his League debut, at Blackburn in April 1949. At 18 years and 71 days he became the youngest-ever Welsh international.

The response was amazing as 20,000 fans turned up for their priceless tickets.

Seven days later the roads to the stadium were clogged up as 53,099 supporters squeezed into Elland Road to watch United dispose of Cardiff 3-1 with goals by Williams, David Cochrane and Ray Iggleden to move into the quarter-finals for the first time in the club's history.

The draw the following Monday handed United a plum tie at First Division big guns, Arsenal.

The city of Leeds seemed to pull up its roots and head for London on 4 March, for the sixth-round showdown at Highbury which attracted an enormous 62,273 crowd.

It proved to be a tremendous end-to-end tussle but the goal which settled it went to Arsenal in the 52nd minute when Reg Lewis toe-poked in a centre from Freddie Cox.

Undeterred, United piled forward in the final 20 minutes and several times they went desperately close to the goal which would have earned them a replay.

Arsenal, with up to eight men packed into their box at the end, hung on and went on to win the FA Cup that year with a 2-0 Wembley success over Liverpool.

However, that sad exit did not signal the end of United's season, for the magic of the FA Cup had rubbed off on their League performances.

Over the second half of the season United soared up the table, their form at Elland Road being particularly devastating.

The highlight came with a thumping 3-0 win over runaway champions Tottenham, goals by Cochrane (2) and Iggleden ending Spurs' 22-match unbeaten run.

There were also a couple of extra League matches at Elland Road as United played good neighbour to Huddersfield Town after the main stand at Leeds Road was destroyed by fire in April.

For United director J.Hilton Crowther there must have been a heavy irony when Town played two First Division fixtures at Elland Road, for he was the man who had tried to take Huddersfield Town 'lock, stock and barrel' to Leeds 30 years earlier.

Huddersfield beat Derby 2-0 on Easter Saturday at Elland Road, then lost 2-1 to Newcastle there three days later.

All the critics were raving about John Charles, who became the youngest-ever Welsh international player – a record now held by Wolves defender Ryan Green – when he turned out with Harold Williams in a goalless draw against Ireland at Wrexham four days after that Cup defeat by Arsenal.

Despite their storming finish, United had left

Goalkeeper Harold Searson joined Leeds for £2,000 in January 1949. He moved to York two years later, after John Scott took over.

themselves too much to do in the race for promotion and eventually finished fifth.

That was good enough to make them favourites to go up the following season in many people's book.

Season of Anticlimax

Predictably Major Buckley made few changes, although Eddie McMorran moved on to Barnsley with reserve full-back Eddie Bannister.

The two new regulars were Eric Kerfoot, a non-stop wing-half picked up for a bargain £3,000 from Stalybridge Celtic, and Peter Harrison, the

Eric Kerfoot, a tireless half-back who signed from non-League Stalybridge Celtic for £3,000 in 1949. He went on to make nearly 350 League and Cup appearances for Leeds.

former Peterborough United winger who had played under Major Buckley as an amateur at Notts County. Harrison took over the number-seven shirt as David Cochrane retired shortly after playing in the opening two games of the 1950-51 season.

The ever-popular Cochrane had joined United in 1937 and although a large chunk of his playing career was lost to the war, he still clocked up 175 League appearances for the club.

But United could not pick up where they started off and by mid-season, Major Buckley was making changes.

John Scott, a former colliery blacksmith, signed from Workington, was given the chance to stake a claim for the goalkeeping job after Harry Searson was dropped.

The Major then recruited one of his former Wolves juniors, inside-left Ernie Stevenson, in an exchange deal which saw Frank Dudley, one of the heroes of the previous season, go to Southampton.

But the most unlikely player to pull on a Leeds shirt that season was an unknown, South African inside-forward, George Miller.

Recommended by a friend of the Major's, he was signed from Arcadia FC, a club in Western Province, and was later followed by fellow countrymen Ken Hastie, Gordon Stewart and John Skene throughout the 1950s, although their contributions proved limited.

Len Browning had a good season up front with 19 League goals, but as promotion hopes gradually slid away, Major Buckley experimented by switching John Charles from centre-half to centre-forward for three games.

The outcome? Three goals for the in-demand youngster. He had so much natural ability it seemed as though he could slot into any position. The possessor of delicate ball skills, Charles was virtually unbeatable in the air, firm in the tackle, neat in distribution, powerful in shot and possessor of a calm temperament.

Charles, still only 21, seemed the complete footballer. He had scouts and agents flocking to Elland Road in their droves, to such an extent, in fact, that United warned clubs off in an editorial notice in the club programme.

United again finished fifth in a season of anticlimax and this time there was no Cup run to excite the fans, even though some players were taking an advanced form of the notorious monkey gland treatment the Major had pioneered at Wolves. United were resigned to the fact that they would lose the talented Charles for some of the 1951-2 season, when he did his National Service in the Royal Tank Regiment.

Charles was virtually irreplaceable, but Roy Kirk, a versatile youngster signed from Bolsover Colliery, did well at centre-half as the young Welsh giant's stand-in.

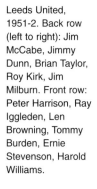

Leeds United, 1951-2. Back row (left to right): Jim McCabe, Jimmy Dunn, Brian Taylor, Roy Kirk, Jim Milburn. Front row: Peter Harrison, Ray Iggleden, Len Browning, Tommy Burden, Ernie Stevenson, Harold Williams.

Kirk was able to play in a variety of positions and relished a brief run in the forward line in the FA Cup, scoring both goals which put out Rochdale at Spotland. United beat neighbours Bradford 2-0 in the fourth round before losing to Chelsea after a second replay.

Kirk wore the number-nine shirt in two of those games against Chelsea as the centre-forward slot proved to be United's problem position.

Six players were tried. Len Browning kicked-off the season as the focal point of the attack, but after he was sold to Sheffield United for £12,000 in November 1951, the position was never filled successfully.

Kirk had a go, new signing Frank Fidler from Wrexham was tried, reserve Ron Barritt had a run out, John Charles had a few games up front, and even full-back Jimmy Milburn played a handful of games as an emergency centre-forward.

It was a problem which Major Buckley failed to resolve by the end of the season and under the circumstances United did well to stage a belated push for promotion to finish sixth, particularly as National Service and a cartilage injury restricted Charles to only 17 League games.

At home United did extremely well, losing only once, to Everton, in September, but on their travels were nowhere near as impressive.

In a season in which United had marked time, there was a bonus in the emergence of a cultured new left-back in Grenville Hair, yet another youngster plucked from non-League football by Major Buckley, who signed him from Burton & District League side Newhall United.

With Hair on the scene, Buckley allowed tough-tackling Jim Milburn to leave the club for Bradford – almost severing the link between the Milburn clan and Leeds United.

Jim, who had also developed into United's penalty-taker and free-kick specialist, departed with over 200 League games to his credit and continued to give excellent service at Park Avenue for a couple more seasons.

Although he joined George and Jack Milburn as former United players, their gangling 16-year-old nephew, Jack Charlton, was now playing for the juniors at the start of an extraordinary soccer career.

Charles turns Goal Stopper to Goal Scorer

United began 1952-3 with Don Mills, originally signed from Cardiff as an inside-forward for £12,000, in the problem centre-forward spot.

Ray Iggleden is challenged by Brentford goalkeeper Alf Jefferies during the 2-1 FA Cup defeat at Griffin Park in January 1953. The Leeds player on the far left is Albert Nightingale.

The job was then handed in turn to Frank Fidler; youngster Barry Smith; one of the South Africans, Ken Hastie; and, finally, John Charles, who became United's fifth centre-forward with only 13 games of the 1952-3 season gone.

United had only scratched a couple of wins in those 13 games and were lying fifth from bottom, but with Charles at centre-forward they looked much more potent in attack.

After an initial outing in a 2-1 defeat at Sheffield United, Charles and Mills both got on the score-sheet in a 4-1 home win over Barnsley the following week, 18 October.

United's other two goals against Barnsley came from Albert Nightingale, who had only just joined the club with diminutive winger George Meek.

Nightingale had been tracked by Major Buckley for several seasons and he finally nailed his man in a £10,000 deal with Blackburn Rovers.

Nightingale was already well known to Leeds fans after his days with Huddersfield Town, but Meek was a surprise package, and a small one at that.

Standing only 5ft 3ins tall, he was signed from Hamilton Academical, and his value to Leeds increased dramatically within weeks of his arrival at Elland Road as Harold Williams broke a leg at Everton in November.

With Nightingale and Meek brought into the forward line to supply Charles with chances, United looked to have more balance up front.

Plugging the gap at the back vacated by Charles was the experienced Irish international Jim McCabe, who was enjoying a new lease of life at centre-half alongside Eric Kerfoot and skipper Tommy Burden.

With Jimmy Dunn and Grenville Hair shaping up well at full-back and John Scott ever present between the posts, United looked a much more solid team. Hair's progress was marked by his selection for the FA XI against the Army in November 1952, whilst the Scottish selectors had run the rule over Dunn several times.

The presence of Charles up front totally transformed the attack as he blasted in 11 goals in his first six games in his new role.

By the end of the season he had chalked up 26 League goals – an astonishing return since he played at centre-half for the opening dozen games.

He adapted so well that the Welsh selectors chose him for their attack against Ireland in Belfast to confirm his status as the most complete young player in Great Britain.

The Major Retreats from Elland Road

By now United were dubbed, unfairly, 'Charles United' by the Press and the pressure continued to mount on United to sell their young colossus, but clubs were given the curt message that Charles was simply not for sale.

Rumours were rife in the newspapers that if Charles did go, he would fetch a British record fee, beating the £34,000 paid by Sheffield Wednesday to Notts County for Jackie Sewell, another of the Major's discoveries.

The Major, now aged 70, had seen United miss out on promotion yet again, so after five years at the club he left in April 1953 to manage Walsall.

Raich Carter, legendary England inside-forward, was appointed the new manager of Leeds United.

He remained at Fellows Park for two more years before leaving the game in June 1955.

When he died in December 1964, aged 81, football had lost one of its most colourful characters. For United fans he was the man that had unearthed the legendary John Charles – and his successor Jack Charlton, who made his debut in the final match of the 1952-3 season against Doncaster Rovers.

The redoubtable Major was going to be a hard act to follow, but United appointed a man who had already stepped into his shoes five years earlier – Horatio 'Raich' Stratton Carter.

Raich Carter had taken charge of Hull City when Major Buckley joined Leeds and now followed him to Elland Road.

Carter was regarded as one of the best inside-forwards England has ever produced, his magnificent ball-control and powerful shooting earning him 13 caps during his great playing days with Sunderland and Derby County. His international haul would have been much greater but for the war and he could also count a League Championship medal (with Sunderland in 1936) and two FA Cup winners' medals (Sunderland in 1937 and Derby in 1946) amongst his honours.

At Hull, Carter helped popularise the role of player-manager and the 'silver-haired maestro', as he was dubbed, took the Tigers to the Division Three North championship in 1949.

A master tactician, he signed future England inside-forward Don Revie for Hull, for £20,000 from Leicester, but Revie, later to build Leeds into a soccer superpower, did not stay too long at Boothferry Park.

Carter, who had also briefly played cricket for Derbyshire, gave up his managerial role at Hull in September 1951, but continued to play until the end of the season when he retired.

He later donned his boots again to assist Cork Athletic for a few months until United chairman Sam Bolton persuaded 38-year-old Carter to run the Leeds show.

Raich Carter's Attacking Policy

Carter ruled out any intention of playing for Leeds, but brought with him his old Sunderland and Hull mate, winger Eddie Burbanks, who became the oldest player to turn out for United, making his 13th and final appearance against his old club, Hull City, three weeks after his 41st birthday.

With little George Meek on National Service, Burbanks started the season on the left wing and, happily, Harold Williams had recovered from his broken leg to line up on the opposite flank as United began the 1953-4 season in style, thrashing

Notts County 6-0 with John Charles, retained at centre-forward, bagging four goals.

The young Welsh giant hit a hat-trick in the second game as Rotherham United were beaten 4-2 and that set the tone for the rest of the season. Later in the season the scoreline against Rotherham was repeated with another hat-trick for Charles.

The emphasis was very much on attacking football, not surprising as Carter had been one of the best attacking inside-forwards in the business.

Charles was unstoppable up front, crashing in power-packed shots from all angles and sending thumping headers ripping past bemused goalkeepers.

He became the scourge of the Second Division and finished as the Football League's highest scorer with a remarkable 42 League goals that season.

That smashed United's previous best, 35, set by Tom Jennings in 1929-30, and no one else has been remotely near it ever since. The only problem with Charles was that there were not two of him!

As he was smacking in goals at one end, his absence at the other saw United's goals-against total mount.

Irish international Jim McCabe, now approaching the veteran stage, was unseated as the pivot by

George Meek, whose career was interrupted by National Service with the Royal Armoured Corps. On his return to Elland Road he played his part in gaining promotion to Division One.

Leeds-born youngster Jack Marsden, who had joined United from Leeds Red Triangle League side, Osmondthorpe YMCA.

John Charles launches a header at Goodison Park in November 1953, with Everton defender Don Donovan in close attendance. Everton, who were on their way to the Second Division title, won 2-1, before nearly 56,000 spectators.

Aerial action around the Leeds goal during the third-round FA Cup replay at White Hart Lane in January 1954. Leeds lost 1-0.

Young Marsden was coaxed along by fellow defenders Eric Kerfoot and Tommy Burden, but the vacuum left by Charles proved difficult to fill and 81 League goals were conceded as United finished tenth for the second season running.

Charles was undoubtedly the leading light at Leeds, shining under the spotlight of United's new £7,000 floodlights, designed and supplied by the London-based General Electric Company.

The first game under lights at Elland Road was a friendly against Hibernian on 9 November 1953, United winning 4-1 in front of 31,500 curious spectators.

Predictably, Charles scored a couple of goals, but just to show he had not lost the knack, Raich Carter had a run out and netted a couple himself.

It was the first of several Monday night games against Scottish sides with Dundee, Falkirk, East Fife and St Mirren among the floodlit visitors.

West Riding Cup and Youth Cup ties were also played under lights, but in midwinter, League games continued to kick-off at either 2.15pm or 2.30pm to ensure that they were completed in daylight.

Further responsibility was heaped on Charles' burly shoulders when the consistent Tommy Burden left the club shortly after the start of the

1954-5 season with over 250 games under his belt.

Burden was a West Country man and had continued to live in that part of England, when he played for United. Weary of all the travelling, he joined a club much nearer home, Bristol City, in a £1,500 move.

He was the second defensive lynch-pin to leave United within months, following the departure of Jim McCabe to Peterborough.

Having lost two of his cornerstones and seeing his team lose five successive games after a 2-0 opening day win at Hull, Carter knew he had to take drastic action as his team wallowed near the bottom of the Second Division.

His solution was to restructure the side around Charles – at centre-half.

The Charles Transfer Crisis
The Welsh wizard dropped back into his old role with aplomb, while Keith Ripley, a youngster from the Wakefield area, was thrown in at the deep end as right-half and hard-running reserve Bobby Forrest, a £500 bargain from Retford Town, took over up front.

The switch worked like a charm as only one of the next 17 matches were lost, but only after United were rocked by a transfer request from

Leeds United, 1954-5. Back row (left to right): Bob Roxburgh (trainer), Harold Brook, Archie Gibson, Jimmy Dunn, Roy Wood, Eric Kerfoot, Grenville Hair. Front row: Andy McCall, Albert Nightingale, John Charles, Bobby Forrest, George Meek.

Charles. Anxious for First Division football, he made his request in writing and immediately Arsenal and Cardiff announced they wanted the versatile superstar.

Cardiff boss Trevor Morris even travelled to Elland Road and waited outside the boardroom as United's directors debated for three hours whether to sell their star man. As United fans bit their nails and Morris waited, chairman Sam Bolton emerged from the meeting to reveal that the board had unanimously rejected Charles' request.

"Why should we sell a brilliant player like Charles. Our aim is to get into the First Division and we cannot do that by selling our star player," said Bolton.

It was like a huge weight had been lifted from the club and the players responded with a hot-streak of form which climaxed with a 2-1 win at leaders Blackburn, Albert Nightingale scoring both goals against his old club, to go joint top.

Two weeks later, United went into their Christmas programme a point clear of Stoke at the top, but a spell of poor away form saw them lose ground and, despite a final flourish, they had to be content with fourth place.

United's leading scorer was Harold Brook, who proved a snip at £600 when he joined Leeds from Sheffield United at the start of the season.

He had shared the job as leader of United's attack with bustling Bobby Forrest, while other newcomers who made an impression in the latter part of the campaign included young Scottish wing-half Archie Gibson, and Jock Henderson, another Scot, who arrived from Rotherham to take over on wing patrol from Andy McCall.

With former Clitheroe goalkeeper Roy Wood proving a fine successor to John Scott, United's defence, in which immaculate full-backs Jimmy Dunn and Grenville Hair were ever present, looked in far better shape than in recent seasons.

Back to Division One

JOHN Charles kicked-off the 1955-6 season where he had finished the previous campaign – at centre-half.

But the same old problem cropped up. With Charles in defence United looked solid, but lacked that vital cutting edge up front.

Carter, who had rejected an offer to manage his old club, Derby County, in the summer, took a calculated gamble. He thrust Charles back up front again and brought in rookie Jack Charlton as centre-half – a move that was to keep United in good stead for many years to come.

Young Charlton, still only 20, was a revelation in a defence in which Grenville Hair looked an even better player after a summer tour with an FA party to the Caribbean.

Roy Wood was now firmly entrenched in goal and Jimmy Dunn continued to be his reliable self with Archie Gibson and Eric Kerfoot looking cast iron alongside new boy Charlton.

Sporting a new strip of dark blue shirts with gold collars, white shorts and blue and old gold hooped socks, United made steady progress despite a series of niggling injuries at the start of the season.

They kept on the fringe of the promotion race, thanks to their wonderful home form, but they suffered badly from travel sickness. Not until the second week in December did United win a second match away from home, victory coming at Blackburn – the only club to win a League game at Elland Road that season.

Blackburn's 2-1 victory on 10 March was the first time United had sampled a League defeat on home soil in 34 games – a tremendous sequence stretching back to 8 September 1954, when Stoke won 1-0. Seven days after Blackburn shattered that proud record, United lost 2-1 at the Victoria

Ground, Stoke, and United's promotion dream seemed to be over for another year, particularly as they were struggling to win away from home.

But the players produced a supreme effort just when it was needed as the promotion bandwagon started to roll with a home win against Plymouth and a rare away win at Fulham.

Defeat followed at Nottingham Forest, but amazingly United stormed through their final six matches, winning the lot to finish as runners-up to Sheffield Wednesday.

Whirlwind Finish

Excitement had reached fever pitch when promotion rivals Bristol Rovers arrived at Elland Road on 21 April. It was United's last home game of the season and only trips to Rotherham and Hull remained.

Rovers came with a two-point advantage, but United had that midweek match at Rotherham in hand.

A huge crowd of 49,274 turned up to see what was billed as United's most important game for a decade.

Leeds fans were stunned when Dai Ward put the West Country team in front after only three minutes, but a classic header from Charles gave United a 17th-minute equaliser.

Ten minutes later the rampant Charles supplied the pass for Jack Overfield, a local lad who had graduated through the ranks after joining from Yorkshire Amateurs, to slam in the winner off the underside of the bar.

That crucial goal saw United move into second place on goal-average from Rovers, five points behind Sheffield Wednesday, who won the championship by beating Bury.

Two days later, United made the short trip to

John Charles scores his 100th goal for Leeds United, beating the Swansea Town goalkeeper John King from the penalty spot at Elland Road in February 1956.

Millmoor where a couple of goals by Albert Nightingale, who had learnt to play the game in local Rotherham leagues, gave United a great 2-0 win.

That set up a tremendous finale as the wheel of fortune turned full circle and took Raich Carter back to Hull, the club he once managed, needing only a draw to take Leeds up to Division One.

About 15,000 Leeds fans made the trip to Boothferry Park and United's travelling army were soon dancing on the terraces as Charles sent a thunderous left-foot shot past goalkeeper Bernard Fisher.

But Hull, bottom of the table and already relegated, silenced the United followers in the 13th minute with a Tommy Martin equaliser.

Just after an hour, George Meek was sent sprawling in the penalty area and the ice-cool Charles blasted in the penalty-kick – his 29th goal of the season. United finished on a high note as veteran Harold Brook added two later goals to give United an emphatic 4-1 triumph.

By winning their last six games, whirlwind United had ended their nine-year exile from the First Division. It was the fourth time they had clinched promotion to the top flight, and each time it had been achieved on a Leap Year.

Once again Charles had been the undisputed star and finished third in the annual poll for the Footballer of the Year, quite an achievement for a player who had never turned out in the First Division.

Raich Carter and his team celebrate promotion in 1956. At the back is a youthful Jack Charlton who came into the side in late September and stayed there for the rest of the season.

Jack Overfield soon established himself in the promotion side after being demobbed from the RAF. He celebrated Leeds' return to Division One with a goal against Everton, after only two minutes of the opening day of the season.

All that would change in 1956-7 as Charles pitted his 6ft 1in, 14st frame against the best players in the land.

He was head and shoulders, sometimes literally, above everyone else in the Second Division. How would he fare at the highest level of the domestic game?

He had no doubts about the team's potential. Speaking after the power-drive to promotion he said: "All the players have fought magnificently. The team has played as one man. To any player who might have slipped, there's always been the consolation that there was somebody else behind him, backing up and pulling out his best.

"The spectators have joined in this team spirit. They have been behind us to a man. It meant a lot to us to know that everybody had such confidence in us. It gave our confidence a boost. It convinced us that we could win promotion.

'Now we feel we can do well in the First Division if we take that team spirit with us. it is the one big thing that can take us far," said Charles.

Any doubts about his ability to produce the goods at the top level were swept away as all-action Charles plundered 38 goals – the best return by any other player in the First Division and bettered only by the prolific Arthur Rowley's 44 for Leicester City.

The first of Charles' haul came in a triumphant opening game in which United marked their first Division One game in nine years with a 5-1 demolition of Everton. But the hero of the day was

Harold Brook, a veteran from Sheffield United, scored twice in the last match in Division Two, then hit a 21-minute hat-trick on the first day of the following season.

Harold Brook, who, at the age of 34, celebrated a 21-minute hat-trick. However, the first goal of the match came after just two and a half minutes from the boot of Jack Overfield.

The lanky winger, who had made great strides in the promotion campaign, went on to be an ever present in his maiden season in the First Division, yet failed to find the net again in any of his other 41 games! His form and that of George Meek on the other wing meant there was no room for veteran Harold Williams, who moved on to Newport County. Williams, a model of consistency in his six seasons at Elland Road, soon returned to Yorkshire with Bradford and after retiring ran a couple of pubs in the Leeds area.

The one black cloud that hung over that great display against Everton was a bad knee injury sustained by Albert Nightingale which ended his career. His number-ten shirt was occupied for much of the season by Bobby Forrest, who slotted in well alongside Charles and Brook.

Disaster as Fire Destroys the West Stand

United were still on a roll from promotion and their hot start saw them in second spot after nine games, tucked in behind leaders Manchester United.

But the heat was nothing compared with the night of Tuesday 18 September 1956 when fire destroyed the West Stand.

The alarm was raised by fish and chip shop proprietor Arnold Price, whose business was opposite the entrance to the Elland Road ground. He ran in his bare feet and pyjamas to raise the alarm but the ferocity of the fire was so great that the roof of the stand had already crashed into the seats below before firefighters could get to the scene.

The fire had been so intense that large sections of the pitch had been scorched by the searing heat.

Damage was estimated at £100,000 as the flames devoured not only the main stand, but all the club's offices, dressing-rooms, boardroom, press box, floodlighting generators, kit, physiotherapy equipment and playing records.

During the week the players helped salvage what they could from the burnt-out wreckage, but after a five-hour emergency board meeting the directors announced that there was no hope of saving the 2,500 seater stand and the club would have to start from scratch.

An appeal was immediately launched to build a new West Stand with assistance from Leeds City Council.

Chairman Sam Bolton boldly declared that the home game against Aston Villa in four days' time would go ahead as planned.

An appeal was made to residents around Elland Road to provide emergency changing accommodation, whilst manager Raich Carter tried to prepare his players as best he could.

He and new coach Ivor Powell, the former Aston Villa, Queen's Park Rangers and Welsh international, immediately ordered 40 pairs of boots for the entire playing squad.

Carter's men were under orders to wear the boots as often as possible to get them broken-in before the Villa game.

With the physiotherapy room wiped out, United turned to former trainer Arthur Campey to treat those players with injuries at his home, where he had set up in private practice.

The fire did not deter the fans from seeing their favourites as 35,388 turned up for the match even though the charred remains of the West Stand were roped-off.

Both United and Villa players, together with referee Mr F.L. Overton of Derby and his linesmen, changed at the Whitehall Printeries sports ground in Lowfields Road before taking a coach for 600-yard trip to Elland Road.

The teams picked their way through the twisted skeleton of metal to reach the pitch where United gained their reward for their determination to play, John Charles scoring the only goal in the 19th minute.

The Lord Mayor of Leeds, Alderman T.A. Jessop, launched a public appeal for £60,000, that sum being the difference between the cost of the new stand and the size of the insurance payment the club were to receive.

Later in the season United were dealt another blow with the death at his Blackpool home of J.Hilton Crowther, the man whose money built United in the 1920s.

Chairman Sam Bolton paid this tribute: "His efforts as a pioneer in The United cause will never be forgotten at Elland Road. He did a lot of spadework for the club and gave it valuable financial aid. He was an esteemed member of the board."

At the time of Crowther's death, United had slipped out of the title race, but with Jimmy Dunn clocking up his 350th appearance and Eric Kerfoot his 250th, they finished a creditable eighth.

Luckily, Carter's men were able to steer clear of injury and no less than five players – Dunn, Kerfoot, Roy Wood, Grenville Hair and Jack Overfield – played in every League game, whilst Charles, Archie Gibson and George Meek missed only two each.

These players provided the backbone of the side, but Raich Carter had been able to blood a handful of youngsters, most notably Chris Crowe.

The Newcastle-born forward had the distinction of playing for Scotland Schools when he lived in Edinburgh and picked up Youth caps for England. He had turned professional in

Grenville Hair, ever-present in 1956-7, the first season back in Division One. Full-back Hair joined Leeds in 1948 and made over 470 League and Cup appearances for United.

John Charles leads out United for the last time before moving to Italy. He would return.

Juventus skipper Boniperti checks that a Juventus shirt will fit the giant frame of John Charles.

Leeds United chairman Sam Bolton and manager Raich Carter wish John Charles the best of good fortune before the player's record transfer to the Italian League.

summer 1956 and his skilful darting runs earmarked him as the brightest young prospect since John Charles had burst on to the scene.

But the Charles era at Elland Road… was about to close in sensational fashion.

United Succumb to the Lure of the Lira

The pressure to sell their great Welsh star had always been immense, but when Italian club Juventus came in with a bid of £65,000 to make Charles Britain's costliest footballer, United, no doubt swayed by their big overdraft, took the money.

The sale of Charles came days after a welcome piece of financial news for all soccer clubs when the Entertainment Tax on clubs was lifted. During 1955-6, United had shelled out £16,041 in Entertainment Tax and £105,665 in the 11 seasons since the war.

The tax was first applied at the start of the wartime 1916-17 season, when it was said to be a temporary measure to help cover the cost of World War One; it took 41 years for it to be abolished.

Clubs estimated that since 1952 about one-fifth of the gross income from gate receipts had been handed over to the Treasury.

Said chairman Bolton: "It is a blessing for the club. At a time when we are head over heels in debt, it is going to be a life-saver and will give us much-needed aid towards the extensive ground improvements we are undertaking."

Having lost potential income from ticket sales of seats in the West Stand, United needed every penny they could get and although Charles was not put up for transfer, the overtures of the Italians proved too great to resist.

Charles, who had first attracted the interest of Juventus president Umberto Agnelli when playing for Wales against Northern Ireland, was also in demand by Inter-Milan, Real Madrid and Lazio.

But Juventus were always front runners and after initial talks with Sam Bolton had failed, the Italian party phoned Bolton at home from their

suite in the Queen's Hotel and a deal was thrashed out.

United agreed to drop their asking price of £70,000 by £5,000 on condition that Juventus brought a side to England to play United. That match went ahead at the start of the following season when United banked £6,000 in receipts.

Charles had signed a two-year contract with Juventus and was reputed to have received £10,000, a salary of about £70 a month, plus win bonuses, a flat in Turin and a car. Not bad for someone who had joined United for £10 as a 16-year-old.

Those were immense riches in the days when footballers were poorly paid by today's standards.

The deal was agreed two days before United's final match of the season, on Easter Monday 1957 as the Welsh superstar signed off in style with a couple of goals in a 3-1 win against Sunderland to take his tally to 38 for the season.

Within days he flew to Turin with Juventus scout Gigi Peronace and was given a hero's welcome by the fans of 'The Zebras'. Charles became an overnight success in Italy, his power and skill tearing apart some of the best defences on the globe.

The 'Gentle Giant' was idolised as he rattled in 109 goals, won three Italian League championship medals, an Italian Cup medal, represented the Italian League and was named Italian Footballer of the Year.

He won further plaudits in 1958 as he played for Wales in the World Cup Finals in Sweden, helping the principality to the quarter-finals.

He made a brief return to Elland Road in 1962, but looked only a shadow of the player who had strode like a colossus through the 1950s.

Because of heavy debts, the Leeds club gave Carter only about half of the Charles cash to spend. The biggest slice of the money went on Charles' replacement, Hugh Baird, the Airdrie centre-forward who had netted 165 goals in six Scottish League seasons.

United paid £12,000 for the man who was the top scorer in Scotland in 1954-5 with 37 goals – marksmanship which earned him international honours the following year.

But replacing Charles was an impossible task and the difficulties were soon underlined when United lost 3-0 at Blackpool on the opening day of the 1957-8 season and went down 2-0 at Aston Villa the following Monday.

While United were getting turned over at Bloomfield Road, their reserves drew 2-2 with Blackpool in the reverse fixture at Elland Road, when the new £180,000 West Stand was in use for the first time.

The following Saturday, new skipper Eric Kerfoot led his side out in front of 26,660 fans and christened the new stand with a 2-1 win, Jack Overfield and a Hugh Baird penalty giving United their first win of the season.

Architect of the new stand was Brian Jackman, of the Leeds firm Braithwaite & Jackman, who had kept roof-supporting pillars down to a minimum so it did not obstruct the spectators' view.

Built by the Leeds building firm of Robert R.Roberts, it housed 4,000 seats and terracing for a further 6,000 supporters at the front. Individual match tickets for the stand cost 7s 6d and 5s 6d.

It was a big improvement and United seemed to win the seal of approval from soccer's hierarchy when they were chosen to host the Football League v League of Ireland game in October.

An added bonus for United fans was the selection of Jack Charlton at centre-half for the Football League team who ran out 3-1 winners in front of 13,000 fans.

Among the Irish forwards who impressed that night was Noel Peyton, a fully fledged Irish international, who joined United from Shamrock Rovers three months later in a £5,000 move.

He took over from the veteran Harold Brook, who moved to Lincoln City, where he wrapped up a long and distinguished career.

Peyton had become the second Irish international to join the club that season, Wilbur Cush, Ulster's Footballer of the Year arriving from Glenavon for £7,000 in November.

But United did not enjoy the luck of the Irish when it came to injuries during 1957-8 with both their stalwart full-backs missing a quarter of the season, Grenville Hair with a cartilage problem and Jimmy Dunn with a knee injury.

Manager Carter had to make do and mend for a while, but United slowly began to slide down the table, despite the arrival of their two new Irish imports.

United finished a disappointing 17th and could not break their FA Cup hoodoo into the bargain.

For the third successive year they were drawn at home to Cardiff City in the third round and each season brought the same result – a 2-1 win for Cardiff.

That remarkable sequence left United seeking their first FA Cup-tie win since 1952, giving them the worst Cup record of any team in the top two divisions.

Following the departure of John Charles it was anticipated that United would have struggled to come to terms with his absence, so it was a surprise when the board decided not to renew Raich Carter's contract when it expired at the end of May 1958.

Carter had paid the price for one bad season and was axed, prematurely, he argued. To make his point he later became manager of Mansfield Town, steering them to promotion from Division Four before three years as boss at Middlesbrough. He left football in February 1966 and become a sports department manager.

George O'Brien joined Leeds from Dunfermline in March 1957 and moved to Southampton two years later, for £10,000. It was at The Dell where his career blossomed; he scored 154 goals in 243 League appearances for the Saints.

Hugh Baird signed for Leeds from Airdrie for £12,000 in July 1957, as a successor to John Charles. A Scottish international and a prolific scorer in the Scottish League, despite scoring 20 goals for Leeds in 1957-8, he could not settle and was transferred to Aberdeen for £11,000 in October 1958.

Wing-half Keith Ripley was a schoolboy star in Normanton and Leeds had to beat off Blackpool and West Brom, both leading clubs of the day, to sign him in April 1952. National Service interrupted his career and in August 1958 he moved to Norwich City.

United's new man at the helm was Bill Lambton, a man Carter had brought to the club as trainer-coach in November 1957 to take over from Bob Roxburgh, who had been trainer since the mid-1950s but had taken on the role of physiotherapist.

Nottingham-born Lambton, aged 43, had no big reputation as a player, but was noted for his unorthodox training methods.

He had been on Nottingham Forest's books as a goalkeeper and after World War Two had a spell with Doncaster Rovers before moving into coaching.

A fitness fanatic, he kept the Great Britain boxing team in trim when he was coaching in Denmark, and on his return to England he coached at Scunthorpe United, introducing trampolining sessions to get players supple and fit.

Lambton was put in temporary charge on Carter's departure and was not officially appointed manager until December 1958.

United won only one of their first nine League games under their caretaker manager, who decided to act quickly to halt the decline.

Hugh Baird, top scorer in 1957-8 with 20 goals, returned to Scotland in an £11,000 transfer to Aberdeen, whilst Bobby Forrest later headed for Notts County.

Fresh faces were little winger Billy Humphries, who joined the growing Irish contingent at Elland Road in a £5,000 move from Ards and centre-forward Alan Shackleton.

United's new leader, Shackleton was signed for £8,000 after three of United's staff saw him in action for Burnley in a Lancashire Senior Cup game against Accrington Stanley.

They immediately rang Elland Road and within minutes transfer negotiations were opened and the deal sealed inside 24 hours in time for him to make a scoring debut in a 2-1 defeat against Manchester United.

Noel Peyton (top) and Wilbur Cush (bottom), two Irish internationals who joined Leeds in 1957.

Shackleton bagged a hat-trick in his fourth game and the following week lined up alongside a man who was to shape the destiny of Leeds United – Don Revie. United pipped Middlesbrough, Revie's home-town team to sign the former England ace in a £12,000 move from Sunderland.

Revie, 31, was nearing the end of a spectacular playing career which had made him one of the most coveted footballers in England.

A master tactician, his services had netted clubs £80,000 in transfer fees, making him the country's most sought-after player. Leicester sold him to Hull for £20,000, he then joined Manchester City, where he developed the deep-lying centre-forward plan, for £25,000.

Capped six times for England, a £23,000 transfer took him to Sunderland, who banked £12,000 when he joined the Elland Road payroll.

Revie, Footballer of the Year in 1955, made his debut in a 3-2 home win over Newcastle, thanks to goals by Jack Overfield, a Chris Crowe penalty and an own-goal by Malcolm Scott.

Things were looking up for United. They had signed a top quality inside-forward, improved results saw them move up the table and Bill Lambton was handed a pre-Christmas bonus by being named the new manager, thus ending weeks of speculation.

At the halfway stage of the season, United were in mid-table, six points behind leaders West Brom and in a good position to make an outside push for the title. But things turned sour as Wilbur Cush quit the captaincy in January because he felt the extra responsibility was affecting his game.

Lambton held a players' meeting and Revie was unanimously elected as the new skipper.

But results failed to improve, including a dismal 4-0 home defeat against Manchester City and rumours soon started to circulate that the players were not happy with Lambton's training methods.

When Jack Overfield, then Grenville Hair slapped in transfer requests, it was clear that something was amiss behind the scenes.

Things came to a head in March when Lambton, the players, chairman Sam Bolton and vice-chairman Percy Woodward met to discuss the unrest. As a result, Lambton handed in his resignation which was accepted by the board.

Lambton, a strict disciplinarian, said: "I have considered this course of action for some time owing to the interference from directors in my training methods." The board hit back with a statement saying that Lambton had their fullest support and they had not interfered.

Billy Humphries from Ards, yet another young Irishman to join Leeds United in the 1950s.

Into the breach stepped Bob Roxburgh, the senior member of the training and coaching staff, who took over team selection and persuaded Hair to withdraw his transfer request. Lambton's three-month term of office was short, but not as brief as his next managerial post at Scunthorpe United, where he lasted only three days during April 1959, although his appointment had only been a verbal one. He later had a spell in charge at Chester.

Meanwhile United continued their search for a new manager and thought they had found one in Arthur Turner, boss of Southern League Headington United (now Oxford United). He was better known from his days as manager of Birmingham City, where he had been a player, taking them to the 1956 FA Cup Final where they lost to a Don Revie-inspired Manchester City.

United were on the brink of appointing Turner and in the official home programme for the match against Blackburn Rovers they introduced Turner to the fans under the heading 'Our New Manager'.

But to United's embarrassment, Turner was persuaded to stay at Headington and played a major role in that club's eventual entry to the Football League.

The Leeds quest for a new chief finally ended in May 1959, when Jack Taylor left Queen's Park Rangers to take over at Elland Road, although he still had a year of his three-year contract to run.

Revie – Taylor-made for the Job

BARNSLEY-BORN Jack Taylor had played under Major Buckley at Wolves, where he formed a solid full-back partnership with his younger brother Frank, who was capped by England. Jack joined Norwich in June 1938, after guesting for Barnsley and Watford during World War Two. In July 1947 he was signed by the Major a second time and moved on to Hull City, staying for three years before becoming player-manager at Weymouth.

He earned his first break in League management at Queen's Park Rangers in June 1952 and was well established when he headed back north to join Leeds.

Taylor went back to his old club for his first senior signing, Bobby Cameron, a bustling Scottish inside-forward who had spent nine years at Rangers.

That was the start of several changes Taylor implemented throughout the course of a difficult season.

Goalkeeper Ted Burgin, a former Sheffield United and England 'B' player, who had joined from Doncaster Rovers, took over the gloves from Roy Wood who retired after playing seven times in this season.

Another senior member of the side conspicuous by his absence was old war-horse Jimmy Dunn, who had joined Darlington after 422 League appearances in the old gold and blue of United. He played very few bad games in those matches and must have considered himself unlucky not to win a Scottish call.

The departure of Dunn was anticipated, but the surprise move came when leading scorer Alan Shackleton was transferred to Everton, after only two games of the 1959-60 season, and a new leader purchased, John McCole.

The Glasgow-born forward was bought for £10,000 from neighbours Bradford City, where he had enjoyed a good scoring record since arriving at Valley Parade from Falkirk.

Taylor's plans were also rocked by a spate of injuries which, at various times robbed him of Don Revie, Bobby Cameron, Jack Overfield, Grenville Hair, Wilbur Cush, George Meek and Chris Crowe amongst others.

The constant shuffling of staff continued when Willie Humphries returned to Ards because he could not settle, but later had a more productive spell in England with Coventry City.

John McCole, a Glaswegian forward bought from Bradford City for £10,000. His 22 goals were not enough to save Leeds from relegation in the 1959-60 season.

During these changes United endured a spell of 14 games where they won only once and plunged deep into relegation trouble by Christmas.

One of the few bright spots of a disappointing season had been the polished displays of young winger Chris Crowe, who was rewarded with an England Under-23 cap against France.

But the ambitious Crowe wanted guaranteed First Division football and after three months on the transfer list was sold to Blackburn Rovers for £25,000.

Part of the Crowe money was spent on Freddie Goodwin, Manchester United's powerful defender, who had come to the fore after the 1958 Munich air disaster.

Goodwin joined a struggling Leeds side that had more than its fair share of youngsters thrust into action because of injuries to senior players.

Bill Lambton had started a successful youth policy, Taylor had kept it running and was rewarded by the emergence of a flame-haired little winger called Billy Bremner.

The wee Scot made his debut in a 3-1 win at Chelsea, a club who had earlier rejected him for being 'too small'. Bremner was 18 at the time and it was clear that Taylor had a stick of footballing dynamite in his hands.

Young Bremner cared little for the lofty reputation of some of his opponents and looked a tremendous prospect as he started his career as a right winger.

But neither the fresh young legs of Bremner, nor the skills of Don Revie and experience of

George Meek, Chris Crowe (middle) and Jack Charlton take to the field for Leeds. Meek and Crowe both left Elland Road in 1960. Crowe had joined Leeds as an amateur in 1954 and turned professional two years later. His career really blossomed at Wolves, though, where he was capped for England.

In his first game for Manchester City after being transferred from Huddersfield Town for a record £55,000, Denis Law crowned a fine display at Elland Road with this goal in March 1960. The United players are Grenville Hair and goalkeeper Ted Burgin. United still won 4-3; earlier in the season the sides had drawn 3-3 at Maine Road.

Freddie Goodwin, could work Leeds out of the rut and they were relegated in 21st place after only three seasons in the First Division.

Inevitably there were more ins and outs before

Don Revie, appointed as player-manager in March 1961. Leeds tottered on the brink of the Third Division before Revie pulled their fortunes around in spectacular fashion.

the start of the new season as Taylor sought the formula that would get United up at the first attempt.

But money was tight, so more emphasis was put on catching more local talent. Scouting had been stepped up in the Leeds district and when the 1960-61 season began United had signed on nearly 50 boys on amateur forms.

Although many fell by the wayside, some broke through to the full professional ranks and took part in the club's tremendous revival in the mid-1960s.

But that was all in the future, Taylor's initial concern was assembling a side good enough to win promotion.

New men included former Scottish international wing-half, Eric Smith from Celtic and St Mirren centre-half Jackie McGugan, who had come close to full Scottish honours.

However, McGugan could not shift the outstanding Jack Charlton from the number-five

berth and made only one appearance before moving on to Tranmere for £12,000 – £3,000 less than Taylor had paid for him.

Colin Grainger, known as 'The Singing Winger' because he was also a nightclub crooner, arrived from Sunderland for £15,000 with Jackie Overfield, now recovered from a cartilage operation, going in the opposite direction.

Another winger to leave was George Meek, whose 'twinkle toes' had danced along both touch-lines in over 200 matches for United. He joined Leicester City for £7,000.

Smith was earmarked to take over from Wilbur Cush, the Irish international wing-half, who had returned to Portadown. But as one Irishman left, another arrived in the form of £7,000 forward Peter Fitzgerald from Sparta Rotterdam, who joined Noël Peyton on international duty.

But the new boys were either hit by injury or loss of form and were only able to make a limited contribution to another spluttering season in which no less than 27 players were used.

To add to Taylor's mounting problems, attendances were dropping rapidly and star man Don Revie was out of form and gave up the captaincy because he did not feel he was a lucky skipper.

The job passed on to Freddie Goodwin, but, like Revie, he was unable to lead the same team out week after week because injuries and illness continued to decimate the squad.

If Revie thought he had been an unlucky captain, then Taylor was certainly an unlucky manager, having to contend with an appalling catalogue of injuries while he was in charge.

After four successive defeats Taylor met the board and was told by director Harry Reynolds, a growing influence at the club, that he was going to recommend that Taylor and the club part company. Taylor handed in his resignation on 18 March 1961 and the search began for a successor.

Revie's Letter of Fate

The board did not have to look far as their man was already at the club, Don Revie.

His appointment as player-manager came a few days after Taylor's departure. Revie was already in the autumn of his playing days and both Chester and Bournemouth had asked if he was available.

Reynolds drew up a letter to send to the Bournemouth club recommending Revie and outlining his qualities as a potential manager. It soon became clear that the answer to United's problem was laid out in that letter which Reynolds promptly tore up and persuaded his fellow directors to put Revie in charge.

Revie was unanimously appointed on a three-year contract, but his first game in charge, on 25 March, ended in a 2-1 defeat at the hands of Sheffield United.

In fact, of the eight games United played under Revie before the close of the season they managed only one win – a spectacular 7-0 thrashing of Lincoln – as they finished 14th.

Generally goals had not been too much of a problem with John McCole bagging 20 League goals to add to his 22 from the previous season.

He also added a further three in a new competition, the Football League Cup, which initially failed to capture the imagination of the supporters. The honour of scoring United's first-ever goal in the tournament fell to Revie in a 3-1 replay success at Blackpool.

A 4-0 win at Chesterfield followed and United hit four in the next round, at Southampton, but still lost in one of the most remarkable games in United's history.

United were 4-0 down to Southampton, Derek Reeves scoring all four goals, before battling back to equalise thanks to Noël Peyton, John McCole, Jack Charlton and a Bobby Cameron penalty.

But 25 seconds from the end Reeves bagged his fifth in a remarkable game which did not finish until 10.10pm because of two floodlight failures, making it the longest-ever match in England.

Both sides also finished with only ten men, Southampton lost goalkeeper Ron Reynolds and United's full-back Alf Jones went off with a knee injury. McCole certainly showed he had a liking for the League Cup by rattling in all four as United beat Brentford 4-1 the following season.

Manager Revie, who used himself sparingly, did not see the Brentford game because he was away scouting for a new forward.

Despite McCole's four-goal haul, a Club record in the competition, he returned to Bradford City the following month. As a temporary measure big Jack Charlton 'did a John Charles' and was thrust up front for the middle of the season while Revie worked to find McCole's successor.

By this time Charlton and Billy Bremner were first-team regulars, Bremner switching from the right wing to inside-right to accommodate the arrival of Preston winger Derek Mayers.

With United strapped for cash, Mayers was Revie's only summer signing as he stood by the players he fielded in his first few weeks in charge.

That crop included a jet-heeled South African winger called Albert Johanneson, who shared the left-wing patrol with York-born youngster John Hawksby, and former Scottish amateur inter-national defender Willie Bell, who had been snapped up from Queen's Park.

In fact, Revie's biggest signings in terms of reputation were the backroom staff he had assembled at Elland Road.

Former Luton and England centre-half Syd Owen, who had a spell as Luton's manager, joined the coaching staff with former Stockport and Accrington Stanley player Les Cocker as trainer and former Everton defender and former Swindon manager Maurice Lindley as chief scout.

Prospects looked good for 1961-2 as the opening two games were won, but a 5-0 thrashing at Liverpool heralded a bleak spell which left United down among the strugglers.

Too many goals were being conceded so Revie recruited former Scottish international goalkeeper Tommy Younger, 31, from Canadian football in September. But United still refused to turn the corner and by November only Charlton Athletic were below Leeds and relegation was been muttered darkly on the terraces.

Revie admitted to the fans that the club was in the throes of a financial and playing depression.

"The long term outlook of this club must be based upon youth. No players, however well intentioned and conscientious, can possibly acquire the loyalty that all clubs need to the same degree as those players who start their life with one club and develop throughout the teams" said Revie.

"We are, therefore, basing our plans upon securing the best youngsters there are available, and to that end all the schools, youth and junior representative matches are being watched and reported upon.

"Already we have a nucleus of talent. You have seen Billy Bremner, the 18-year-old forward whom I regard as the man most likely to succeed me as schemer of the forward line. It may be that I shall continue to play until Billy is ready to take over, but I regard his promise as so great that I do not consider that date far advanced."

They were prophetic words and the junior side in the Northern Intermediate League was packed with youngsters that were to become household names in the near future.

One of them, goalkeeper Gary Sprake, made his League debut as a 16-year-old in remarkable circumstances.

The blond-haired apprentice was in bed in Leeds before a junior match as the first team were down in Southampton for a League game.

Then Tommy Younger fell ill with tonsillitis, second-string Alan Humphreys was unfit, so Sprake was taken by taxi to board a chartered flight to the South Coast.

The Football League had given special permission for the game to kick-off late. Sprake was sick on the plane, but after another taxi dash

Gary Sprake made his debut as a 16-year-old, after a spectacular dash by air and road to Southampton where he played as a last-minute replacement for the illness-stricken Tommy Younger.

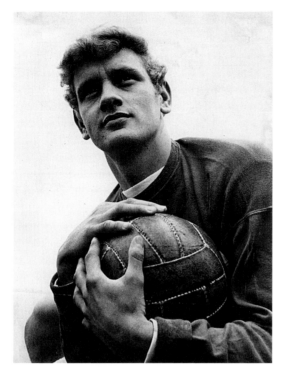

to The Dell arrived just before 3pm, the game starting at 3.15pm.

Sprake did little wrong, but Southampton won 4-1, United's goal coming from Ian Lawson, a £20,000 centre-forward signed from Burnley.

Wee Scot Bobby's Final Fling

Lawson was one of four new men in the Leeds line-up as Revie broke the bank in an effort to steer Leeds out of trouble.

The United boss knew he could not rely on youngsters alone and the season had reached such a critical stage that some old hands were needed to stave off relegation.

Deeply in debt, United raised more than a few eyebrows when they paid £25,000 for the veteran Scottish international midfielder Bobby Collins. It proved an inspired gamble, however.

Lawson teamed up with centre-forward Billy McAdams, an Irish international who had earlier joined from Bolton, having previously played with Revie at Manchester City.

A further £10,000 was spent on experienced Sheffield United left-back Cliff Mason, but the biggest purchase of them all, £25,000 for veteran Scottish international schemer Bobby Collins, raised several eyebrows.

With United reputed to be £150,000 in debt it was an enormous risk in forking out so much money on Collins, a brilliant inside-forward-in his day but, at 31, considered by many to be past his best. Collins had sparkled with Celtic before three years at Everton confirmed his status as one of the best post-war inside-forwards, or as they were becoming known, midfield players.

Many critics could not understand why Revie had spent such a large amount on a player approaching the end of his career, while others were puzzled why the multi-capped little Scot should leave a big club like Everton for struggling Second Division Leeds.

But the big gamble paid off. Only one game out of the last 11 – that match at Southampton – was lost, although it needed a win at Newcastle on the final day of the season to guarantee Second Division safety. Despite an extremely difficult first season, Revie and his backroom staff had been backed to the hilt by new chairman Harry Reynolds, the man who had argued the case for Revie to be appointed in the first place. Reynolds had taken over the chairmanship vacated by Sam Bolton in a mid-season boardroom reshuffle.

Bolton had become one of the top soccer administrators in the game. He was an FA councillor, FA life member, Football League management committee member and an England Under-23 selector.

As chairman of the FA Cup committee he was a familiar figure as the man who pulled numbered balls out of the famous velvet bag while the nation was glued to their transistors tuned in to the FA Cup draw.

Bolton felt the time was right to step down from the chair, He was renowned for his sense of timing and punctuality. One story told among Football League officials was that after a management committee meeting in London, his wife turned up to meet him a few minutes late, only to discover he had set off back to Leeds without her.

Big Sam now had more time to spend on the golf courses at South Leeds and Moortown, whilst remaining on the board.

Harry Reynolds was in the same, big bluff Tyke, mould as Bolton, A self-made millionaire who headed the engineering and steel stockholding firm of H.L.Reynolds, he set his keen business mind to work on turning around United's finances.

The son of working-class parents from Holbeck, he worked as a flour boy with Leeds Co-op, a railway cleaner and fireman before founding his steel stock-holding company.

Rumoured to be a millionaire by the late 1950s, he lived at Hough Top, Bramley, went hunting with the Bramham Moor Hunt, played polo and became a familiar face at the captains' tables on the liners *Queen Mary* and *Queen Elizabeth*.

Despite mixing in high circles, Reynolds never lost sight of his roots and even visited tenement flats in Glasgow with Revie to recruit up-and-coming Scottish youngsters for Leeds,

But it was not just at the top where there were changes. Stanley Blenkinsop stood down after 27 years as a director and joined John Bromley as a vice-president.

On to the board came three new directors, Albert Morris and Manny Cussins, two Leeds businessmen who were also to assume the role of chairman in future years, and Sidney Simon.

To complete the changes, the Earl of Harewood, a regular supporter of the club, was elected the first president of Leeds United, a position he holds today. As the winds of change were blowing through the boardroom, gales were also blowing through Elland Road, damaging the Lowfields Road stand to such an extent that it was closed for the final two and a half months of the season – robbing United of vital revenue at a time when they could ill afford to lose money.

That Famous All-White Strip

On the field United had firmly nailed their new colours of all-white to the mast of youth, although the intention was to blood the talented youngsters gradually.

The change from old gold and blue to white was Revie's idea as he announced he wanted his team to become as good as the great Real Madrid, whose all-white strip had dominated European soccer.

Outsiders sniggered, but within the club Revie was already making progress with his talented youngsters in the Northern Intermediate League.

The new directors had helped ease United's debts and also helped Revie fork out a record £53,000 to Juventus to bring John Charles back to

Don Revie watches John Charles sign again for Leeds United, for a record £53,000. Alas, the move back to Elland Road did not really work out and Charles returned to Italy with AS Roma. Leeds, though, made a handsome £17,000 on the short-term transfer.

August 1962 and a
suntanned John
Charles is pictured
on his return to
Leeds United,
although he only
stayed for 11
matches.

Elland Road and £15,650 for Airdrie's prolific scorer Jim Storrie,

Storrie marked his debut with the only goal in United's 1962-3 opening-day win at Bury, but United made only a moderate start with the return of Charles failing to have the desired effect.

Big John did not seem to be the same powerful player who had dominated the 1950s and after only 11 matches and three goals of his comeback, United snapped up a handsome £17,000 profit as AS Roma came in with a £70,000 bid,

The Welsh giant returned to Britain less than 12 months later to join Cardiff City, where he took his tally of full caps to 38 before being appointed Hereford United's player-manager, helping to lay the foundations of their successful bid for Football League membership.

The sale of Charles, plus the summer departures of Billy McAdams for £8,000, Derek Mayers to Bury and Bobby Cameron to non-League Gravesend & Northfleet helped generate much needed cash.

It was a game at Charles' home town of Swansea which proved to be the turning point of United's season.

Revie's plan had been to ease in a clutch of young players alongside the knowledgeable Bobby Collins, but United's uninspired start to the season saw those plans brought forward.

At Swansea on 8 September 1962, Paul Reaney, Norman Hunter and Rod Johnson all made their first senior appearances, while Gary Sprake came in for only his second match.

The rookies were an instant hit, Johnson scoring in a 2-0 win, whilst Sprake, Reaney, Hunter became permanent fixtures, not just for the rest of that season but for about the next ten years.

Three weeks after that Swansea game, another teenager took his first steps to soccer fame – Peter Lorimer, who had been at the club for only four months.

He was sweeping the Lowfield Road terraces when he heard that he was going to play for the first team against Southampton, because Billy Bremner was injured.

Dundee-born Lorimer was such a prolific scorer in schoolboy football that he earned the nickname 'The Cannonball Kid' for his power-packed shooting which had brought him nearly 176 goals in one season for Stobswell School.

No fewer than 28 clubs wanted to sign Lorimer, and Revie was in such a hurry to get the youngster to Leeds that he was booked for speeding on his way north to sign him.

At 15 years 289 days, the precocious Lorimer became United's youngest-ever player, beating the previous youngest, Gary Sprake.

United's young team was starting to take shape around the skills of Bobby Collins and their move up the table gained further momentum with the arrival from Rotherham of Don Weston, who celebrated with a hat-trick on his debut as United beat Stoke City 3-1 at Elland Road.

Stoke were also beaten 3-1 in the FA Cup, United's first win in the competition for nine years, ending the worst record of any League side.

That third-round game was not played until 6 March because soccer had been put in cold storage by one of the worst winters on record, with no play possible for two months.

The Stoke tie attracted 36,873 sports-starved fans and many made the journey up to Middlesbrough ten days later to see United win 2-0 with goals from Albert Johanneson and Jim Storrie, who finished the season with 27 goals.

The mini-FA Cup run ended at the hands of Nottingham Forest in the fifth round, but by this time United were pushing strongly for promotion with Stoke, Chelsea, Sunderland, Huddersfield and Bury.

Three successive defeats in May snuffed out United's brave challenge as they finished fifth behind champions Stoke and runners-up Chelsea.

But there was no doubt that Don Revie had built a launching pad ready for promotion take off the following season and his hard work was rewarded with a new three-year contract, even though he still had ten months of his existing one to run.

Swinging in the Sixties

WHEN Don Revie filled in the team-sheet for the start of the 1963-4 season, the names Bremner, Charlton and Hunter occupied shirts numbered four, five and six. It was only the second time that the trio had played together in what was to become one of the most famous combinations in football (they had already lined up like that against Bury on 18 September 1962).

It eventually rivalled, then surpassed the great Edwards-Hart-Copping half-back line of the 1930s. Revie had tipped young Billy Bremner to take over as the schemer of the team – a role he shared with the evergreen Bobby Collins.

United's vibrant youth policy was paying dividends and allowed Revie to release Noël Peyton to York City for £4,000, whilst another former international, Tommy Younger, retired.

Revie started the new season with this line-up at Rotherham: Gary Sprake; Paul Reaney, Willie Bell, Billy Bremner, Jack Charlton, Norman Hunter, Don Weston, Ian Lawson, Jim Storrie, Bobby Collins and Albert Johanneson.

Weston bagged the only goal of the game against his old club, but three days later a new face trotted out in the all-white of United at Elland Road for the game against Bury – Johnny Giles.

Only a few weeks earlier, Irish international Giles had picked up an FA Cup winners' medal with Manchester United, but the right winger had no qualms about dropping into Division Two with Leeds. The £33,000 transfer for the Dublin-born 22-year-old was yet another astute piece of business by Revie, who was rapidly building his reputation as an outstanding manager.

Giles came in for Lawson and his craft helped Leeds to a 3-0 victory over Bury, courtesy of goals from Collins, Storrie and Johanneson.

Albert Johanneson joined Leeds United from South African football in April 1961. When they swept to the Second Division title in 1963-4, Johanneson was joint top scorer with Don Weston.

Giles was on target in the 4-1 win at Southampton at the end of October, when United powered to the top of the table with goals from Lawson (2) and Johanneson completing a great display.

Success brought big crowds flocking back to Elland Road as United were locked in a tremendous battle with Sunderland and Preston in the race for the title.

Leeds United, Second Division champions 1963-4. Back row (left to right): Billy Bremner, Paul Reaney, Gary Sprake, Jack Charlton, Norman Hunter, Willie Bell. Front row: Johnny Giles, Don Weston, Bobby Collins, Alan Peacock, Albert Johanneson.

United kept their noses in front for most of the season and even when they lost 2-0 at rivals Sunderland in the final game of 1963, United still held top spot.

It was to the North-East that Revie turned to find the final piece of his promotion jigsaw by signing centre-forward Alan Peacock from Middlesbrough in a club record £50,000 deal.

Peacock, a superb header of the ball, had won four caps at Ayresome Park where he played alongside the prolific Brian Clough.

Although he had over a century of goals under his belt, some doubted Peacock's fitness following a cartilage operation on his left knee.

But Peacock proved up to the job, showing the Leeds fans his aerial prowess as United marched towards the title in superb style, his contribution of eight goals in 14 appearances, helping keep Don Revie's boys ahead of the pack.

Records Tumble in Promotion Push

Club records were broken as United reached the home stretch. Goals by Don Weston and Johnny Giles gave United a 2-1 home win over Leyton Orient on 4 April, leaving them needing only a point from their final three games to secure promotion.

It came the following Saturday at relegation-haunted Swansea, where two Peacock goals and one from Giles had the champagne flowing on the

train journey back to Yorkshire as the 3-0 win sent United up.

Revie's burgeoning 'grow-your-own' policy was blossoming at such a rate that he had no hesitation in naming 19-year-old Terry Cooper on the left wing for his debut in the crucial Swansea match.

Other youngsters like Paul Madeley and Jimmy Greenhoff were given a taste of first-team football during the memorable 1963-4 campaign and both went on to carve out illustrious careers in the game.

After a 1-1 home draw with Plymouth, United wrapped up the Second Division title on the final Saturday of the season with a 2-0 win at Charlton, Peacock snapping up both goals.

That success completed United's best-ever season to date.

They were unbeaten at home, lost only three of their 42 games, won away from home a dozen times and clocked up 63 points – the best by any Second Division side since Tottenham were promoted in 1920.

Success breeds success and United's magnificent season did not go unnoticed on the international scene. Johhny Giles soon added to his collection of Eire caps, Paul Reaney and Billy Bremner were capped at Under-23 level for England and Scotland respectively, whilst Gary Sprake etched his name into the record books by becoming Wales' youngest-ever goalkeeper when he donned

Above: Bobby Collins weaves his way through the West Ham defence at Elland Road in April 1965. Bobby Moore (6) and Ken Brown (5) are the Hammers' defenders. *Below*: West Ham goalkeeper Jim Standen is put under pressure from United's Alan Peacock. Billy Bremner is number-four.

the gloves in a full international against Scotland, the first of his 37 Welsh caps.

These were among the first steps on the road to stardom and it was not long before others in Revie's academy of all stars were making the same journey.

United's young warriors had already had a taste of what to expect in the First Division by giving champions Everton a run for their money in the FA Cup.

United had already won 1-0 at Cardiff in the third round, in a match marred by broken legs for United centre-half Freddie Goodwin and Cardiff winger Alan McIntosh in separate accidents.

In the next round, 48,826 fans at Elland Road saw United take Everton every inch of the way in a 1-1 draw. The replay at Goodison Park attracted a staggering 66,167 crowd and despite a virtuoso display by the evergreen Bobby Collins against his old club, United went down 2-0.

United were to cross swords with the Blues again in 1964-5, but this time as First Division opponents.

Runners-up – at the Double

With more star youngsters coming off the conveyor belt, Revie was able to allow Grenville Hair to join Wellington Town as player-manager, whilst former Scottish international Eric Smith returned north of the border with Morton.

Hair was to return to Yorkshire as trainer to Bradford City in 1967, taking over as manager the following year. He had been in charge at Valley Parade for only a matter of weeks when he collapsed and died at the age of 36, when supervising a training session. His loss was particularly felt at Elland Road where he had been an outstanding performer, clocking up 443 League games. A true sportsman, Hair was an outstanding athlete and would probably have been in line for an England cap had he been with a more fashionable club than United in the 1950s.

The quest to make United a more glamorous club began at Villa Park as United set off on a memorable, and sometimes controversial 1964-5 campaign.

When Welsh international Phil Woosnam put Villa ahead after only three minutes, it seemed as though Revie's rookies could be in for a hiding.

But United roared back with goals from Albert Johanneson and Jack Charlton for a 2-1 win and the best possible start to the new campaign.

When champions Liverpool were sent packing from Elland Road after a 4-2 hiding from United four days later, the rest of the First Division sat up and took notice.

Two goals from Jim Storrie and another from

Charlton made it three wins from three games for United as they beat Wolves 3-2.

Although Liverpool soon gained their revenge with a 2-1 win at Anfield, United's marauders had set out their stall for an attack on the Championship, even though centre-forward Alan Peacock had yet to play because of injury and Ian Lawson was out of action with cartilage trouble.

They were soon joined by Don Weston on the treatment table, but once again Revie had no hesitation in turning to youth to plug the gaps as Rod Belfitt and Rod Johnson were given their chance to lead the attack.

However, sections of the Press dubbed United a dour, over-physical side and matters came to the boil in a bruising encounter at Everton when referee Ken Stokes, of Newark took the teams off for five minutes after a flare-up which prompted missiles to be hurled on to the Goodison Park pitch.

The United board seemed convinced that sections of the press were determined to smear the club following a notorious article in the *FA News* which labelled United as a 'dirty team'.

United were undoubtedly a hard, uncompromising side and it took the club several years to bury their 'dirty Leeds' tag.

When order was finally restored at Goodison, United won 1-0 with a Willie Bell goal. That bitter game came in the middle of a hot streak as United rattled up seven straight wins to equal a club record set up in 1923-4.

Victory soon followed at Old Trafford against Manchester United and on 2 January 1965 the Red Devils were knocked off the top as goals by Jack Charlton and Norman Hunter at home to Sunderland sent United shooting to the top of the First Division for the first time in the club's history.

The race for the title developed into a three-cornered fight between Chelsea and the Uniteds of Leeds and Manchester.

The London club eventually lost ground, but the match which decided the destiny of the League title was fought out at Elland Road on 17 April.

Leeds, unbeaten in 18 League games and with the fit-again Alan Peacock back in attack, were chasing a double after winning 1-0 at Old Trafford earlier in the season with a Bobby Collins goal.

This time Matt Busby's team turned the tables in front of 52,368 fans at Elland Road, John Connelly scoring the only goal of a tense, taut match.

When Leeds crashed 3-0 at Sheffield Wednesday two days later the title dream lay in tatters, but Leeds won the return match against the Owls 2-0 the following day, then triumphed 3-0 over

Sheffield United at Bramall Lane to take the race right up to the finishing line.

Leeds travelled to already-relegated Birmingham as leaders, knowing that nothing less than victory would do.

The men from Manchester were only one point behind with a game in hand and the additional bonus of a better goal-average.

Leeds had to win at St Andrew's and hope Manchester slipped up in either of their final games against Arsenal and Aston Villa.

When it came to the crunch Leeds could not handle the tension and were 3-0 down after 55 minutes. Although they produced a storming fight-back to draw with goals by Johnny Giles (penalty), Paul Reaney and Jack Charlton, a point was not good enough as Manchester beat Arsenal 3-1 at Old Trafford,

In the end the Red Devils lost their final game but had pipped Leeds to the Championship by 0.686 of a goal, thus gaining revenge over Don Revie's boys for their FA Cup semi-final exit.

Only five days after the League Championship slipped away. Leeds suffered another disappointment as they lost the FA Cup Final in extra-time to Liverpool. To reach the Final was an achievement in itself as United were still saddled with an abysmal FA Cup record, having reached the last eight only once in their 45-year history.

But 1964-5 was an exceptional season and Revie possessed an exceptional side.

After Southport were eliminated, United gained revenge over Everton for their 1964 Cup defeat with a stunning replay win, then swept aside Shrewsbury to go through to the sixth round at Crystal Palace.

Alan Peacock, recently restored to the attack, scored twice as Leeds roared to a 3-0 win and booked a semi-final spot for the first time.

Their opponents at neutral Hillsborough were deadly rivals Manchester United, but a bruising encounter on a heavy pitch failed to produce a goal. Tempers were restored for the replay at the City Ground, Nottingham, Leeds snatching a dramatic 1-0 victory with a twisting backward header by Billy Bremner, 90 seconds from the end.

Bremner was also on target in the Final at Wembley but it was not enough as Liverpool put their name on the Cup for the first time with a 2-1 extra-time victory.

It was billed as one of the greatest days in United's history, but by the high standards they had set themselves the men from Elland Road failed to spark in a disappointing game.

Leeds seemed to freeze on a surface made slippery by rain, and only cool handling by Gary Sprake and superb defending by Norman Hunter and Jack Charlton kept the Anfield raids at bay.

The Final went into extra-time for the first time since 1947 and Liverpool proved the stronger.

Roger Hunt put the Merseysiders in the lead, but Bremner thrashed in the equaliser eight minutes later with a tremendous rising shot.

The sodden Wembley turf sapped the strength from tired limbs, but Liverpool summoned one more deadly raid nine minutes from the end as Ian St John headed in the winner from Ian Callaghan's right-wing cross.

The teams for United's first FA Cup Final appearance were:

Leeds United: Gary Sprake; Paul Reaney, Willie Bell, Billy Bremner, Jack Charlton, Norman Hunter, Johnny Giles, Jim Storrie, Alan Peacock, Bobby Collins, Albert Johanneson. **Liverpool:** Tommy Lawrence; Chris Lawler, Gerry Byrne, Geoff Strong, Ron Yeats, Willie Stevenson, Ian Callaghan, Roger Hunt, Ian St John, Tommy Smith, Peter Thompson.

It was heartbreak for United who had lost the title on goal average and the FA Cup in extra-time, but had announced to the rest of the soccer world that Leeds United had arrived as a force to be reckoned with.

They did not finish the season altogether empty-handed. At 34, the remarkable Bobby Collins earned a Scotland recall and was named Player of the Year.

The runner-up in the voting was Jack Charlton, who was amply compensated with his first England cap against Scotland at Wembley when Collins was on the opposite side.

The following month Bremner joined the international ranks by playing his first game for Scotland in a goalless draw against Spain.

These honours cushioned the blow of double disappointment and there was also a new venture to look forward to in 1965-6 – European football.

Gary Sprake dives at the feet of Liverpool's Roger Hunt in the 1965 FA Cup Final. Ian St John rushes in; Jack Charlton looks back.

Leeds defenders can only look on in dismay as Liverpool find the net during extra time in the 1965 FA Cup Final.

Into Europe

Revie, meticulous as ever, flew out to Italy with his chief coach and master spy Syd Owen to run the rule over first Inter-Cities Fairs Cup opponents, Torino.

But no amount of planning could prepare United for such a violent introduction to European soccer. Goals by Billy Bremner and Alan Peacock, who had fought back bravely from injury to recapture his England place, saw United take a slim 2-1 advantage to Turin.

The second leg ended 0-0, but Leeds were dealt a shattering blow as a 50th-minute tackle by Italian defender Fabrizio Poletti broke Bobby Collins' thigh. Although substitutes had been introduced for the first time in the Football League, they were still not used in European competition, but United hung on to their slender advantage.

United also won their second-round tie against Locomotive Leipzig by a 2-1 aggregate to set up a confrontation with Spanish side, Valencia.

The Valencia game at Elland Road became so violent that referee Leo Horn sent off Spanish players Francisco Vidagany and Sanchez Lage and United's Jack Charlton. Towards the end, a bitter running brawl saw police come on to the pitch and referee Horn took the teams off for an 11-minute cooling off period.

The game ended 1-1 and inevitably there was talk of a blood bath in the second leg in Spain. This time the game passed without problems and United upset the odds by grabbing the only goal from Mike O'Grady, a Leeds-born winger who had joined United from neighbours Huddersfield Town in a £30,000 deal in October which saw Don Weston go in the opposite direction.

O'Grady was a player who had slipped through United's net as a youngster at Corpus Christi School. Instead of joining Leeds, he turned professional with Huddersfield and went on to win an England cap with the Town.

Hungarian outfit Ujpesti Dozsa were swept aside 5-2 on aggregate in the next round to put United through to a semi-final against Real Zaragoza.

Having already suffered against one Spanish club, Valencia, United found themselves in another

bruising tussle which saw Johnny Giles and Violetta sent off by referee Marcel Bois.

United had relied on solid defence but were beaten by a penalty from Carlos Lapetra after hand-ball by Bremner.

In the second leg, United won 2-1 with goals from Albert Johanneson and man-of-the-match Jack Charlton. The 'away goals count double' rule had yet to be introduced so the replay venue was decided on the toss of a disc.

Charlton, who had taken over as captain from the stricken Collins, called correctly and Elland Road would stage the replay on 11 May.

Despite having home advantage United were blasted out of the competition as Real surged into a 3-0 lead inside 13 minutes to stun Elland Road into near silence. Charlton pulled a goal back but it proved academic as United ended the 1965-6 season without a trophy.

Revie's team had made early exists from the FA and League Cups, but had harboured genuine Championship hopes for much of the season until Blackpool pulled off a shock double at the end of March. Starring for Blackpool was midfielder Alan Ball, a player whom Revie had tried to sign at the start of the season.

United eventually finished runners-up on goal-average over Burnley, six points behind runaway Champions Liverpool.

However, United were winners on the financial front, banking a £59,028 profit and wiping out their debts and overdraft which had stood at around £250,000 three years earlier.

Throughout the season Revie had made adjustments to his squad. He covered the loss of Collins, by switching Johnny Giles to midfield where he struck a formidable partnership with Billy Bremner.

The arrival of O'Grady and the emergence of more young players like Peter Lorimer, Eddie Gray, and Paul Madeley certainly strengthened the first-team pool.

The teenage Lorimer responded to an extended run in the senior side by finishing joint leading scorer with Jim Storrie, Fellow Scot Gray, a silky skilled winger, marked his debut with a goal in a 3-0 win over Sheffield Wednesday, whilst Leeds-born Madeley, a signing from non-League Farsley Celtic, proved his worth by filling a variety of positions.

Although the defence was settled the attack was continually changed. Revie was not helped as injury once more ruled out Peacock for half the season but his ever-ready youngsters filled the breach well.

Norman Hunter had built up a fearsome reputation for his tremendous tackling and he deservedly won the first of his 28 caps when he came on as substitute – England's first-ever – in Spain. A few weeks later he played alongside Jack Charlton against West Germany at Wembley.

Charlton also made the line-up against the Germans in the World Cup Final on that never-to-be-forgotten afternoon of 30 July 1966, when England lifted the trophy in a thrilling 4-2 win at Wembley.

Hunter, although a member of the World Cup squad, could not get in the side because of the brilliance of skipper Bobby Moore, but for whom Hunter could possibly have doubled his tally of caps. Moore was a natural leader and Charlton

Gary Sprake chases a loose ball at Stamford Bridge in November 1965. Paul Reaney is the Leeds defender on the goal-line. Barry Bridges is the Chelsea forward. Leeds went down by 1-0.

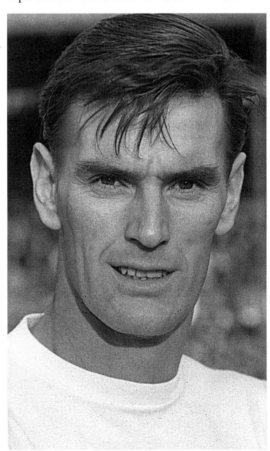

Alan Peacock joined Leeds from Middlesbrough for £53,000 in February 1964 and his goals helped to lift United into Division One.

Jim Storrie was joint top scorer with Peter Lorimer when they returned to the top flight.

also seemed the natural choice to skipper the Leeds team in the absence of broken thigh victim Bobby Collins. But Charlton did not like doing the job because he had a superstition about being last to run out on to the field – not the ideal situation to lead the side out.

The 35-year-old Collins returned to action for the final game of the season and the following season, skippered United on an opening day 3-1 defeat at Tottenham, where the thermometer touched 81°F.

Collins' comeback was cruelly cut short by a ligament injury in United's opening home fixture of 1966-7, a 2-1 win over West Brom.

Charlton reluctantly took on the role as skipper again, this time only for a brief period as the honour of leading Leeds was passed on to Billy Bremner.

Making Bremner skipper was a Revie masterstroke, The little red-haired Scot often found himself in hot water with referees and in the headlines for the wrong reasons because of his fiery temperament.

With extra responsibilities on his shoulders, Bremner matured as a leader, driving his men on in their pursuit of victory.

The injury to Collins was just one of a string to disrupt Revie's plans, particularly in the first half of the season. Once again it was the attack which had to bear the brunt of the chopping and changing. Ian Lawson, no longer able to command a first-team place, had been sold to Crystal Palace

for £9,000 and it was no secret that Revie was scouting round for a new forward but no new man was found during the season.

The Leeds boss was lucky that he could call on versatile youngster Paul Madeley to fill a variety of roles. Play-anywhere star Madeley played in every position but goal for Leeds and in 1966-7 turned out in eight different shirts – excluding number-12. United made only a moderate start to the season and in mid-November the vultures were circling as they crashed out of the Football League Cup, thrashed 7-0 at West Ham where young Leeds-born reserve goalkeeper, David Harvey, was making a rare appearance.

Twelve days later, United crashed 5-0 in a League game at Liverpool where Gary Sprake had the misfortune of scoring one of the most spectacular own-goals ever seen, throwing the ball into his own net as he shaped to toss it out to a colleague. The Kop, in its own inimitable style sang *Careless Hands*, a popular song at the time.

Fortunately neither Sprake nor Leeds were - thrown off line by such disappointments and by the end of the season had moved up the table and were driving towards Wembley once more,

Crystal Palace and West Brom were swept aside in the early rounds of the FA Cup, but Sunderland proved a tougher nut to crack. After a 1-1 draw at Roker Park, a record 57,892 crowd squeezed into Elland Road.

The masses were packed so tightly in one corner of the Lowfields Road terrace that a crash-barrier gave way and fans spilled on to the pitch.

Eighteen people were taken to hospital in a fleet of ambulances suffering from shock and crush injuries. The game resumed after a 15-minute break and finished in another 1-1 draw.

The replay at Boothferry Park, Hull, was a highly-charged affair, Sunderland players George Herd and George Mulhall were sent off after United clinched a 2-1 win three minutes from the end with a controversial Johnny Giles penalty.

The sixth-round 1-0 home win over Manchester City was much calmer, but the semi-final at Villa Park against Chelsea ended in uproar after a United 'goal' was disallowed in the dying minutes.

With Chelsea leading 1-0 thanks to a Tony Hateley header, United lay siege to the London club's goal at the end. They thought they had equalised when Terry Cooper blasted the ball past Peter Bonetti, only to have the goal ruled out on a marginal offside decision.

Then with two minutes remaining United were dealt another gut-wrenching blow. They won a free-kick outside the Chelsea box, Giles touched it on and substitute Peter Lorimer blasted a scorch-

Jack Charlton was voted Footballer of the Year in 1967, the year after he had gained a World Cup winners' medal with England.

In the humidity of Zagreb, United's attackers are Jack Charlton, Rod Belfitt, Norman Hunter and Mike O'Grady. The Fairs Cup Final was held over until the start of the 1967-8 season

Dinamo Zagreb's goalkeeper fists the ball over the bar during another Leeds attack at Elland Road in the second leg in September 1967.

ing shot past Bonetti. But United's joy was premature as referee Ken Burns ruled 'no goal' because he had not been ready and signalled that the kick should be retaken.

This time Chelsea cleared and United's dreams of a second FA Cup Final appearance lay in ruins.

United could not find any solace in Europe, although they did reach the Inter-Cities Fairs Cup Final.

After clobbering DWS Amsterdam 8-2 on aggregate United were drawn against Valencia and visions of a repeat of the physical battle of the previous season was predicted.

After being held 1-1 at Elland Road, an injury-ravaged United were given little chance in the return leg in the Mestalla Stadium.

But, against all odds, they stormed to a 2-0 victory with goals from Lorimer and Giles, the latter having just heard minutes before the kick off that his wife had given birth to a baby girl.

Giles kept his nerve in the next round to score the penalty at Elland Road to give United victory over Italian side, Bologna, and tie the aggregate at 1-1. This time there was to be no third meeting and the tie was decided on the toss of a coin with United skipper Billy Bremner calling correctly.

But there was no luck involved in the semi-final as United blitzed Kilmarnock 4-2 with reserve centre-forward Rod Belfitt bagging a hat-trick and then Leeds defended in depth in the second leg in Scotland to reach their first European Final.

They came up against Yugoslavian side Dinamo Zagreb, who turned in a well-drilled performance to win 2-0 in the first meeting which had been carried forward to the start of the following season. That left Leeds facing an uphill task at Elland Road and despite non-stop pressure they were thwarted by the woodwork and an inspired display by international goalkeeper Zlatko Skoric.

The game ended goalless, leaving United without a trophy for a third successive season, despite pushing hard on several fronts.

One of the main reasons had been a lack of bite in attack, where only Johnny Giles reached double-figures in the League and a third of those had come from the penalty-spot.

Injury restricted Peacock to only half a dozen League appearances, Jim Storrie, whose goals had established Leeds as a force in the First Division had moved on to Aberdeen while big money signing Mike O'Grady was another laid up on the treatment table for most of the season.

Revie searched high and low for a striker of the right calibre but refused to spend for the sake of it and continued to patch up his side with an ever-increasing number of youngsters which now included Mick Bates and Terry Hibbitt, two more teenagers who had shot up from the junior ranks.

Once again the defence was ultra-efficient. Gary Sprake, despite occasional lapses of concentration cemented his international career, Paul Reaney continued to press his claims for an England cap, whilst Willie Bell joined Billy Bremner as a fully-fledged Scottish international.

Norman Hunter and his famous left foot proved an admirable foil to the aerial skills of centre-half Jack Charlton, now firmly established as England's top number-five, a fact confirmed by his election as Footballer of the Year.

Yet despite all the glittering array of talent, Revie still had to win some silverware for Leeds' trophy cabinet in the three seasons since promotion. United, though, were soon to change their label of eternal bridesmaids.

Cups of Cheer

Leeds United at the start of the 1967-8 season. Back row (left to right): Paul Madeley, Alan Peacock, Jack Charlton, Norman Hunter, Mike O'Grady. Middle row: Rod Johnson, Rod Belfitt, Willie Bell, Gary Sprake, David Harvey, Albert Johanneson, Eddie Gray. Front row: John Giles, Jimmy Greenhoff, Paul Reaney, Terry Cooper, Billy Bremner, Mick Bates, Terry Hibbitt, Peter Lorimer.

DON Revie's long, hard search for a new striker ended in October 1967 just a few miles south of Elland Road when Sheffield United's Mick Jones was signed for £100,000 – a record for both clubs.

Jones, an immensely strong front runner, shot to prominence with the Blades as a youngster and won a couple of England caps in 1965.

He had failed to make the World Cup squad but his short move to Leeds was to benefit both United and the player. He was another excellent header of the ball and seen as an ideal replacement for the injury-prone Alan Peacock, who had left on a free transfer to Plymouth but was forced to retire the following year.

Although Peacock's career hit a stop-start-stop period at Leeds, his goals in the run-in to the 1964 Second Division championship had proved vital.

Injury was also to cut Jones' career short, but not before he had given the club eight years outstanding service.

Ironically Jones was not a part of United's first senior success under Revie – winning the Football League Cup. He was Cup-tied and could only watch from the sidelines as United moved relentlessly towards Wembley. A Peter Lorimer hat-trick had already dispatched Luton in the opening round before Bury, Sunderland and Stoke were beaten without the loss of a goal.

The Bury game saw the return to Elland Road

He was able to pass on his knowledge and experience to Revie's bright young players and had even recaptured his place in the Scotland midfield.

After helping Bury, he joined Morton as player-manager, then spent some time playing in Australia before returning to England with Oldham. Collins remained a familiar figure on the Yorkshire soccer circuit, managing Huddersfield, Hull and Barnsley, and also returned to Elland Road for a spell as United's youth coach in the mid-1970s.

Collins and his Bury side were treated with great respect but United eased through 3-0, then beat Sunderland 2-0 and Stoke 2-0 to progress in comfort.

United had a single-minded look about them and their odds of reaching Wembley were slashed when they were drawn with Second Division Derby County over two legs in the semi-final.

Derby were managed by Brian Clough, who had carved out a reputation as a free-thinking manager with Hartlepool and was now moulding Derby into a side to be reckoned with. The Rams piled on the pressure in the first leg at the Baseball Ground, but United virtually put one foot on the Wembley turf by sneaking a win via a Johnny Giles penalty.

of Bobby Collins, who had joined the Shakers on a free transfer in February 1967.

The little midfield general had made an enormous contribution to United's fantastic rise.

In October 1967, Don Revie signed Sheffield United striker Mick Jones for £100,000 – a record fee for both clubs. Already an England international, Jones was to give Leeds eight years' fine service, although his career was to be cut short by injury, just like that of Alan Peacock, the man he had replaced at Elland Road.

Bates, Madeley and Bremner outnumber Nottingham Forest's Bob McKinlay at the City Ground in November 1967. Leeds won 2-0.

If United had relied on all-out defence in the first meeting, it was all-out attack in the second as they won 3-2 to book a Cup Final place against Arsenal at Wembley on 7 March.

Cooper's Wembley Dream

The League Cup Final against the Gunners was a dour affair punctuated by ugly scenes as tempers frayed during several flashpoints.

United, driven on by Billy Bremner's thirst for hard work, never looked like losing a game settled by a controversial goal.

It came after only 18 minutes, when the young Scot, Eddie Gray, hoisted a corner into the Arsenal box. The Gunners' defence were only able to clear the ball just beyond their own penalty area, where Terry Cooper thundered a shot into the net.

Furious Arsenal claimed that goalkeeper Jim Furnell had been baulked by Jack Charlton and Paul Madeley as he went for Gray's cross, but the goal stood.

It was literally a dream come true for Cooper, the winger-turned-full-back, who, for three nights leading up to the big game, had dreamed of scoring the winning goal.

Cooper was now established as one of the First Division's outstanding attacking full-backs and his progress had been so rapid that Revie had been able to release Scottish international Willie Bell to Leicester City for £45,000. Bell had been an important part of Revie's early strategy and after his playing days were over he managed Birmingham City and Lincoln City.

Once in front, United's cast-iron defence made sure they were not caught and the first major trophy in United's history was won with Cooper's solitary goal.

The teams on that important March afternoon in United's history were: **Leeds United:** Gary Sprake; Paul Reaney, Terry Cooper, Billy Bremner, Jack Charlton, Norman Hunter, Jimmy Greenhoff, Peter Lorimer, Paul Madeley, Johnny Giles, Eddie Gray (Rod Belfitt). **Arsenal:** Jim Furnell; Peter Storey, Bob McNab, Frank McLintock, Peter Simpson, Ian Ure, John Radford, David Jenkins (Terry Neill) George Graham, Jon Sammels, George Armstrong.

It was a vital psychological breakthrough for United who finally shook off the tag of perpetual runners-up.

The nature by which they had won the Final certainly did not gain them any friends, but the nearly men from Elland Road had finally come good. The Football League Cup was paraded through the streets of Leeds the following day, which must have proved a particularly sweet one for the ailing Harry Reynolds.

He was the man who had backed Revie to the hilt in the dark days of the early 1960s, but was now suffering from arthritis and had resigned as chairman, a role taken on by Albert Morris, the club's financial director.

Reynolds was appointed as a life president and despite his illness was determined to see United on their big day. He travelled to London by rail in a wheelchair and carrying crutches but was unable to take his seat at Wembley.

Morris, a director of Morris Wallpapers Ltd, was a member of one of the most notable Jewish families in Leeds, going on to be president of the Leeds Jewish Board of Guardians and a founder member and former treasurer of the Leeds Jewish Housing Association.

A United director since November 1961, his chairmanship was a brief one, lasting eight months. Just four weeks after that glory day at Wembley he died in Leeds General Infirmary.

His death saw the club's vice-chairman Percy Woodward step up to become chairman, and United enjoyed some famous successes under his stewardship.

Woodward had supported United as a youngster on the terraces and was vice-president of Leeds Wanderers before joining the United board in 1946.

Within a year, Woodward, who ran a successful packing company in Hunslet, was appointed United's vice-chairman, a position he held for over 20 years.

Woodward's daughter, Jacqueline, married a United reserve player, Terry Duffy, and his son, Brian was also a part-time professional on United's books after World War Two. Brian

A scuffle develops during the Wembley Final between Ian Ure and Frank McLintock of Arsenal and Jack Charlton and Norman Hunter, with Billy Bremner as peace-maker!

Gary Sprake and Jack Charlton provide support for Billy Bremner as he holds aloft the League Cup, won after a stormy Wembley Final against Arsenal in March 1968.

Woodward later went on to play first-team football for York City and Hereford United,

Three weeks after Morris's death, United's hopes of becoming the first side to reach the Football League Cup and FA Cup Finals in the same season were shattered by Everton,

United put out Derby, Nottingham Forest and Bristol City in the early rounds of the FA Cup to set up a sixth-round meeting with Sheffield United at Elland Road. A single goal from Paul Madeley was good enough to cut the Blades down to size and send United on to their third FA Cup semi-final. But United went down 1-0 to Everton in front of a 63,000 crowd at Old Trafford, after a howler by goalkeeper Gary Sprake. Just before half-time his poor clearance travelled just 20 yards, straight to Jimmy Husband whose direct shot was handled by Jack Charlton, leaving Johnny Morrisey to score from the resulting penalty.

It was a bitter disappointment to miss out on another Wembley appearance, particularly as United had done the double over Everton in the League.

United had made a slow start to their 1967-8 programme, but the arrival of Jones saw an upsurge in their fortunes which included a tremendous unbeaten run of 26 matches in all competitions.

They roared to the top, but defeat at Tottenham on Good Friday proved a shattering blow and as the heavy fixture backlog created by success in the Cups took its toll United ran out of steam.

In a real neck-to-neck race, Manchester City lifted the title ahead of their neighbours Manchester United. Leeds' only home defeat came against Liverpool in May, a result which saw the Reds squeeze United into fourth place – the same position which they had achieved the previous season.

It had been a gruelling campaign but United's side were no longer looked upon as a promising crop of youngsters. They had matured quickly into a well-drilled highly efficient side, one of the best in Europe.

Outside the city of Leeds, United's style had its critics particularly in London, but at Elland Road they had a huge following and the cash created from soaring attendances was pumped into ground improvements.

For years the Spion Kop at the Geldard Road end of the ground had remained virtually unchanged. 'But towards the end of the 1967-8 season work began on a new roofed Kop costing £250,000.

As the rest of the clubs in the Football League headed off for their summer break, United still had some unfinished business to attend to in Europe.

The quest for Inter-Cities Fairs Cup honours began in humble surroundings at Spora Luxembourg, where United set a new club record by winning 9-0, Peter Lorimer scoring four of them.

Lorimer, whose reputation as a top-quality marksman was growing, was also on target in the second leg as United cantered to a 7-0 – and 16-0

Leeds goalkeeper David Harvey collects the ball as Liverpool's Peter Thompson and Roger Hunt follow up. The 2-1 defeat on 4 May 1968 was Leeds' only home reverse of the season.

Eddie Gray, scorer of the only goal, in action against Dundee in the 1968 Fairs Cup semi-final. Work had already started on roofing the Kop at Elland Road, hence the empty end.

aggregate – win with Albert Johanneson scoring a hat-trick.

Partizan Belgrade offered a much stiffer task in the second round as United squeezed through 3-2 on aggregate.

It was then a case of taking the high road to the Final as three Scottish sides crossed swords with United. Hibernian were the first tartan opponents and stretched United who had to work hard for their overall 2-1 victory.

That set up a blockbusting showdown with Rangers in round four. The game at Ibrox pulled in 80,000 fans but the Scottish supporters were frustrated as United gave a magnificent defensive display to ensure they started the second leg at 0-0.

The two matches with Rangers attracted so much interest that both games were shown on closed circuit TV at each away ground.

United, playing in front of an Elland Road crowd of 50,498, silenced the noisy travelling Rangers support with one of their best European displays which saw a Johnny Giles penalty and a goal by Peter Lorimer yield a 2-0 victory.

That put United into their third successive Fairs Cup semi-final with Eddie Gray's lone goal nine minutes from time against Dundee at Elland Road proving decisive as United reached the Final 2-1 on aggregate. The home attendance for the Dundee game was half that of the Rangers match, chiefly because only three sides of the ground were open as work had begun on roofing the Kop.

That home tie against Dundee was United's 64th game of an incredible season, but at least they had a couple of months rest before pitting their wits against the mighty Hungarian side, Ferencvaros.

Despite the close attention of several opponents, Mick Jones (dark shirt) scores against Ferencvaros in the home leg of the 1968 Fairs Cup Final. Billy Bremner is in the background.

Leeds United players and manager Don Revie with the Fairs Cup after the goalless draw in Budapest. Mick Jones's goal from the first leg was enough to give United their second trophy of the season.

Mick Bates provided cover for Billy Bremner and Johnny Giles in the great Leeds teams of the 1960s and 1970s.

Set Fair for European Glory

Because of the tremendous backlog of games, the European authorities ruled that the final should be played in August.

Despite a Final of such importance, the game surprisingly attracted only 25,268 fans. United officials cited the annual Leeds holidays and the live TV coverage of the game as the reasons for such a poor attendance.

The Hungarians relied on a blanket defence to keep United at bay and on their star centre-forward Florian Albert to hit Leeds on the break.

Frustrated United chipped away at the Ferencvaros defence but their only breakthrough came just before half-time, thanks to a famous, and controversial, Leeds tactic.

Mick Jones won a corner and United sent up lanky Jack Charlton to stand on the goal-line in front of goalkeeper Istvan Geczi, obscuring the goalkeeper's view.

Lorimer sent the ball across and Charlton rose to nod the ball down for Mick Jones to force it over the line from close range as the Hungarians appealed for a foul by Charlton.

Jones was later carried off after a collision with Geczi and Don Revie was left to ponder whether

had been limited since the arrival of Jones. Greenhoff accepted a £100,000 move to Birmingham City, thus achieving the unusual feat of being transferred during a Cup Final.

The tension in the Nep Stadium, packed with 76,000 excited Hungarians, was enormous, but Revie's boys showed nerves of steel to keep Ferencvaros out and become the first British winners of the Inter-Cities Fairs Cup.

It was nerve-jangling stuff, but goalkeeper Gary Sprake, so often a target for the critics, gave an inspired performance as United held on by his fingertips to a goalless draw.

United gave a superb defensive display and always looked dangerous on the counter-attack, Mick Jones clipping the bar with a header in the 33rd minute. As time ticked away Revie had nearly bitten his finger nails down to the quick as he watched agonisingly from the bench.

Republic of Ireland international Johnny Giles joined Leeds from Manchester United for £33,000 in August 1964, when the club were still in the Second Division. He went on to make nearly 500 senior appearances, taking over from Bobby Collins the role of midfield general.

the 1-0 score-line would be sufficient to take United to glory in Budapest.

Revie later admitted: "I did not admit the doubts I had and I tried everything I knew to inject confidence in the players. But, privately, I was more than a little worried about the outcome of the second game."

Missing from the United squad as they jetted off to Budapest was Jimmy Greenhoff, whose chances

"When we got into those final few minutes my heart nearly stopped beating. As the final whistle drew nearer every minute seemed like an hour." he said. United had richly deserved their rewards in the Fairs Cup and in the Football League Cup and soon the Football League Championship trophy itself would be proudly displayed in the Elland Road trophy cabinet.

Champions, Champions

UNITED had been desperately close to the ultimate prize of the League Championship in each of the four seasons since their return to Division One. Each time their challenge had run out of steam as they became overwhelmed by a backlog of fixtures.

United had continually fallen between too many stools and perhaps they had sacrificed the League Championship as they strived for success on all fronts.

The 1968-9 season was different, however. Early exits from the FA Cup and the Football League Cup and only moderate progress in Europe left United to train their sights firmly on the League title. More games inevitably meant more injuries, but United, with a less strenuous programme, kept a relatively clean bill of health and proved untouchable as they stormed to the title in a record-breaking season.

The first four League games were won – against Southampton, Queen's Park Rangers, Stoke and Ipswich – but United's sizzling start was stopped in its tracks at Nottingham Forest on 24 August, when fire swept through the dressing-rooms at the City Ground, forcing the game to be called off at half-time with the score at 1-1.

The teams had just trooped back into the dressing-rooms ready for Don Revie's interval pep talk when goalkeeper Gary Sprake smelled smoke.

Revie immediately ordered the team out to safety as the flames spread. The police evacuated the stand as the fire devoured much of the structure, including the United players' clothes and personal effects.

On the following Wednesday, United dropped their first point of the season when they were held 1-1 by Sunderland, Rod Belfitt scoring the Leeds goal.

Arsenal took advantage of that slip to move to the top of the table, but United regained top spot on 21 September by outplaying the Gunners in a 2-0 win with goals from Jack Charlton and Mike O'Grady. After that they never really looked back.

Revie had seen no need to buy new players during the summer and his faith in the existing squad was justified as they continued to amass points left, right and centre.

United's super start was eventually ended at Maine Road, where Manchester City ran out 3-1 winners to halt United's nine game unbeaten start to the season. This was no surprise to the statistically minded because United had not won at Maine Road in 32 years.

More of a shock was a 5-1 thrashing at Burnley three weeks later, when the Turf Moor side played some irresistible football.

But that was to prove United's last defeat of the season as they powered through the rest of the League campaign, 28 matches, unbeaten.

United's supreme start to the season prompted the board to award Revie a new contract which bound him to Elland Road for a further seven years until 1975.

The defeat at Burnley signalled the start of a sticky patch in which United suffered a 'bout of drawitis'. Goals dried up, but although they were not scoring too many, United were hardly letting any in at all at the other end.

United's defence, apart from that poor day at Burnley, were on peak form and scoring a goal against Leeds United was a major achievement for most sides.

By Christmas, United were back in the groove and a 6-1 thrashing of Burnley at Elland Road was not only sweet revenge but also served notice to leaders Liverpool that United were back on song.

Above: Eddie Gray gets ready to ride a tackle from Liverpool ironman Tommy Smith in the title decider at Anfield. *Below*: Jack Charlton gets into the attack as Geoff Strong slides in.

Gradually the pressure from United on the men from Anfield began to tell as United reeled in their lead.

Goals by Rod Belfitt and Mick Jones gave United a 2-0 home win over Ipswich to leap-frog Liverpool during February and they were never headed again.

International Aces

On 8 March, United gave a stunning performance to win 5-1 at Stoke, with Mike O'Grady and Billy Bremner bagging a couple of goals each.

That confirmed O'Grady's status as the in-form winger in the country and he deservedly gained an England recall for a friendly against France at Wembley the following Wednesday.

O'Grady was winning only his second cap, his first coming in his Huddersfield Town days in 1963, when he scored twice in a 3-1 win over Northern Ireland.

Billy Bremner, the
commitment and
steel in the midfield
that carried Leeds
United to great
deeds. Bremner's
never-say-die
attitude and
leadership were
complemented by
great passing skills.
He made 587
League
appearances for the
club after his debut
at Stamford Bridge
in January 1960 and
was Footballer of
the Year in 1970,
when Leeds
narrowly missed
what would have
been a unique treble
of League
Championship, FA
Cup and European
Cup.

O'Grady was also on the mark against the French in a runaway 5-0 win, but was never selected again as Alf Ramsey opted for his 'wingless wonders' formation for the 1970 World Cup. Three United men were in the England line-up which decimated France, Jack Charlton playing at centre-half and Terry Cooper earning his first senior cap at left-back. In addition, Paul Reaney and Norman Hunter were also in the squad.

It was the first time that United had three players in the same England side; even that famous trio of the 1930s, Willis Edwards, Ernie Hart and Wilf Copping, never played as an England trio.

Billy Bremner was now ensconced as Scotland's captain and his tartan colleagues Peter Lorimer and Eddie Gray were pressing their claims for regular international selection, while goalkeeper Gary Sprake was an automatic choice for Wales, and Johnny Giles pulled the midfield strings for the Republic of Ireland.

Such strength merely emphasised United's dominance of the season and the rest of the League were left trailing in their wake.

Liverpool clung on to United's coat-tails and it was fitting that United should wrap up the title on Merseyside. A goalless draw at Goodison Park proved priceless as on the same night title rivals Liverpool were held to a 0-0 draw at Coventry.

That sent United to Liverpool on Monday 28 April 1969 needing only one point to lift the League Championship for the first time.

Anfield was packed with 53,750 fans with thousands more locked out and the atmosphere tingled as the two teams clashed in one of the most famous theatres in sport.

United's defence had been magnificent throughout the season and did not buckle as they faced up to the ultimate test in a fast and furious battle. Liverpool enjoyed the bulk of possession, but were thwarted by some fine Sprake saves and were stretched by some speedy counter-attacking United play.

Norman Hunter and Jack Charlton were superb in the centre of the Leeds defence and as the minutes ticked away Liverpool became more frustrated. United kept their cool in the heat of the night and when Harlow referee Arthur Dimond signalled the end of the game, United's players punched the air with joy. The Championship-winning goalless draw was celebrated by United's huge travelling support and the Liverpool fans also paid United the ultimate accolade.

As Billy Bremner took his troops towards the Kop, the huge terracing behind the goal fell silent for a split second before acknowledging United's

Leeds United, League champions 1968-9. Back row (left to right): Paul Reaney, Norman Hunter, Allan Clarke, Mike O'Grady, David Harvey, Gary Sprake, Paul Madeley, Eddie Gray, Rod Belfitt, Jack Charlton. Front row: Mick Jones, Terry Cooper, Terry Hibbitt, Billy Bremner, Johnny Giles, Mick Bates, Peter Lorimer.

feat by booming out the chant "Champions! Champions!" It was a magnificent gesture and proved to United that they had finally carved their niche in English soccer history.

Record-breaking Champs

Two nights later it was party time at Elland Road against Nottingham Forest as the squad was presented with the League Championship trophy by Len Shipman, president of the Football League.

United could not find a champagne performance to match the occasion but a late, long-range goal from Johnny Giles was enough to give United a 1-0 win and set or equal a host of records:

- Most points (67), beat the previous Championship best by Arsenal (1930-31) and Spurs (1960-61) of 66 points
- Most home points (39)
- Most wins (27)
- Most home wins (18)
- Fewest defeats (2) beating Arsenal's previous best of four in 1930-31
- Only two away defeats is also a record
- Unbeaten at home equalled United's best, set in their 1963-4 Division Two championship season
- Only 26 goals were conceded
- Only nine of those goals were let in at home

Those statistics alone paint a picture of a side fitting to be called Champions and guaranteed Don Revie was named Manager of the Year.

Consistency had been United's watchword in the League with Sprake, Reaney, Bremner and

Hunter all ever-presents, Charlton missed only one game and Jones two.

Backroom Boys

Revie, whose services were now sought by the likes of Juventus and Torino, also had the benefit of a magnificent backroom staff whom he was always quick to praise for their dedicated work for United's cause. Revie's first lieutenant was Stockport-born Les Cocker, who joined his home-town team from school in 1938. After joining the Army four years later, he re-signed for Stockport in August 1947, alternating between centre-forward and outside-right.

Cocker was transferred to Accrington Stanley in August 1953 where he finished his playing career and took up coaching, becoming a fully qualified FA coach.

After being spellbound by the mighty Magyars of the 1950s, Cocker became a keen student of Hungarian methods of training and left Stockport to be assistant trainer-coach at Luton in 1958.

He worked in tandem with Syd Owen at Luton and the pair both joined Leeds in July 1960 after playing a key role in Luton's run to the FA Cup Final the previous year. Cocker was also highly regarded by England manager Sir Alf Ramsey and assisted England trainer Harold Shepherdson during England's 1966 World Cup triumph.

Helping with training duties was Cyril Partridge, a native of neighbouring York. Like Cocker, he had been a forward in his younger days, but failed to reach the senior team after signing for Queen's Park Rangers in August 1954.

He moved on to Rotherham, where he played a handful of League games on the right wing before being appointed second-team trainer at Elland Road by Revie.

Physiotherapist Bob English was another for whom a full-time career failed to materialise. Despite a trial with Swindon Town in 1936, he opted to continue his life in the Army. He spent nearly 25 years in khaki, serving with the Army Physical Training Corps from 1938.

English played soccer and hockey for the Army and also represented his unit at boxing, fencing and basketball.

A preliminary FA coach, he joined Queen's Park Rangers in 1958 and arrived at Leeds when former QPR manager Jack Taylor was in charge at Elland Road.

One of the most important roles at the club was held by Maurice Lindley, the chief scout and assistant manager. A centre-forward with Keighley Town, he joined Bradford City as an amateur at 16 but it was with Everton with whom he turned professional. He was a centre-half with the Goodison Park club either side of World War Two, during which he appeared once for Leeds as a guest. Lindley retired in 1953, when he was appointed manager-coach at Swindon.

That move did not pay off and after spells at Barry Town and Crewe Alexandra he was appointed southern area scout for Newcastle United. Lindley first joined Leeds as trainer-coach in 1958 but the following year had moved on to Sheffield Wednesday before returning to Elland Road in July 1960.

The final member of Revie's 'Famous Five' was Syd Owen, one of the most well known and astute men in the game, who had won three caps for England. Born in Birmingham, he worked as an engineer in a factory before enlisting in the RAF in 1941, serving with a mobile radio unit in Egypt, Palestine, Sicily, Italy and Austria.

Owen, a tall commanding type, had played representative soccer in the forces and on demobilisation played a trial game with Birmingham City and was immediately signed.

His stay at St Andrew's was brief, for he moved to Luton Town for £1,500 in June 1947, where he became a pillar of the Hatters' defence for 12 years, nine as captain.

His distinguished career ended in fairytale fashion, playing his last game for Luton in the 1959 FA Cup Final, when they lost 2-1 to Nottingham Forest. Luton did not have a manager on the big day and were led out by their chairman, Thomas Hodgson, although Owen had been earmarked as their new boss.

He held the manager's job for a year and was quick to leap at the chance to join Leeds as chief coach to Revie's young team in July 1960.

He arrived at Elland Road with Les Cocker and after United's meteoric rise up football's ladder, Owen and Lindley became known as Revie's eyes and ears as they travelled throughout the Continent preparing reports of United's European opponents.

But secret dossiers did not help United on the domestic cup scene in 1968-9 as a third-round FA Cup replay exit against Sheffield Wednesday and a shock 2-1 defeat at Crystal Palace in the League Cup left Leeds to concentrate on League success.

Although the League Cup had been wrenched from their grasp, there was no way United were going to let go of the Fairs Cup so easily.

Just a week after winning the trophy, United started their defence with a goalless draw in Belgium against Standard Liege.

The return leg at Elland Road looked a formality but Revie's boys were staring defeat in the face when they trailed 2-0 with 51 minutes gone.

Digging deep into their reserves, United fought back to 2-2 through Jack Charlton and Peter Lorimer, but still looked as though they would go out on the away goals ruling when, minutes from time, tireless skipper Billy Bremner popped up with the winner.

Two Jack Charlton goals gave United the edge as they travelled to Naples for their second-round second-leg game, but in a rugged game in which the Italians used some strong-arm tactics to square the tie at 2-2, United had to rely on the toss of a coin to go through to the third round.

German side Hanover proved easy meat in the next round as United won 5-1 at home and 2-1 away for a comfortable passage into the quarter-finals, although victory was marred by the dismissal of Terry Cooper in the second leg.

Cooper was missing from the Leeds line-up when Hungarian side Ujpesti Dozsa arrived at Elland Road for the first leg of the quarter-finals. They joined Sheffield Wednesday as the only team to win on Leeds soil during 1968-9, with a 1-0 victory through Antal Dunai.

That left United a mountain to climb in the second leg, when a weakened side missing the likes of Reaney, Charlton and O'Grady were well beaten 2-0.

Despite that bitter disappointment Don Revie and his men now had a new goal for 1969-70 – the European Cup.

The Impossible Treble

CHAMPIONS Leeds showed they were not going to rest on their laurels by smashing the British transfer record to snap up goal-poacher Allan Clarke from Leicester City.

United forked out £165,000 for the free-scoring striker hailed as the best penalty-area goal thief since Jimmy Greaves first arrived on the scene.

Slender and stealthy, Clarke first hit the goal trail with Walsall and Fulham before a £150,000 move saw him go to Leicester City in June 1968.

His goals helped the Filberts to the FA Cup Final which they lost 1-0 to Manchester City but he could not prevent them from dropping into Division Two.

Leeds quickly stepped in to make Clarke the costliest footballer in Britain and paired him with Mick Jones in attack. It was a devastating partnership, with the rapier-like Clarke proving a perfect foil for the all-action hard running Jones.

The new-look spearhead was paraded in front of United fans for the first time at Elland Road when Leeds beat FA Cup holders Manchester City 2-1 in the FA Charity Shield with goals by Eddie Gray and Jack Charlton.

United began their 1969-70 League campaign with a 3-1 win over Spurs, courtesy of goals by Bremner, Clarke and a Giles penalty.

That victory was followed by a goalless home draw against Arsenal which equalled Burnley's record 30-match unbeaten run in the First Division which had stood since 1920-21.

United broke that record in style with a thumping 4-1 win at Nottingham Forest and stretched it to 34 with a 1-1 draw at Burnley – a match which saw 33-year-old Jack Charlton make his 500th appearance for United.

That record run came to a halt at Goodison Park, where United lost 3-2 to high-flying Everton. Goals by Joe Royle (2) and Jimmy Husband sent Everton into a 3-0 lead with 50 minutes gone but United showed true champion quality to fight back through Billy Bremner and Allan Clarke.

While Everton continued to set a hot pace at the top of the table, United took time off for their first venture into the European Cup, and what a dramatic start they made.

The draw had paired them with Norwegian amateurs SK Lyn Oslo who were buried under a landslide of goals in the first leg at Elland Road.

United took only 35 seconds to register their first goal, through Mike O'Grady, as they demolished the part-timers 10-0 – the biggest victory in United's history. Mick Jones finished the game with a hat-trick while Clarke, Bremner and Giles chipped in a couple apiece.

The arrival of Clarke had left Revie top heavy with attackers, so he allowed O'Grady to go to Wolves in a £80,000 deal, leaving Eddie Gray and Peter Lorimer as the United widemen.

United made several changes for the second leg but still ran out 6-0 winners to establish a record 16-0 aggregate win.

Despite a rapid exit at the hands of Chelsea in the League Cup, Revie felt there was no need to spend the O'Grady cash on strengthening his first-team pool.

Two-horse Race

Gradually United began to get their act together and rolled off some impressive results, including a 6-1 thrashing of Nottingham Forest which saw a Lorimer hat-trick. By Christmas it was shaping up into a two-horse race between United and Everton for the title.

Jack Charlton (dark shirts) and Martin Chivers of Spurs challenge for a high ball at White Hart Lane in February 1970. The result was a 1-1 draw.

United were hell-bent on avenging their League defeat at Goodison Park and two Mick Jones goals gave Leeds a 2-1 win in front of 46,770, the best of the season at Elland Road.

That helped whittle down Everton's lead and a fortnight later United scored an emphatic 5-2 win at Chelsea which helped nudge Everton off the top.

But United were victims of their own success and the last quarter of the season saw them surrender the Championship to Harry Catterick's team from Goodison as Revie's treble-chasing warriors ran out of steam.

United were not only battling it out on the League, FA Cup and European Cup fronts but also regularly had men on international duty.

No less than four players – Cooper, Charlton, Hunter and Jones – played in England's goalless draw against Holland, whilst a fifth, Paul Madeley, was on the bench, and Allan Clarke had to pull out of the squad with a shin injury.

It all added up to extra pressure for Revie's men and a season which had promised so much blew up in United's faces during a heartbreaking April.

Everton continued to keep winning while Leeds' increasingly tired players began to drop a few points on their travels. Slowly daylight appeared at the top with Everton in the driving seat and United having to rely on the Toffees coming unstuck. Six League games remained when United, unbeaten at Elland Road, went into their home game against Southampton three points adrift of Everton, who also had a game in hand.

That match against the Saints proved to be a disaster. Illness and injury forced Revie to leave out Bremner, Hunter and Giles. For once United's reliable reserves could not plug the gaps as the proud unbeaten home record was shattered by a stunning 3-1 smash and grab win by Southampton, whose goals came from a Ron Davies penalty and own-goals by Jack Charlton and young Welsh defender Terry Yorath, another product of United's youth policy.

Meanwhile Everton were thumping Chelsea at Goodison to put one hand firmly on the title.

Two days later, on Easter Monday, the crown was as good as in Everton's hands as they won at Stoke while a team of United reserves crashed 4-1 at Derby. The Leeds side was straight out of the Central League: David Harvey, Nigel Davey, Paul Peterson, Jimmy Lumsden, David Kennedy, Terry Yorath, Chris Galvin, Mick Bates, Rod Belfitt, Terry Hibbitt, Albert Johanneson.

Leeds United manager Don Revie after receiving his OBE at Buckingham Palace. With him are his wife Elsie and children Duncan (15) and Kim (10).

Revie, who had been awarded an OBE at the New Year, claimed that he could not field his first-teamers because of injury and had been warned by the club doctor that at least five senior players were mentally and physically drained by the demands of a gruelling season.

That cut little ice with the FA who fined United £5,000 for failing to field their strongest side.

Two days after the Derby debacle, United's European Cup and FA Cup dreams were dealt a shattering blow as Paul Reaney broke a leg in a now meaningless 2-2 League draw at West Ham.

Celtic Showdown

Fate, it seemed, was conspiring against United as they prepared for the FA Cup Final against Chelsea and their European Cup semi-final against Celtic.

The route through Europe had been smooth. After hammering Lyn Oslo in the first round, United turned on two scintillating exhibitions to thrash Ferencvaros of Hungary 3-0 both home and abroad. Incidentally, a trip to see the game in Budapest with Leeds-based coach firm Wallace Arnold would have cost 33 guineas.

In the quarter-finals, Belgian champions Standard Liege were beaten 1-0 in both legs, so United had reached the semi-finals of Europe's top competition without conceding a goal.

The showdown with Celtic was billed as the 'Battle of Britain' but jaded Leeds could not do themselves justice in either game. The first leg saw Elland Road packed with hordes of Scots, confident that the green and white hoops of Celtic would triumph. The travelling tartan army were not disappointed. Inspired by a

Jack Charlton is just wide with a header during the 'Battle of Britain' European Cup game against Celtic.

The camera sometimes lies – Allan Clarke appears to have just received a boot up the bottom from Celtic goalkeeper Evan Williams.

dazzling performance by winger Jimmy Johnstone, they snatched a goal after only 85 seconds from George Connelly and were able to take a 1-0 advantage back north of the border as Leeds struggled to find their form.

Just to rub salt into their wounds, Everton beat West Brom 2-0 on the same night to wrap up the League title in blue and white ribbons.

That first-leg game against Celtic was staged on 1 April but, despite the loss of their Championship crown, there was still the FA Cup to play for.

United had to switch off from their European campaign and channel their thoughts into lifting the FA Cup against Chelsea at Wembley.

The early European rounds had seen United sweep all before them, but the FA Cup was less trouble-free. Indeed, Leeds were nearly brought down to earth by Fourth Division Swansea in the third round as they trailed 1-0 at home to a David Gwyther goal.

With 30 minutes left, Swansea defender Mel Nurse was sent off after clashing with Allan Clarke and United squeezed home 2-1 against the ten-men opposition with a Johnny Giles penalty and a Mick Jones header. Clarke hit the headlines in the next round with a four-goal haul against Isthmian League club Sutton United, in one of the competition's most romantic ties.

United won 6-0 at the charmingly-named Gander Green Lane ground, but had more difficulty beating Mansfield Town in the fifth round, surviving a disallowed goal for the Stags before winning 2-0.

Clarke took his FA Cup tally to seven with both goals in United's 2-0 sixth-round win at Swindon to set up a mouth-watering semi-final meeting with Manchester United.

Battling Billy's Honour

Because of the World Cup in the summer, the Football League season was ending earlier than normal to allow Sir Alf Ramsey to prepare his squad for Mexico, putting further pressure on United's players. The semi-finals were earmarked for 14 March and at that stage United were still going full tilt for the treble. But they needed two energy-sapping replays before the Old Trafford side were beaten 1-0 at Burnden Park, Bolton, in a thrilling tussle.

Once again the Leeds match-winner was Billy Bremner, whose last-gasp goal against Manchester United in 1965 took Leeds through to their first FA Cup Final.

This time he struck early on and turned in a tremendous performance which fully justified his selection as the 1970 Footballer of the Year.

Bremner and his boys had little time to rest as the big fixtures were coming thick and fast now.

The week after booking their place at Wembley against Chelsea, weary United suffered that morale-shattering European Cup first-leg defeat against Celtic.

Jack Charlton heads Leeds in front in the 1970 FA Cup Final. The two Chelsea defenders on the line misjudged the bounce of the ball on the wet, sandy pitch.

Mick Jones restores United's lead in the 1970 FA Cup Final with an 84th-minute goal. But Chelsea fought back again and the game went to a reply.

But they showed no signs of flagging in the FA Cup Final, when they turned in a superb display, only to be clawed back by the Londoners twice and held at 2-2.

Eddie Gray, who had scored two memorable individual goals against Burnley the week before the Final, turned in a blistering display, running his marker, David Webb, ragged.

On a sand-covered Wembley pitch, both sides produced a game oozing with bright attacking football, yet it needed two defensive errors to get the scoreboard moving.

United took the lead when Jack Charlton headed in a corner as two defenders on the line misjudged the bounce of the ball on the beach-like turf. Just before the interval, United goalkeeper Gary Sprake made a crucial error, allowing a speculative long shot from Peter Houseman slip from his grasp and over the line. United, with Johnny Giles spraying the ball around the field, looked the better side and struck the woodwork twice but could not shake off a brave Chelsea side.

Leeds looked to have the Cup in the bag when Mick Jones drilled in an 84th-minute goal after Allan Clarke's header came back off a post. But United lost concentration two minutes later and Ian Hutchinson stole in with a fine equalising header. Extra-time failed to find a winner and United fans were to wonder when the season would end.

Allan Clarke lurks as Peter Bonetti covers his post during the 1970 FA Cup Final replay.

In the case of the European Cup, the answer was four days later. United were already trailing 1-0 to Celtic as they headed north to take on Jock Stein's Scottish champions. The destination was not Parkhead but Hampden Park as so many people wanted to see the game. A staggering crowd of around 136,000 – the biggest attendance of any European Cup-tie – were jammed in to witness the second stage of the 'Battle of Britain'.

Leeds weathered an early storm of non-stop Celtic pressure to break out and score in the 14th minute with a fierce drive by Billy Bremner, the little man for the big occasion.

That put the tie level, but things turned sour for United just after the interval. First John Hughes sent a diving header past Sprake, who was then carried off after a collision with the same player. The first thing Sprake's replacement, David Harvey, did was to pick the ball out of the back of the net as Bobby Murdoch's 15-yard drive flashed past him.

That gave Celtic a 2-1 win on the night and a comfortable 3-1 aggregate win to send them through to the European Cup Final, where they lost to Dutch side Feyenoord.

Final Heartbreak

United still had a final to contest themselves – the FA Cup Final replay against Chelsea.

It was a case of two down and one to go for Revie's troops as they went into battle for the last time in a marathon season.

The game was held on 29 April, a fortnight after United's demise in Glasgow, and Leeds seemed to have benefited from their rest.

In a physical encounter they enjoyed the bulk of possession and shot ahead after 35 minutes with a thumping drive by Jones after a superb crossfield dribble by Allan Clarke.

But once again Chelsea illustrated their remarkable capacity for survival, grabbing an equaliser via the head of Peter Osgood 12 minutes from the end.

United continued to take the game to Chelsea in the extra period but saw the Cup disappear when David Webb, the man given such a roasting by Eddie Gray at Wembley, headed in to give Chelsea a 2-1 extra-time victory.

United, regarded by many as the best team in the country, had ended a momentous season with nothing. For broken-leg victim Paul Reaney the loss was even greater.

He missed out on a trip to Mexico with Sir Alf Ramsey's England squad.

Paul Madeley was considered by Sir Alf as a replacement, but the shattered Madeley, having played eight games inside 18 days for trophy-chasing Leeds, turned down the chance.

Apart from being exhausted and in need of a break, Madeley reckoned he would probably not be selected anyway. He believed he made the right decision for United and England.

Terry Cooper, Jack Charlton, Norman Hunter and Allan Clarke did all link up with the England squad, the latter scoring coolly from the spot to give England a 1-0 win over Czechoslovakia in his debut game. That match proved to be the last time Jack Charlton pulled on an England shirt.

His 35 appearances make him Leeds United's most capped England international and although the lanky centre-half's international career was at an end, he still looked forward to more honours with Leeds United – even at the age of 35.

Putting on the Style

SINCE winning the title there had been signs that United had added more flair to their play.

They had often been dubbed a 'method' side, a highly efficient ultra-professional footballing machine but not a particularly entertaining one.

The spirit running through the club was tremendous – encapsulated by the motto 'Keep Fighting' in the dressing-room at Elland Road.

United were a close-knit unit with Revie seen as the head of the family. On away trips he organised games of bingo and carpet bowls to relax the players whom he looked upon with great pride and protectiveness.

They were among the best paid players in the country and during the 1968-9 Championship season seven players were earning between £10,000 and £12,500 a year.

Now Revie felt it was time to let his boys off the leash.

During the momentous 1969-70 season, United seemed to play with more adventure and for the next few years adopted a more cavalier spirit which won new friends. It was as though United had been released from a strait-jacket and their gifted players began to express themselves.

This was apparent in the start to the 1970-71 season as United confounded their critics to make a blistering start.

Some of the World Cup players barely got any rest during the summer and there were grave doubts about whether Revie's players could

pick themselves off the floor after such a shattering finish to the previous season.

When the players reported back for pre-season training, one familiar face was missing – Albert Johanneson. His speed and skill had endeared him to United's fans during their rise in the mid-1960s but his appearances had only been spasmodic in the last couple of years and he started a new chapter in his career after joining York City on a free transfer.

Revie gave the rest of his squad a vote of confidence by keeping out of the transfer market and they responded by rolling up their sleeves ready for another all-out assault on the League Championship.

In the early weeks they seemed unstoppable, reeling off five straight wins starting with a 1-0

Norman Hunter shoots for goal, beating the outstretched leg of Southampton's Jimmy Gabriel at Elland Road in September 1970. United won 1-0, recovering from a 3-0 defeat by Stoke City the previous week.

Gary Sprake is left to reflect after Ray Crawford scores Colchester United's second goal in the FA Cup shock at Layer Road in February 1971.

win at Manchester United through a Mick Jones header – his 100th League goal.

Soon afterwards United enjoyed a sweet 3-2 win over champions Everton on a freshly-seeded Elland Road pitch to christen the completion of the West Stand extension.

United lost their 100-per-cent record in a goalless draw at Highbury against Arsenal, failing to break down a determined Gunners side which had been reduced to ten men when Eddie Kelly was sent off for striking Terry Cooper in the 23rd minute. But five successive wins was still United's best start to the season and included a 3-0 success at Burnley, where Allan Clarke's goal inside 21 seconds was reckoned to be the fastest in the club's history.

Although they were brought down to earth in September when they crashed 3-0 at Stoke and were surprisingly eliminated from the Football League Cup at Sheffield United, Revie's aces looked unstoppable in the League.

Even injuries to Giles (fractured cheek-bone) and Eddie Gray (broken ankle) failed to halt United's charge to the top and by Christmas the Championship race was between United and Arsenal with United overwhelming favourites with the bookies.

Just as United seemed to be pulling away from Arsenal they suffered consecutive home defeats against Tottenham and Liverpool and were sensationally knocked out of the FA Cup by Fourth Division Colchester United.

A catalogue of defensive errors saw Colchester build up a 3-0 lead and although United fought back to make it 3-2, they could not prevent the U's pulling off one of the biggest giantkilling acts in the history of the competition.

It was a shattering blow but United bounced back with four straight wins to re-establish their supremacy over Arsenal and when Allan Clarke scored all four goals in the 4-0 thumping of Burnley in April, United held a six-point advantage over the Gunners who needed to win all their games in hand.

The West Brom Invasion

Gradually Arsenal kept chipping away at United's lead and had reduced the gap to two by 17 April – a day which was to prove one of the blackest in United's history. While Arsenal were beating Newcastle 1-0 with a Charlie George goal, tense United were struggling against lowly West Brom at Elland Road. West Brom, without an away win for 16 matches, were leading with a Tony Brown goal when Elland Road erupted as Albion scored a highly controversial second.

Match of the Day cameras caught Colin Suggett yards offside as Tony Brown collected a pass. He even stopped to look around, but referee Ray Tinkler waved play on.

Brown ran on unchallenged before slipping the ball to Jeff Astle to net a simple goal.

Fans howled in anger, Tinkler was surrounded by United players and even Revie went on to the field to plead his team's case, but Tinkler would not be moved.

It was too much for some supporters to take and a handful of them dashed on to the field to manhandle the under-fire referee. Tinkler was jostled by several people before police restored order and the match could be restarted. Although Clarke pulled a late goal back, the damage had been done.

Arsenal, with two games in hand, had taken over at the top on goal average and guaranteed a nail-biting finish to a tremendous campaign.

Nine days later the Gunners arrived at Elland Road having won 23 points from their last 13 games and United knew they had to win to keep their faint Championship hopes alive.

United managed it with an 89th-minute goal from Jack Charlton but Arsenal staged their own last-ditch heroics to finally win the title.

United completed their campaign with 64 points – one more than Arsenal, whose last game in hand was at North London rivals Tottenham.

An Arsenal victory and a goalless draw would give the Gunners the title, but any other scoreline, including a 1-1 draw would give United the Championship on goal-average.

Nearly 52,000 fans crammed into White Hart Lane and they saw Arsenal clinch the title for an eighth time with a header from Ray Kennedy in the dying seconds.

In December 1970, Leeds beat Sparta Prague 6-0 at Elland Road and 3-2 in Czechoslovakia to move into the fourth round of the Fairs Cup. *Above*: Vaclav Masek nips through the Leeds defence. *Below*: Rod Belfitt scores Leeds' third goal in Prague.

Arsenal's 1-0 win gradually filtered through to Boothferry Park, Hull, where United were playing in a testimonial for striker Chris Chilton, and messages of congratulations were sent down to Highbury. It had been a fantastic fight to the finish and to underline their claim to be the best team in the country, Arsenal beat Liverpool at Wembley the following Saturday to become the first team to win the 'double' since Spurs in 1960-61.

United, who had held a six-point lead with eight games to go, could reflect on what might have been but Arsenal had richly deserved their reward, built on a sensational run of nine successive wins.

More Fairs Cup Glory

But United were not to finish the season empty-handed as they had been 12 months earlier. This time they created a little bit of history of becoming the first British club to win the Inter-Cities Fairs Cup for a second time.

United used the first-round second-leg against Norwegian side Sarpsborg to reintroduce Reaney to senior action for the first time in 27 weeks as Leeds cruised through 6-0 on aggregate.

East German side Dynamo Dresden offered a much stiffer task in the next round. United won the first leg 1-0, thanks to a Lorimer penalty, and although they lost a bruising return leg 2-1 – a game which saw Mick Bates and Geyer sent off – they scraped through on the controversial away goals rule.

The third round saw United turn on a vintage performance to thrash Sparta Prague 6-0 and they were given a tremendous ovation in Czechoslovakia as they won 3-2 to set up a quarter-final tie with Vitoria Setubal from Portugal. Setubal were stubborn opponents and were incensed with the penalty scored by Johnny Giles late on which gave United a 2-1 win.

United protected their lead superbly in the second leg, Peter Lorimer scoring in his seventh successive match, to earn United a 1-1 draw.

United did not have far to travel for their semi-final – just across the Pennines to Liverpool, United's arch rivals in domestic soccer.

Revie took a big gamble by giving Billy Bremner his first start in three months following injury. It proved a masterstroke as Bremner, playing upfield, demonstrated his love of the big occasion with a

Top: Billy Bremner races for the ball on a waterlogged Stadio Comunale pitch in the abandoned Fairs Cup Final first leg against Juventus. *Bottom:* This time it is Mick Jones who finds it almost impossible to move the ball on the rain-soaked surface.

diving header which gave United a priceless 1-0 win.

Liverpool were locked out in a goalless draw at Anfield to put United through to their third Fairs Cup Final.

This time Juventus, the club which had lured John Charles away from Yorkshire 14 years earlier, were the opposition.

The opening game in Turin was abandoned after 52 minutes because of a waterlogged pitch, but two nights later the match went ahead after the Stadio Comunale pitch had recovered from its soaking.

The Italians took the lead through Roberto Bettega with a swift counter attack, but United stormed back with a deflected Paul Madeley shot.

Franco Causio made it 2-1, but Mick Bates, a substitute for the injured Mick Jones, drilled in a second equaliser against a side Revie described as 'the best team we have ever met in Europe'.

Allan Clarke struck early in the Elland Road return on 3 June and although Pietro Anastasi equalised, United, inspired by a superb display by Terry Cooper, lifted the trophy on the iniquitous away-goals ruling.

For once luck and the rule book had favoured United whose efforts for another hard season had finally been rewarded. There were also notable individual successes. Paul Reaney successfully

Jack Charlton challenges in the 1971 Fairs Cup Final second leg at Elland Road.

battled back from his broken leg to earn his first full England cap in a 1-0 European Nations win in Malta. Paul Madeley, who had turned down the chance to go to the World Cup in Mexico, won the first of his 24 full England caps against Northern Ireland in May. Terry Yorath, still largely confined to reserve-team football, joined Gary Sprake in the Welsh team.

Yorath was still finding his feet as a utility player and illustrated United's strength in depth, as did Bates, an admirable stand-in for the injured Bremner in midfield.

Many people believe the controversial West Brom game had cost United the 1970-71 Championship crown and some even went as far to say it cost them the title the following season.

The FA Disciplinary Commission held an inquiry into the pitch invasion and after considering the post-match

Leeds United pictured with the Fairs Cup. Back row (left to right): Rod Belfitt, Norman Hunter, Gary Sprake, David Harvey, Joe Jordan, Terry Yorath. Middle row: John Faulkner, Chris Galvin, Mick Jones, Paul Madeley, Allan Clarke, Jack Charlton. Front row: Paul Reaney, Mick Bates, Peter Lorimer, Johnny Giles, Billy Bremner, Nigel Davey, Terry Cooper.

Don Revie with the Fairs Cup and the Manager of the Year trophy.

comments of chairman Percy Woodward and manager Revie, who had said Tinkler's decision was the worst he had ever seen, came down hard on United.

Elland Road was shut down for three weeks from the start of the 1971-2 season, the club was fined £500 and ordered to pay visiting clubs for the loss of cash through the gate during the period of ground closure.

Revie was severely censured and warned as to

his future conduct for his remarks and Woodward was also censured, although both men apologised to the Commission.

United in Exile

United gleaned six points out of a possible eight from those games in exile, although if one more point had been achieved, it would have given them the title. For the record, United drew 0-0 with Wolves at Huddersfield, drew 1-1 with Spurs in the first-ever First Division game played at Hull, thrashed Newcastle 5-1 at Hillsborough and beat Crystal Palace 2-0 at Huddersfield.

United returned from exile with a Lorimer goal giving them a sweet 1-0 win over Liverpool as normal service was resumed at Elland Road. Indeed, United were all but invincible on their home patch, surrendering only two more points throughout the rest of the season.

The only blip was a spectacular one – an amazing 4-0 reverse against Belgian side Lierse in the UEFA Cup (formerly the Fairs Cup). United had already won 2-0 in Belgium and Revie, thinking the tie was as good as in the bag, opted to field a weakened side at Elland Road.

It was to prove a rare Revie mistake as United crashed in sensational style. They also lost the chance to hold the old Fairs Cup trophy outright, losing 2-1 to Barcelona in a special game between the current holders, United, and the first holders, Barcelona.

Although the rest of Europe could not see United's new-found style, the First Division certainly did.

United's football reached dizzy heights with many games televised on *Match of the Day* winning them legions of new fans who were captivated by a series of spell-binding performances.

In February, Manchester United were hammered 5-1, Mick Jones bagging a hat-trick in a superb team display. The next home match, against Southampton, was even better as Revie's aces tore the Saints apart in a 7-0 blitz that is regarded as the best exhibition ever seen at Elland Road.

Peter Lorimer knocked in three goals in that game and finished the season with 23 League goals in his best-ever season.

With Lorimer, Clarke and Jones settled in attack, Terry Hibbitt joined Newcastle for £30,000 and Rod Belfitt went to Ipswich for £40,000.

These were the main departures. during the season, although there should have been another player coming in to Elland Road – Asa Hartford.

The West Brom midfielder was signed for £177,000, terms were agreed and everything looked set to go ahead until a medical revealed that Hartford had a hole in his heart.

Revie, although anxious to strengthen his squad with such a quality player, believed he could not take the risk of completing the deal because of Hartford's condition.

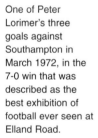

One of Peter Lorimer's three goals against Southampton in March 1972, in the 7-0 win that was described as the best exhibition of football ever seen at Elland Road.

Arsenal goalkeeper Geoff Barnett is helpless to prevent Allan Clarke's header taking the FA Cup to Elland Road in 1972.

In fact, Hartford went on to play for Scotland 50 times and proved an excellent servant to West Brom, Manchester City and Everton in a long and healthy career.

The Hartford affair did not deflect United from their title target as they continued to turn over teams at Elland Road. Champions Arsenal were beaten 3-0 and Nottingham Forest obliterated 6-1 as Leeds tussled with Manchester City, Derby and Liverpool for top spot.

Had United been able to show the same form away from home, then the title would have been a formality. But their willingness to attack on their travels saw them exposed at the back and nine games were lost on opposition soil.

But their invincible Elland Road form kept them on track for the League and FA Cup 'double' as the season reached its thrilling climax.

Wembley Wonders

The whole campaign boiled down to two games in three days – the FA Cup Final and the last League game as United sought to join the elite of 'double' winners.

The FA Cup trail began with Bristol Rovers being beaten 4-1. Liverpool were knocked out 2-0 in a titanic fourth-round replay at Elland Road and two goals by Johnny Giles put paid to Cardiff.

In the sixth round, Spurs were beaten 2-1 and the semi-final saw Second Division Birmingham outclassed 3-0 in a one-sided match at Hillsborough.

Between the posts for United in that semi-final was David Harvey, whose patient wait as understudy to the erratic Gary Sprake finally gained him reward.

By the time the Final came around, Leeds were still in with a great chance of the 'double' and Revie had decided to stick with Harvey, who played in the Centenary FA Cup final against the holders, Arsenal.

Harvey proved Revie's decision was correct with an immaculate display as United ended their long quest for the FA Cup with a 1-0 win.

Man-of-the-match Allan Clarke scored the only goal of the game with a tremendous diving header from a Mick Jones cross in the 53rd minute. It was the most famous goal in Leeds United's illustrious history.

United really opened up after that goal and were unlucky not to add to their lead as a succession of sweeping, attacking waves towards the tunnel end had the Gunners back-pedalling.

United's players danced with glee at the final whistle as they lifted the FA Cup for the first time in the club's history after going so close in recent seasons.

The first leg of the 'double' had been achieved – but at a price.

In the run in to the Championship, United had already lost England fullback Terry Cooper, who broke a leg in a 3-0 win at Stoke.

Now, on one of the greatest days in United's history, they lost striker Mick Jones, who had

dislocated an elbow in a last-minute challenge with Arsenal goalkeeper Geoff Barnett.

United's players had already collected their winners' medals and Arsenal's team their losers' mementoes when Jones, swathed in bandages, was led gingerly up to the Royal Box by Norman Hunter for the gentlest of handshakes from the Queen. The teams for the Final were: **Leeds United:** David Harvey; Paul Reaney, Paul Madeley, Billy Bremner, Jack Charlton, Norman Hunter, Peter Lorimer, Allan Clarke, Mick Jones, Johnny Giles, Eddie Gray. Sub: Mick Bates. **Arsenal:** Geoff Barnett; Pat Rice, Bob McNab, Peter Storey, Frank McLintock, Peter Simpson, George Armstrong, Alan Ball, Charlie George, John Radford(Ray Kennedy), George Graham.

The 'Double' Slips Away

United had no time for mass celebrations as they had to play at Wolves on Monday night in a game which could have sealed the 'double'.

The FA had ruled that United and Liverpool should both play their outstanding games that night – a decision which drew considerable criticism in the press.

Brian Clough's Derby, the surprise packet of the First Division, had finished their games and had been taken abroad for a holiday, whilst Leeds and Liverpool concluded their unfinished business.

United needed only to draw at Wolves to win the title, but Revie's leg-weary troops went down 2-1 in front of 53,379 fans, although United were twice denied a clear-cut penalty near the end.

The atmosphere at Molineux was white hot as Leeds took to the field backed by a huge army of travelling fans. Clarke, hurt in the Cup Final, defied injury to play but United did not really play at their best against a Wolves side inspired by the occasion.

Scottish international Francis Munro gave Wolves the lead and when Derek Dougan added a second, United's 'double' dream lay in tatters.

Battling Billy Bremner gave his

Allan Clarke, scorer of the winning goal, doesn't want to let go of the trophy. Substitute Mick Bates shares his delight.

"Let me hold it…"
Don Revie's hands
are outstretched as
Billy Bremner hands
over the FA Cup
following Leeds'
Wembley victory
over Arsenal.

troops a lifeline when he pegged a goal back and, although they piled on the pressure at the end, Wolves somehow survived the Leeds onslaught.

United had two loud penalty appeals rejected but the efforts of Wembley had left too many of United's players jaded and they fell at the final hurdle again with the Championship within their grasp.

Liverpool also failed to cash in on their final throw of the dice, drawing 0-0 at Arsenal, so the holidaying Clough and his Rams won the Championship, Derby looking back to see how vital their victory over Liverpool in their last game of the season had proved.

It was a shame that another magnificent season for United should end on a low note, but nothing could ever erase the glory of that Wembley triumph from the memory.

Revie's Legacy

DURING the summer of 1972 Don Revie made a double raid on neighbours Huddersfield Town to sign central defenders Trevor Cherry (£100,000) and Roy Ellam (£35,000).

With Terry Cooper still recovering from a broken leg and Jack Charlton having reached the venerable age of 37, the new recruits were evidence that Revie was slowly beginning to rebuild his side.

He had already started to introduce young Joe Jordan from Morton to the attack as a natural successor to Mick Jones and another raw Scot, centre-half Gordon McQueen, was to join the club for £30,000 from St Mirren.

Jordan and McQueen were ones for the future, but circumstances forced Revie into playing his new men from Huddersfield in the opening game of the 1972-3 campaign, at Chelsea.

Cooper's place went to Cherry, Ellam came in at centre-half to partner Paul Madeley, who wore the suspended Norman Hunter's number-six shirt, whilst suspension also ruled out Allan Clarke.

It proved to be a disastrous start. David Harvey, now preferred to Gary Sprake in goal, went off with concussion, Mick Jones was carried off with a twisted ankle, Peter Lorimer took over between the sticks and a disorganised ten men went down 4-0.

Harvey recovered to play at Sheffield United the following Tuesday as Leeds, with Charlton restored to centre-half, won 2-0.

It was business as usual for Leeds, who quickly got into their stride, including a 5-0 drubbing of the reigning Champions, Derby, but it was Liverpool who were to emerge as the biggest threat to United's title ambitions.

A goal from their new striking star Kevin

Revie's double raid on Leeds Road: Trevor Cherry (left) and Roy Ellam (right) joined United from Huddersfield Town in time for the start of the 1972-3 season.

Billy Bremner nets a last-minute winner against Southampton in August 1972.

David Harvey had won his place over Gary Sprake but was carried off with concussion in the opening game of 1972-3. He was back for the next game, however.

Keegan eliminated United from the Football League Cup and they also achieved the double over Leeds in the League.

Despite a spectacular overhead kick from Mick Jones, the Reds won 2-1 at Elland Road and their 2-0 win over United in April virtually clinched the Championship.

United had not managed to reach the heights of the previous season but still finished third, playing a brand of attractive soccer.

Jordan, a £15,000 bargain from Morton, was emerging as a striker of true quality when he stood in for both Jones and Clarke, who finished the season with 18 League goals to his credit. Lorimer weighed in with 15 and Jones and Jordan nine apiece. Apart from Jordan, defender McQueen was being groomed as a replacement for Jack Charlton and Frank Gray, brother of Eddie, marked his full League debut with a goal in a 4-0 thumping of Crystal Palace. Although the Championship had just proved beyond United's grasp once more, they were making plenty of headway on the FA Cup and European fronts.

The defence of the FA Cup began against Norwich, who were destroyed by a brilliant Allan Clarke hat-trick in a second replay at Villa Park as United stormed home 5-0. Plymouth, West Brom and Derby were knocked out as United moved into the semi-final against Wolves at Maine Road.

Once more Billy Bremner showed he was the man for the big occasion by grabbing the only goal of the game to take United to Wembley again.

United fans danced on the terraces as news filtered through that Second Division Sunderland had beaten Arsenal in the other semi-final at Hillsborough.

Sunderland Shocker

United were made the shortest-ever favourites to win the FA Cup with no one outside Wearside

The 32nd minute of the 1973 FA Cup Final and Sunderland's Ian Porterfield stuns Leeds with a volleyed goal.

believing that Sunderland could pull off the impossible.

But the men from Roker Park, inspired by their manager Bob Stokoe astounded the football world by beating Leeds 1-0 to become the first Second Division side to win the FA Cup for 42 years.

Their golden moment came in the 32nd minute when Ian Porterfield smacked in a crisp volley to stun United.

Gradually United stirred themselves into belated action and only a miraculous double-save by goalkeeper Jim Montgomery – from Trevor Cherry then Peter Lorimer – denied United an equaliser.

Sunderland goalkeeper Jim Montgomery denies Peter Lorimer. It was the 'keeper's wonderful double save that fans remember more than Porterfield's winning goal.

More action from the Cup Final. Trevor Cherry gets the ball into the Wearsiders' net but his effort was disallowed for a foul on Sunderland goalkeeper, Jim Montgomery.

Eleven days later United's cup of woe ran over as they lost a controversial European Cup-winners' Cup Final against AC Milan in Greece.

It was the first time that United had contested the Cup-winners' Cup and they progressed calmly past Turkish side Ankaraguku, Carl Zeiss Jena and Rapid Bucharest in the early rounds.

Allan Clarke scored the only goal in the first leg semi-final against Hajduk Split at Elland Road and was then sent off, leaving United a difficult job in Yugoslavia.

But they turned in one of their classic European away performances to force a goalless draw and book their place in the Final in Salonika.

But United arrived in Greece under a cloud. Not only had they lost the FA Cup to Sunderland, Clarke and Bremner were suspended, Giles was injured and rumours were rife that Revie was to leave Leeds for Everton.

The Goodison Park club had put in a massive offer for Revie's services the day before the Final against Milan.

United's board, now chaired by Manny Cussins, were quick to slap in a counter-offer to hang on to the manager.

Cussins, a millionaire head of a chain of furniture shops, had replaced the colourful Reynolds at the end of the previous season, Reynolds remaining as vice-chairman.

A native of Hull, Cussins started work at 13 by pushing a handcart around to collect furniture to launch a new business. Such early planning paid off as in 1954 he sold the Cussins Group for £1 million and began the John Peters chain of furniture stores which was to expand to over 100 retail outlets, a dozen clothing factories and a building business by 1975.

He had been co-opted on to the United board in 1961 and now faced one of the club's toughest fights – keeping Revie.

The Leeds boss said he wanted time to consider Everton's offer, but first wanted to concentrate on plotting the downfall of AC Milan.

Greek Tragedy

But no amount of planning could have prepared United for their clash with the tough Italians during an infamous Final played out in heavy rain, thunder and lightning.

Milan took a fourth-minute lead when Luciano Chiarugi drilled in a deflected free-kick to give AC the lead. After that they packed their penalty area and adopted any tactic they could think of to keep Leeds out.

United had three genuine penalty claims turned down and virtually every decision went the Italians' way.

Frustration boiled over at the end with Norman Hunter and Sogliano were ordered off by Greek referee Christos Michas.

But it did not alter the 1-0 win for the Italians, who, along with the referee, were booed off whilst United received all the cheers. Michas was so inept that he was suspended by UEFA and his own federation, but no inquiry was ever held to discover why he had been so bad.

United had been the moral victors and were soon to win another major victory as Revie announced he would be staying at Elland Road.

He wanted one last crack at winning the League Championship but would have to do so without the towering presence of big Jack Charlton.

'The Giraffe' had spent 21 years at Elland Road, through thick and thin, and at the age of 38 knew it was time to quit.

His contribution to the United effort was enormous. His 629 League games are a United record and late in his career he was transformed from a run-of-the-mill Second Division centre-half into one of the best stoppers in international football.

He played for England 35 times, his most memorable international appearance coming in the 1966 World Cup Final. He was named Footballer of the Year in 1967.

Elland Road would never quite be the same without Big Jack. On the pitch he looked awkward and ungainly, but his aerial command and ability to pull off telescopic tackles made him one of the best-ever post-war centre-halves.

Charlton went straight into management with Middlesbrough and he proved to be a good pupil under his old master Revie. He took 'Boro to the Second Division title by a record points margin in 1973-4 and was named Manager of the Year – a title Revie had won three times himself.

Charlton later became a national hero in the Republic of Ireland as he revitalised that country's footballing fortunes by taking them to the 1990 World Cup quarter-finals and then to the 1994 finals in the USA, where they beat eventual runners-up Italy 1-0.

While Charlton made a sensational entry into the world of management, Revie showed he had lost none of his old managerial magic by taking United to their second Championship in brilliant style.

Charlton's successor in the centre-half berth was 20-year-old Gordon McQueen, the towering 6ft 3½ Scot – but he was not the biggest thing around Elland Road during 1973-4.

United threw the switch on their new 250ft-high floodlights, the tallest in Europe, which had been assembled for £50,000. Although only three pylons were ready for the start of the season, United were soon operating on full power.

The Magnificent Seven

Everton were beaten 3-1 on the opening day of the season with goals by Billy Bremner, Johnny Giles and Mick Jones.

Wins at Arsenal and Spurs followed before the new lights were christened with a sparkling 4-1 demolition of Wolves.

Peter Lorimer then thumped in a hat-trick as Birmingham were sent packing 3-0, whilst victories at Wolves and Southampton brought United's tally to seven successive wins.

Leeds were in seventh heaven, but Manchester United brought the winning streak to an end by defending in depth to force a goalless draw at Elland Road.

October saw United lose their first game of the season when a scratch side lost at Ipswich in the League Cup.

It was also the month which saw United part company with Gary Sprake, who had played more games for United than any other goalkeeper.

As he headed for Birmingham, who paid out £100,000 – a British

Paul Reaney clears off the line at White Hart Lane in September 1973, as goalkeeper David Harvey looks beaten by Martin Chivers of Spurs. Billy Bremner is also on the goal-line. Spurs' Alan Gilzean looks on.

January 1974 and Terry Cooper, back in the Leeds first team for the first time since breaking a leg in April 1972, goes past Peterborough United's Dave Llewellyn at London Road. Leeds won this fourth-round FA Cup tie against Fourth Division Peterborough, 4-1. By the end of the year, Cooper was being recalled to the full England team by none other than Don Revie.

record fee for a goalkeeper – United snapped up Ayr United's Scottish Under-23 international David Stewart for £30,000 as cover for David Harvey.

United were bursting at the seams with international stars. Although Sprake left, Stewart was to prove such an able deputy for Harvey that he followed Harvey into the Scotland team. Leeds-born Harvey qualified to play for Scotland because his father was born north of the border.

United had a strong Scottish international contingent: Billy Bremner was skipper of his country, Joe Jordan was making an impact at the highest level, Peter Lorimer and Eddie Gray had seen plenty of Scottish action, Gordon McQueen was on the verge of full honours, whilst Gray's brother, Frank, was another international in the making.

Allan Clarke, Paul Madeley, Terry Cooper, Mick Jones, Paul Reaney and Norman Hunter had also been capped by England at some stage, whilst Terry Yorath was soon to be joined in the Welsh international side by two up-and-coming United juniors, Carl Harris and Byron Stevenson.

Midfield maestro Johnny Giles was also a permanent fixture in the Republic of Ireland side.

The Scottish contingent had plenty to cheer as they reached the 1974 World Cup Finals in West Germany, Joe Jordan scoring the vital goal in the crunch qualifier against Czechoslovakia at Hampden.

Jordan's joy was in sharp contrast to Norman Hunter's misery as he shouldered responsibility for a mistake which allowed Poland to pinch a 1-1 draw at Wembley and grab a place in the Finals at England's expense. Even his election of the first PFA Player of the Year was little consolation to the crestfallen Hunter, who with, Bremner, enjoyed an ever-present League season.

With such international power at their disposal it was not surprising to see United sweep all-comers aside, including the Champions, Liverpool, who succumbed to a Mick Jones goal at Elland Road.

United were producing some really entertaining football even without two of their long-term injured stars Johnny Giles and Eddie Gray – injuries which enabled Terry Yorath to make his presence felt in the midfield engine room alongside Billy Bremner.

Few clubs could have survived the lengthy loss of such key players, but United's reserve strength kept the Championship charge at full tilt.

A 2-1 win at Chelsea with goals from Joe Jordan and Mick Jones gave United a new record – the longest-ever unbeaten post-war run from the start of a season.

Liverpool held the previous best of 19, set in 1949-50, but United stretched that record to a remarkable 29 matches – beating the previous all-time best of 28 set by Liverpool in 1893-4 when they completed their 28-game season undefeated.

United's fantastic run ended in sensational style at Stoke on 23 February. United cruised into a 2-0 lead through Billy Bremner and Allan Clarke and it seemed as though the odds were going to shorten on United remaining undefeated through the season.

They were nine points clear of the field and looked like collecting maximum points from the Victoria Ground, but Stoke staged a tremendous fight-back to win 3-2 with goals from Mike Pejic, Alan Hudson and Denis Smith.

That triggered a mini-wobble as United

collected just one win from a seven-match spell which included successive defeats against Liverpool, Burnley and West Ham.

United's lead was now down to four points with nearest rivals Liverpool having three games in hand.

Champions Again

Goals by Lorimer and Bremner gave United a 2-0 win over Derby to steady the nerves and goalless draws at Coventry and at Elland Road against Sheffield United on Easter Monday saw Leeds edge closer to the title as Liverpool also dropped points.

The return game the following night against the Blades saw United triumph 2-0 with a couple of Lorimer goals but Liverpool were still in contention.

United's last home game of the season saw them beat Ipswich 3-2, Clarke scoring a late winner. At Anfield, the Merseyside derby finished goalless, leaving Liverpool needing to win their last three games to stand any chance of overhauling United.

Four days later Liverpool lost at home to Arsenal and the title was Leeds United's.

They were determined to complete their programme in style and thousands of United followers made their way to London to swell Queen's Park Rangers' Loftus Road attendance to a record 35,353.

United did not let their army of followers down, turning in a champion performance which saw a typical clinical piece of finishing by Allan Clarke put the icing on United's championship cake.

Clarke finished with 13 League goals, one behind Jones and one ahead of Lorimer, while Bremner chipped in with ten from midfield.

It had been a tremendous season with the only blemishes coming in the cup competitions where United made early exits – the FA Cup defeat against unfancied Bristol City in a replay at Elland Road being one of the shocks of the season.

In Europe several understrength sides were fielded and in the circumstances did well to get through a couple of rounds before losing 3-2 on aggregate to Portuguese side, Vitoria Setubal.

Don Revie with the Football League championship trophy which Leeds won in 1974. United took the title by finishing five points ahead of Liverpool. Honours between the clubs were even, however, each winning their home game by 1-0. In July that year, Revie left Elland Road to become manager of England.

If directors of Hibernian had their way, United would have been booted out of the UEFA Cup anyway.

After easing past Norwegian part-timers Stromgodset in the first round, United were paired with Hibs who forced a goalless draw at Elland Road.

Because of a goalkeeping crisis United fielded reserve John Shaw (19) in the second leg at Hibs, but when he was injured just before half-time United were forced to put on Welsh youth international Glan Letheran.

The game finished 0-0 after extra-time and United went into their first-ever penalty competition with a rookie goalkeeper between the posts. United won the penalty drama after Hibs skipper Pat Stanton drove his first kick on to a post.

The extraordinary game also had a sting in the tail as Hibs accused United of breaking the rules as Revie and Les Cocker were coaching during the shoot-out.

Two Hibs directors flew to Zurich to lodge their protest with UEFA, who ruled that the result should stand. However, United were ordered to forfeit £400 and Revie was barred from acting in an official capacity in the first leg of their next round against Setubal.

Revie for England

But Revie was to look beyond European horizons as he was appointed the successor to Sir Alf Ramsey, who had been sacked following England's failure to qualify for the World Cup finals. Former Manchester City boss Joe Mercer had been doing the job on a caretaker basis for a few months, but Revie took charge in July 1974 and took the faithful Les Cocker as his second in command.

Revie had spent 13 years at Leeds. Initially it had been hard work, but a highly successful youth policy saw him develop one of the greatest club sides. Magically, he had transformed a mediocre Second Division club into one of the superpowers in world football.

He stood by his players in the early days when United were dubbed a 'method side' and 'dirty'. Gradually the criticism mellowed to 'ultra-professional' and finally his side were acknowledged to be one of the best ever seen in British soccer. Perhaps if he had allowed his players to express themselves on the pitch more often then United would have won more silverware – but few success-starved fans at Elland Road were complaining.

With more luck, Leeds could have won more trophies. Revie was eternally superstitious. He wore a lucky blue suit on match days and even brought in a gypsy to remove a curse from the Elland Road ground after United had yet another of their 'so-near-yet-so-far' seasons.

He was the head of a footballing family whose managerial influence spread beyond Elland Road. Jack Charlton, Norman Hunter, Johnny Giles, Terry Yorath, Billy Bremner, Trevor Cherry, Allan Clarke, Bobby Collins, Joe Jordan, Willie Bell, Grenville Hair , Eddie and Frank Gray all went into management, but none could match Revie's ability at club level.

His place in Leeds United's history assured, Revie was the obvious successor to Ramsey, but he was unable to recapture the club atmosphere he had generated so successfully at Elland Road.

He was seen as the man to take England to the 1978 World Cup Finals in Argentina, but after some poor results in key qualifying matches, criticism began to mount.

In July 1977, Revie astonished the soccer world by quitting to become coach to the United Arab Emirates on a tax-free contract reported to be £60,000.

Revie's decision to walk out on England was blasted by the Football Association and the Press. He was suspended from working in England until he was willing to face a charge of bringing the game into disrepute.

There were some startling allegations in newspapers about matches involving United when Revie was in charge and his popularity just about everywhere outside Elland Road plunged to an all-time low.

Revie later won a High Court case against the FA and was granted an injunction quashing the ban on him from working in England. However, the mud had been flying throughout the case and many considered it a hollow victory as Justice Cantley criticised aspects of Revie's character in his summing up.

Revie, who had a street named after him in Leeds, was still guaranteed a special place in United's history. Although he never returned to full-time football, his court victory did briefly allow him to take up a consultancy post at Elland Road. His career in English football may have ended in ignominy, but he finished his Leeds United days in glory.

He left the club after guiding them to undreamed of riches when he was first appointed in those dark Second Division days of 1961.

His reign brought United two League Championships, the Fairs Cup twice, the FA Cup, League Cup, Second Division title, FA Charity Shield, numerous semi-finals and a place in the top four in each of Revie's ten years as a First Division manager. The big debate was who would succeed the maestro Revie in the quest for European Cup glory?

The Strife of Brian

UPON his departure, Don Revie recommended the United board appointed Johnny Giles as his successor. For once the club's directors did not agree with Revie and the position was left vacant before they came up with their own man.

Maurice Lindley, Revie's assistant manager, was put in temporary charge until the identity of the new man was revealed.

In July 1974, that new man was announced as Brian Clough, the Brighton manager, who had previously led Derby to great success.

For many it was a surprising choice as Clough, still only 39, and undoubtedly one of the most skilful managers around, had often been a critic of the United style. United chairman Manny Cussins, however, was convinced United had appointed 'an ideal manager for Leeds'.

Clough and Revie were like chalk and cheese – but they did share a distinguished playing pedigree.

Like Revie, Clough was born in Middlesbrough and played for his home-town club. A prolific scorer with both Middlesbrough and Sunderland, Clough won two England caps in 1959 before injury terminated his playing career. His 251 League goals in 274 games is still the highest ratio since World War Two.

Clough was hungry as a player and proved equally hungry as a manager, impressing sufficiently at lowly Hartlepools to earn the chance at a higher grade with Derby. Together with his assistant, Peter Taylor, the former Middlesbrough goalkeeper, Clough transformed a moribund Derby into a League Championship-winning side in 1971-2, when they denied United the 'double'.

Brian Clough and his trainer Jimmy Gordon on the bench at Elland Road. They looked happy enough but Clough's reign at Leeds was to be spectacularly short-lived.

Always outspoken, Clough's remarks on television and in newspapers led to a row at Derby which saw him and Taylor move to Brighton.

When Clough left his job at Brighton, where he was reported to be on a five-year contract worth £20,000, Taylor remained at the Goldstone Ground and was elevated to manager.

In July 1974, Clough arrived at Elland Road, bringing with him trainer Jimmy Gordon, another former Middlesbrough player, who replaced Les Cocker.

Clough was charged with the task of winning the European Cup, and wasted little time in bringing in new blood ready for the 1974-5 campaign.

He paid out £250,000 to Nottingham Forest, a record for both clubs, for the highly skilful striker Duncan McKenzie, and went back to his old club, Derby, to sign striker John O'Hare and midfield man John McGovern for £125,000.

Clough's first game in charge took him to Wembley which was staging the annual pre-season FA Charity Shield game for the first time.

United, as League Champions, took on FA Cup holders Liverpool, who were led out by Bill Shankly, just days before he retired as manager of the Anfield club.

What was a televised showpiece game turned out to be a niggling match which exploded when Billy Bremner and Kevin Keegan were sent off for fighting by referee Bob Matthewson.

The game ended at 1-1, Trevor Cherry scoring for United and Phil Boersma for the Reds. Usually the trophy would have been shared, but this time a penalty shoot-out was used for the first time to determine the winners.

In the sudden death spot-kick drama Liverpool won 6-5 after United goalkeeper David Harvey, reputed to have an even harder shot than Peter Lorimer, hit the ball over the bar.

Bremner and Keegan were handed unprecedented punishments for their displays of temper. Both were banned until the end of September and fined £500.

But the loss of the influential Bremner, who along with Harvey, Lorimer and Jordan, had shone with Scotland in that summer's World Cup, was just the start of Clough's problems.

He looked on helplessly as United crashed 3-0 on the opening day of the League season at Stoke, where former Leeds man Jimmy Greenhoff was among the scorers.

A home defeat against Queen's Park Rangers and a scratchy 1-0 win over Birmingham at Elland Road with an Allan Clarke goal followed, but the Champions were looking a pale shadow of their former selves.

Bremner's number-four shirt was taken by new boy John McGovern, but he suffered a nightmare start to his career as a Leeds player and was soon barracked by the boo-boys on the terraces at Elland Road, who were also turning against Clough.

Defeat at Manchester City and a disappointing 1-1 home draw with Luton left United in 19th place with only one win in six games. Anti-Clough chants were already coming from some sections of the Elland Road terraces.

United, the team that had outclassed everyone the previous season, were simply failing to produce the goods with what was essentially the same side.

Rumours were rife about discontent in the dressing-room and that the players had held a meeting with chairman Manny Cussins and vice-chairman Sam Bolton and given Clough a 'vote of no confidence', although that was later denied by Cussins.

Black clouds were hanging over the United camp and the gloom deepened when United needed a last-minute Peter Lorimer goal to force a 1-1 draw in the League Cup at Huddersfield Town, who were languishing near the foot of Division Three.

Two days later, at a special board meeting, Clough was sensationally sacked after just 44 days in office. It had been a remarkable U-turn by the United board, who, having made the decision to appoint Clough, failed to stand by him.

Cussins held a four-hour meeting with Clough and his solicitor before an agreement on compensation was reached. The sum was said to be £20,000 tax-free.

The phrase 'player-power' was bandied about in the Press as Cussins outlined why the board had taken the shock decision.

He said that the directors had detected from the feelings of the players a certain amount of unrest and apprehension. That prompted the special board meeting at which the club and Clough agreed to part company.

Said Cussins: "Everyone seems sympathetic towards Brian Clough that he was not given a true chance. The directors believe he was given a chance and it was their opinion that there should be a parting.

"They had to be big enough, honest enough to admit they had made a mistake. Brian Clough was not the man to manage Leeds United. The decision the board took was made in the best interests of the club – long and short term."

Cussins' statement was soon followed by one by the players who strenuously denied the 'player-power' allegations reported in the Press.

On the way out? Brian Clough steps from the Elland Road trainer's box. His eventual departure after only 44 days was cushioned by a 'golden handshake'.

"We gave the same support to Mr Clough as we did to Don Revie," they said.

Whatever the background to the affair, Brian Clough departed richer and probably a bit wiser after his seven weeks at Leeds.

"I think it is a very sad day for Leeds and for football," said the departing manager, whose trainer, Jimmy Gordon, also left Elland Road.

Gordon's departure left United short-handed on the training staff, so Eddie Gray, laid low by a career-threatening thigh injury, started to coach United's juniors.

Scottish international winger Gray's career hung in the balance at the age of 26, as he awaited two specialists' reports.

Syd Owen took first-team training and reverted to the sort of sessions the players had gone through during Revie's reign. The Clough affair

Allan Clarke just fails to connect as Peter Lorimer's pass goes across the face of the Luton Town goal at Elland Road in September 1974. The sides drew 1-1 in what was the last League game with Brian Clough in charge.

split United's supporters right down the middle. There were those that thought Clough should have been given a proper chance and those who felt the directors had made a brave decision and swallowed their pride.

Whatever the rights and wrongs of the issue, it reflected little credit on United. It proved a shambolic and expensive, episode in United's history.

Clough was later to emerge with Nottingham Forest and, together with his old sidekick Peter Taylor, took them to European Cup, League Championship and League Cup glory while United went through a fallow period.

What would have happened if he had remained at Elland Road is anyone's guess.

Amid all the accusations and counter-accusations during the Clough saga, the death of former Leeds chairman Harry Reynolds during the ill-fated month of September 1974 went almost unnoticed.

Reynolds had been the man who had urged the board to appoint Revie and had laid the foundations for the modern Leeds United.

After seven turbulent weeks United were back to square one – still searching for a manager to replace Revie.

United's immediate problem was preparing for their next game, a trip to Burnley. The squad for that match was picked by assistant manager Maurice Lindley, chief coach Syd Owen and suspended skipper Billy Bremner. Clough's three signings, McGovern, O'Hare and McKenzie were not included in the squad. McGovern and O'Hare later left Leeds in a £35,000 deal to link up with Clough again at Nottingham Forest, where they played key roles in Forest's spectacular revival.

To add to their problems, United lost 2-1 at Turf Moor in a game which saw Gordon McQueen and Burnley's Ray Hankin, later to join Leeds, sent off.

The turmoil was no way to prepare for a European Cup tie, but United called on all their experience to beat FC Zurich 4-1 at Elland Road in the first-round, first-leg tie.

That was the first bit of good news United had enjoyed for several days but there was more around the corner on the following Saturday as Sheffield United were thrashed 5-1 at Elland Road.

The message was clear to the rest of the First Division – Leeds United were still alive and kicking. Lindley was in charge when United travelled to Switzerland for the second leg of their European Cup tie and, although they lost 2-1, their overall aggregate lead was never under threat.

Eventually, three weeks after Clough's shock

departure, Jimmy Armfield was named as United's new boss. Armfield, a former England skipper who had served Blackpool splendidly as a right-back in a distinguished career at Bloomfield Road, was reckoned to be a steadying influence.

At 38 he was relatively short of managerial experience, but had done well at Bolton, whom he had taken to the Third Division title in 1972-3.

'Gentleman Jim', possessor of 43 England caps, was the man with a 'nice guy' image brought in to ease United's current troubles.

The quiet, pipe-smoking Armfield, was far removed from the style of Clough, but he was the man the board believed could provide much-needed stability to the club.

With nearly a quarter of the season gone, United were already so far behind leaders Ipswich that thoughts of retaining the First Division title had vanished.

But Armfield arrived at Elland Road in a positive frame of mind.

"I see the club's priority as winning League points. After the difficult start to the season your priorities have got to be that – but if we can stay clear of injuries, we'll be going out to try and capture a bit of the icing on soccer's cake too. We're still in the European and League Cups – and the FA Cup is still to come.

"Take it from me, there's still a lot more to be won at Leeds United – and we're going to try to win it," said Armfield as he prepared for one of the greatest challenges in his life.

Rebuilding
After Paris

SLOWLY but surely, Jimmy Armfield got United back on the right track. In the League they made steady, if unspectacular, progress to finish ninth. That was their worst standing since gaining promotion in 1964, but in the aftermath of the Clough affair it was no mean achievement.

With Mick Jones ruled out for the entire 1974-5 season by a knee injury, Eddie Gray's future still on the line and Norman Hunter laid low with a cartilage injury, the likes of Joe Jordan and Terry Yorath continued to seize their opportunity to make a big impression in the first team.

United, despite all their early season troubles were still feared and respected. On 20 November 1974 no less than ten United players were on international duty in European Championship qualifying games.

Allan Clarke, Paul Madeley and Terry Cooper, now happily recovered from his broken leg, played for England in a goalless draw against Portugal at Wembley; Billy Bremner, David Harvey, Gordon McQueen, Joe Jordan and Peter Lorimer played in Scotland's game against Spain; Terry Yorath was a scorer in Wales' 5-1 romp over Luxembourg, whilst Johnny Giles starred in the Republic of Ireland's 1-1 draw in Turkey.

Cooper had been recalled by Don Revie for his first England cap for just over three years but limped off after 23 minutes for what was to be the last of his 20 international appearances.

The Elland Road career of the attack-minded full-back Cooper was also drawing to a close and he was sold to Jack Charlton's Middlesbrough for £50,000.

Cooper, whose League Cup Final goal of 1968 had given United their first major trophy, had been

a marvellous servant for United, clocking up around 350 competitive appearances for the club.

Like many of Revie's side he entered management and enjoyed a fair amount of success with Bristol City, Exeter City and Birmingham City.

Armfield had felt able to do without Cooper because Eddie Gray's brother, Frank, still only 21, had turned in some sparkling displays at left-back after being converted from midfield.

The departure of Cooper was the first sign that Armfield was preparing to dismantle Revie's aging side, but he played a key role in reviving the career of one of Revie's stars – Eddie Gray.

The talented Scottish wingman seemed on the verge of quitting because of injury, but he was coaxed back into action by Armfield after a spell coaching the juniors and marked his return in sensational style against Cardiff in the FA Cup third round.

With Yorath out through suspension, Armfield brought back Gray for his first game since the FA Charity Shield match in August and the wizard of the dribble triggered United's 4-1 win with a goal inside three minutes.

It was a tremendous comeback by Gray and began a bizarre FA Cup run by Armfield's team.

The fourth round pitted them against Southern League Wimbledon at Elland Road. Dubbed 'The Wombles' after a popular children's TV programme, Wimbledon proved they could play more than kids' stuff by eliminating First Division Burnley at Turf Moor in the third round.

United had already come a cropper in the League Cup against Fourth Division Chester that season when they were outplayed at Sealand Road 3-0 in one of the greatest shocks in the competition, so Leeds could not afford to take Wimbledon for granted.

Leeds defender Frank Gray cannot stop Ipswich Town's David Johnson getting in a cross at Portman Road in March 1975. This was the first game in a marathon quarter-final FA Cup tie which went to four matches before Ipswich won 3-2 at Leicester.

A 46,230 crowd turned up at Elland Road expecting a landslide but the brave non-Leaguers kept United at bay, with goalkeeper Dickie Guy the hero, saving a Peter Lorimer penalty in front of the Kop towards the end.

Champions United also struggled in the replay at Selhurst Park, needing an own-goal by Dave Bassett, who later managed Wimbledon, to put them through to a fifth-round meeting with Derby.

Once again United won 1-0 thanks to an own-goal, this time by England defender David Nish, to set up four titanic ties with Ipswich.

It took three replays to find a winner, the East Anglians edging home 3-2 in a tremendous third replay after an injury time goal by Duncan McKenzie salvaged the second game at Elland Road.

£500,000 South Stand Unveiled

The new look South Stand had only been open a few days before that nail-biting first replay with Ipswich at Elland Road.

Costing £500,000, the South Stand, which had replaced the old outdated Scratching Shed, was designed by Leeds architects Braithwaite & Templar. It was the most costly and largest building phase ever done at Elland Road, providing seats for 3,300 spectators and standing accommodation for a further 4,400.

Those Ipswich games were spread over 19 days and came as United were tackling Belgian champions Anderlecht for a place in the European Cup semi-finals.

United had clearly set their sights on the European Cup. For many of the team it would probably be the last chance to have a crack at the biggest prize Europe could offer.

After easing past FC Zurich, United took on the experienced Hungarian team Ujpesti Dozsa in the second round.

Despite having Duncan McKenzie sent off for retaliation after only 15 minutes, United won 2-1 in Budapest with goals by Lorimer and McQueen. It could have been more had Lorimer not missed a penalty minutes before the Hungarians had Harsanyi sent off.

The return leg saw Billy Bremner back in midfield following his lengthy suspension after the Charity Shield bust-up with Kevin Keegan and he

celebrated with a goal in a comprehensive 3-0 win.

Anderlecht were left mystified at Elland Road, crashing 3-0 in such thick fog that the teams had to be taken off for 15 minutes in the first half.

The Belgians seemed content to defend, but United kept pushing forward and were rewarded by goals from Jordan, McQueen and Lorimer.

In the mud at Brussels, United negotiated the second leg with little fuss, Bremner's delicate lob giving a 1-0 victory and a 4-0 aggregate.

United, with many of their players into their 30s, were dubbed 'Veteran United' by some sections of the Press but they continued to rise to the occasion in Europe.

The semi-finals paired United with Spanish giants Barcelona and their star Dutchman Johan Cruyff with United enjoying home advantage in the first leg, their seventh game in a fortnight.

Record receipts of £90,000 were taken at Elland Road which witnessed a tense battle. Bremner, yet again scored in a semi-final, blasting the ball into the net after only ten minutes.

Dogged Barcelona defended in depth but stunned United with an equaliser from Asensi. With time running out and pressure mounting on the Barcelona goal, Jordan headed the ball on to master marksman Clarke who rifled in a 77th-minute winner.

United took a 2-1 advantage to Spain and could not have made a better start in the huge Nou Camp Stadium when Lorimer stunned the huge crowd with a fearsome right-foot volley.

Goalkeeper David Stewart, in for the injured David Harvey, who had broken a foot in a car crash, frustrated the Spaniards with a string of fine saves.

Barcelona started to dish out some heavy tackling but United kept their cool until the final quarter of the game when Clares equalised and

McQueen was sent off for a rash challenge on the Spanish scorer.

Ten men United were indebted to some wonderful Stewart saves at the end as United's memorable performance earned them a place in their first European Cup Final on 28 May 1975.

United were only the second English side to reach the Final, following Manchester United, who won the tournament in 1968.

Their opponents were to be the crack West German outfit Bayern Munich, the holders of the trophy.

Despite a moderate season by their own high standards, United started as fractional favourites against a Bayern club which had also sacked its coach during the season.

Tears in Paris

The Final was held at the Parc des Princes in Paris and thousands of Leeds fans crossed the Channel to invade the French capital for the biggest game in United's history.

What could, and probably should, have been the greatest night in United's history turned sour on and off the pitch.

Armfield, deprived of suspended centre-half Gordon McQueen, opted to keep the unpredictable talents of Duncan McKenzie and the dribbling skills of Eddie Gray on the bench at the start, whilst Bayern looked to their skipper Franz Beckenbauer for inspiration.

The teams were: **Leeds United:** Stewart, Reaney, F. Gray, Bremner, Madeley, Hunter, Lorimer, Clarke, Jordan, Giles, Yorath (E. Gray). **Bayern Munich:** Maier, Durnberger, Andersson (Weiss), Schwarzenbeck, Beckenbauer, Roth, Tortensson, Zobel, Müller, Hoeness (Wunder), Kapellmann.

United set the early pace against a German side happy to contain.

United had two strong penalty appeals turned down by French referee Marcel Kitabdjian, both against Beckenbauer. One was for handball and the other saw the Bayern skipper bring down Allan Clarke.

With Joe Jordan continually outwitting his marker, United carved out the chances but were denied by the acrobatic Sepp Maier in goal.

Those disappointments were nothing compared to the one United faced in the 67th minute as Lorimer sent a full-blooded volley screaming past Maier. After consulting with a linesman, the referee disallowed the goal because of offside, although no one seemed to be interfering with play.

Peter Lorimer (7) finds the back of the Bayern Munich net in the 1975 European Cup Final in Paris, but the effort was disallowed because Billy Bremner (right) is offside. Many believe he was pushed by Franz Beckenbauer (5).

Leeds United in the 1975-6 season. Back row (left to right): Jimmy Armfield (manager), Duncan McKenzie, Joe Jordan, Gordon McQueen, David Harvey, David Stewart, Paul Madeley, Norman Hunter, Paul Reaney. Front row: Terry Yorath, Frank Gray, Peter Lorimer, Trevor Cherry, Billy Bremner, Allan Clarke.

After that things fell apart for United on the field whilst anarchy reigned on the terraces.

A handful of United supporters clashed with security officers and French riot police patrolling perimeter fencing. It was the heavy hand of the security men, rather than the disallowed goal, which sparked a full-scale riot among a section of United fans.

The game was played out with fans and baton-wielding police fighting behind one of the goals while the action on the pitch was confined to the other end.

Bayern, sensing United had shot their bolt, crept out of their defensive shell and scored twice with two classic counter-attacks through Roth and Gerd Müller.

Once again the big prize had proved just beyond United's grasp.

Throughout the presentation the fighting continued. Seats were ripped out and as Bayern foolishly attempted a lap of honour they were bombarded by missiles.

Trouble then spilled over into the streets as windows were smashed and cars attacked by a rampaging mob.

It was a sad end to a sad night.

In the cold light of the following day there was sympathy for United's players, but not for the fans whose actions had put the club in the UEFA Disciplinary Committee's dock.

The following month UEFA meted out their punishment. United were banned from European competition for four years, although that was later reduced to two after a well-argued appeal by manager Armfield.

Paris was a watershed for Leeds United.

It was the club's last appearance in a major Cup Final and is always remembered in some quarters for its hooliganism rather than football.

That mindless element attached itself to United for over a decade and the club which had worked so hard to rid itself of its mid-1960s dour image had become saddled with a new, more frightening label as the club with the biggest hardcore of yobs in the country.

Years of hard work which had helped popularise Leeds United were undone in one night of madness.

Paris also signalled the beginning of the end for Revie's magnificent team as Armfield went about the difficult task of rebuilding a superb side piece by piece.

Giles departs, Jones retires

The summer of 1975 saw the first key departure as Johnny Giles, the man tipped by Revie to be his successor, moved to West Brom for £45,000 to become player-manager at The Hawthorns.

Predictably Giles, 34, made a success of the job and later managed the Republic of Ireland and coached Vancouver Whitecaps before moving into journalism.

Quick-thinking Giles was a master craftsman, the best passer of a ball that ever pulled on a United shirt, who dove-tailed perfectly with the sheer drive of Billy Bremner in midfield for nearly ten years.

The season also saw another link from the past severed, but this one stretched way back before the Revie era.

Bob Roxburgh, the popular North-Easterner, who had been United's coach for over 20 years before and after World War Two, died.

As a full-back he played for Newcastle and Blackburn and when injury cut short his career he spent some time coaching in Holland before joining Leeds United.

It had been a season for United to mourn their losses.

Although the Paris riot had left a nasty taste in the mouth, Armfield still had plenty to look forward to as he entered 1975-6, his first full season as United's chief.

Although Giles had gone, Armfield had a ready made replacement in Terry Yorath, a growing influence both at Leeds and with Wales, despite being barracked by sections of the Elland Road crowd.

Another Welshman, speedy winger Carl Harris was pushing hard for a place and was called into the Welsh squad at the age of 19, despite having played only one full game for United. The individual talent of Duncan McKenzie was also starting to blossom alongside experienced campaigner Allan Clarke, who had moved beyond 200 career League goals, and the powerful Joe Jordan.

Clarke's old striking partner Mick Jones finally succumbed to a knee injury and announced his retirement in October 1975.

The fearless Jones was a magnificent leader of the front line. Superb in the air, chaser of lost causes and no mean performer on the ball, Jones was the perfect foil for Clarke and scored his fair share of goals in the most successful striking spearhead United have ever had.

Said Jones: "If I have one regret it's that I didn't link up with Allan Clarke at Leeds earlier. I often feel that we would have won even more than we did had we played together earlier.

"We played together tremendously well, I took the knocks, he finished it off."

The curtain also came down on Billy Bremner's international career when he was banned from international football for life by the Scottish FA following an alleged row in a Copenhagen nightclub following Scotland's win over Denmark.

Bremner, holder of 54 Scottish caps, together with Willie Young, Pat McCluskey, Joe Harper and Arthur Graham (later to join Leeds from Aberdeen) had the book thrown at them at a Scottish FA disciplinary committee. Although the ban was lifted in July 1977, it proved to be Bremner's final appearance in a Scotland jersey.

It was a shattering end to an illustrious international career as Bremner was only one short of equalling Denis Law's record number of caps at the time. He was an inspirational leader for his country and his displays in the 1974 World Cup confirmed him as one of the globe's best midfield players.

United, whose own disciplinary record was under scrutiny from the FA, reprimanded Bremner and warned him of his future conduct.

As Bremner's international career closed, Trevor Cherry's opened with England when he was capped against Wales in March 1976, the first of 27 appearances for his country.

Centre-half Gordon McQueen's hopes of building on his fine start with Scotland were wrecked by leg and Achilles injuries for most of the season, although Armfield had a ready-made replacement in versatile Paul Madeley.

McQueen's anguish was also felt by Mick Bates, the man who had faithfully understudied midfield greats Bremner and Giles for a decade.

Bates was the forgotten man of Elland Road after injury wiped out two years of his career. He finally clawed his way back to full fitness, but not a regular first-team spot and was eventually sold to Walsall for £25,000. United were written off at the start of the 1975-6 season as being over the hill.

But despite subtle changes in personnel by Armfield, United kept in the race for the title until the final weeks of the season before finishing a creditable fifth. However, the Wembley trail was cold as United crashed at home to lowly opposition, losing to Notts County in the League Cup and Crystal Palace in the FA Cup.

There was also a significant change among the backroom staff as coach Syd Owen left after 17 years to join former United star Willie Bell, who was manager at Birmingham.

His replacement was another former England defender, Don Howe, who had coached Arsenal to the League and Cup double in 1970-71 when the Gunners pipped Leeds to the title.

One of Howe's former clubs, West Brom, arrived at Elland Road to start the 1976-7 season with old Leeds maestro Johnny Giles the driving force behind the Baggies.

In his first season as Albion's player-manager he steered them to promotion and he stepped out on the First Division stage once more on his old stamping ground. The honours were even, goals from Carl Harris and Allan Clarke ensuring a 2-2 draw for United.

Tony Currie joined Leeds from Sheffield United in August 1976 and went on to make well over 100 appearances, winning 10 of his 17 full England caps with United. In 1979 he moved to QPR for £400,000.

Occupying the number-ten shirt graced by Giles for 12 years was a new United hero, Tony Currie, a £240,000 summer signing from Sheffield United.

Like Giles, Currie was a master passer of a ball which coupled with his powerful shooting made him a real crowd pleaser.

He already had seven caps to his name when he joined Leeds and added ten more as he struck a rich vein of form with his new club.

The arrival of the skilful Currie compensated for the departure of another gifted player, striker Duncan McKenzie who wanted to try his luck abroad and moved to Anderlecht in a £200,000 deal.

Welsh midfielder Terry Yorath, although good enough to skipper his country, had become a target for the Elland Road boo-boys and went to Coventry for £125,000. Yorath, who later starred for Tottenham, had spells of management in the lower divisions before being appointed the full-time manager of Wales in 1991.

Both Yorath and United were to share tragedy in May 1992. Just weeks after signing YTS forms with United, Yorath's son, Daniel, died of a rare heart disease, collapsing during a game of football with his father in their garden.

Both were magnificent servants for the club. Bremner's sheer drive, commitment and skill hallmarked him as one of the greatest post-war midfield players.

Hunter, the gin-trap tackler with a superb left foot, was both feared and respected by his fellow

Exit Bremner and Hunter

The break up of the old Revie side continued during the early months of the 1976-7 season as Armfield sold skipper Billy Bremner to Hull City for £25,000 and Norman Hunter to Bristol City for £40,000.

Terry Yorath (left) and Norman Hunter (right), continued the break-up of the great Revie team as the 1976-7 got under way. Yorath moved to Coventry for £120,000. Hunter went to Bristol City for £40,000. Billy Bremner also departed, for Hull.

professionals who voted him their first-ever Player of the Year in 1973. Bremner, the very epitome of Leeds United, was later to return for a spell in the manager's chair, while 'Bites Yer Legs' Norman also trod the managerial path at Barnsley after successfully winding up his career at Bristol City.

Despite the departure of such luminaries, Armfield only pulled out the cheque book once more during the season, snapping up Ray Hankin from Burnley for £172,000 after Allan Clarke picked up a hip injury. However, after only four games Hankin was himself was hit by a knee injury and missed the rest of the season.

Instead of relying too much on big-money signings, Armfield allowed the Elland Road youngsters to have their fling.

Peter Hampton looked comfortable at left-back, allowing Frank Gray to slot back into midfield, while Scottish Under-21 international David McNiven and Welsh youth international Gwyn Thomas were given a chance up front.

Armfield was taking the necessary steps to build for the future, but it was not an overnight success and United struggled at times, particularly at home where attendances dipped alarmingly.

With no Europe, an early exit from the League Cup and only a mid-table position, United set their stall out for the FA Cup.

They launched their bid with a spectacular 5-2 thrashing of Norwich, all the United goals coming in the first half, including a rare effort from Paul Reaney, who had now taken on the mantle of the club's senior citizen.

Goals by Jordan and Clarke brought a 2-1 win at Birmingham while a late goal by new skipper Trevor Cherry beat Manchester City 1-0 in the fifth round. A rare headed goal by Eddie Gray at Wolves steered United into the semi-finals, but at Hillsborough they were caught cold by two early goals by Manchester United. Although Allan Clarke pulled one back from the spot, Armfield's men had left it too late.

Two of United's Scottish stars, Gordon McQueen and Joe Jordan did find FA Cup success later in their careers, with Manchester United.

Joe Jordan in action against Manchester United's Jimmy Nicholl in October 1976. Jordan joined Leeds for £15,000 from Morton in October 1970. In January 1978 he moved to Old Trafford for a record £350,000. Jordan scored 35 goals in 169 League appearances for Leeds. He won a League championship medal at Elland Road and scored the goal which took Scotland, for whom he won 52 caps, to the 1974 World Cup finals.

Leeds United, 1976-7. Back row (left to right): Paul Reaney, Norman Hunter, Byron Stevenson, Neil Firm, Gordon McQueen, Keith Parkinson, Billy McGhie, Joe Jordan, Gary Liddell. Middle row: Geoff Ladley (physiotherapist), Jimmy Armfield (manager), Don Howe (coach), David McNiven, James Wright, George Boyd, Glan Letheran, David Harvey, David Stewart, Tony Currie, Frank Gray, Peter Willis, Gary Felix, Jim McAnearney (coach), Bob English (trainer), Bobby Collins (coach). Kneeling: Peter Hampton, Carl Harris, Eddie Gray, Peter Lorimer, Trevor Cherry, Paul Madeley, Allan Clarke, Billy Bremner, Terry Yorath, Neil Parker, David Whyte, Gwyn Thomas. On ground: Chris Hope, Duncan Reynard, John McPhee, David Reed, Tony Rowe, Bob Skilling, Peter Daly, Sean Sturman,

The brothers Frank and Eddie Gray. Frank (right), who won 32 Scotland caps, moved to Forest for a Leeds record fee of £500,000 and enjoyed his best years under Brian Clough. Eddie (left) was more talented than his brother but won only 12 caps, often being hit by injury. Eddie Gray later managed Leeds.

Both left Leeds for Old Trafford in big-money deals during a troubled 1977-8 season.

Goalscoring had been a problem in the previous campaign, but a fully-fit Hankin blossomed as he teamed up with Jordan early on.

Allan Clarke was fighting an uphill battle for fitness, so Armfield twinned the powerful Hankin and Jordan together.

They were fed a succession of crosses from Carl Harris, soon to graduate to the full Welsh side and new £100,000 Scottish Under-23 winger Arthur Graham from Aberdeen.

The big guys were then joined by one of the smallest players in the Football League, 5ft 3ins Brian Flynn, a £175,000 signing from Hankin's old club, Burnley.

Little Flynn came in to forge an effective partnership with Tony Currie, who was winning many plaudits for his displays in the middle.

Graham and Dave Stewart both earned Scottish caps, taking United's roll call of tartan internationals to a staggering seven, David Harvey, Joe Jordan, Gordon McQueen, Peter Lorimer and Eddie Gray having already won their international spurs.

Double Scots Departure Hard to Swallow

Everything at Elland Road looked rosy and by January 1978 United had worked their way into a position to make a major assault on the League title when Armfield's plans were shattered by a double blow.

First, Jordan was transfer-listed and almost immediately sold to Manchester United for £300,000 and the following day Leeds crashed out of the FA Cup at the hands of Manchester City in one of the blackest days in the club's history.

When Peter Barnes, later to join Leeds, made it 2-0 to City in the 72nd minute, visiting goalkeeper Joe Corrigan turned to the Kop with his arms raised in salute.

The City goalkeeper was pelted with missiles and then confronted by a fan who had got on to the pitch. Hundreds of others poured on to the field and referee Colin Seel took the players off as mounted police restored order.

Seel broadcast a public-address message to the crowd saying he would complete the game even if it took until midnight. After a delay of 15 minutes, order was restored and the game restarted, Frank Gray netting a consolation effort from the spot.

After the game United, in an effort to pre-empt any action by the FA, decided to fence off the Kop, but it was a case of closing the stable door after the horse had bolted.

The FA dished out a three-year ban on Elland Road staging FA Cup ties, although that was later reduced.

For Armfield there were more problems. During the game David Harvey and Gordon

Eddie Gray tangles with Aston Villa's John Robson at Elland Road in December 1976.

McQueen scuffled with each other as City prepared to take a first-half corner.

McQueen was fined for his part in the incident, had a transfer request granted and was soon on his way to join Jordan at Manchester United in a British record £450,000 deal.

The loss of Jordan and McQueen were hammer blows, particularly in the eyes of Leeds diehards as they had joined the old enemy, Manchester United. Leeds made a thumping profit of £750,000 on the deals but to some supporters it meant that Leeds had slipped out of the elite by selling their stars to their rivals.

The replacement for the talented McQueen was Blackpool's Paul Hart, who was signed for £330,000.

But by the time Hart arrived in March 1978, the last rites on a bitterly disappointing season had been administered by old boss Brian Clough.

United had been going great guns in the League Cup, beating Rochdale, Colchester, Bolton and Everton on the way to a semi-final meeting with Clough's Nottingham Forest.

Clough's team outplayed United, winning 3-1 at Elland Road with a magnificent display, then hammering them 4-2 at the City Ground. United, who finished a mediocre ninth in the League, had slipped badly by their own high standards, but Armfield's new-look team needed more time to knit together.

Paul Hart joined Leeds from Blackpool, as a replacement for Gordon McQueen. After a shaky start he became a rock at the centre of United's defence, making over 220 appearances before moving to Nottingham Forest in the summer of 1983. Hart moved around the League before going into management at Chesterfield. Eventually he returned to the City Ground as manager.

Managerial Merry-go-round

THERE was a great deal of speculation about Jimmy Armfield's future following the disappointments of 1977-8.

The side was still being reshaped by Armfield who continued his rebuilding programme during summer 1978.

Two more men from the Revie era, Paul Reaney and Allan Clarke, left, while Hull City goal-grabber John Hawley arrived with a £81,000 price tag.

'Speedy' Reaney had been one of the most underrated of Revie's men. A superb defender, he specialised in goal-line clearances and was reckoned to be one of the best man-for-man markers of his day. Three England caps was a poor reward for a player of great calibre who clocked up around 750 appearances for Leeds, a figure bettered only by Billy Bremner and Jack Charlton. Reaney joined

Bradford City on a free transfer in a deal which created a bit of history as he became the first player in the country to transfer himself following the introduction of the new freedom of contract policy. Clarke, who bagged 151 goals in United colours, accepted the job as player-manager at Barnsley, where he showed he had lost none of his old predatory penalty box skills.

During the summer of 1978, Paul Reaney (left) and Allan Clarke were two more of the Revie side to leave Elland Road.

Leeds United in the 1978-9 season. Back row (left to right): John Hawley, Paul Madeley, Paul Hart, David Stewart, Ray Hankin, David Harvey, Keith Parkinson, Tony Currie, Byron Stevenson. Front row: Frank Gray, Eddie Gray, Peter Lorimer, Brian Flynn, Trevor Cherry, Carl Harris, Arthur Graham, Peter Hampton.

Despite the rumours, Armfield looked safe, then, with the 1978-9 season just over a month away he was given the chop.

Manny Cussins was still chairman, but younger men like Brian Roberts, Rayner Barker, Jack Marjason and Brian Woodward, many with family links with previous directors, had been added the previous year. Barker had taken over as vice-chairman following the death of the legendary Sam Bolton, at the age of 82, in December 1976.

Armfield's four-year reign had been ended because of lack of success. Many felt he was on the right path, having pulled the club round after the Brian Clough fiasco, steered United to the European Cup Final and then rebuilt the side piece by piece.

Some argued that the mild-mannered Armfield was too nice and lacked the ruthless streak necessary in top management. After his sacking by Leeds he never ventured into management again but became a successful journalist and radio commentator.

The United job was a big managerial plum and Southampton boss Lawrie McMenemy and Don Howe, the former United coach, who had returned to Highbury as Arsenal's coach, were reckoned to be at the top of the tree. However, neither could be lured to Elland Road.

When United kicked-off their season with a 2-2 draw against Howe's Arsenal at Highbury, the new man had still to be named and United were being run by caretaker-boss Maurice Lindley.

The following day, United named Celtic legend Jock Stein as manager.

Stein had recently been pushed upstairs' by Celtic and was unhappy in his new role. A great friend and admirer of Don Revie and his methods, Stein seemed a wise choice.

"I did not want to stay at Celtic as a director. I feel I have too much to offer football and I wanted closer involvement," he said.

Stein was revered at Parkhead where he had led Celtic to their greatest triumph, lifting the European Cup in 1967 to add to a stack of domestic honours.

His experience and United's stature seemed to go hand-in-hand, but the honeymoon lasted only 44 days, exactly the same length of time Brian Clough had spent at the club.

Jock Stein was appointed Leeds United manager but, like Brian Clough, he too spent only 44 days at Elland Road.

Jimmy Adamson had turned down the chance to manage England back in 1963, but he took over at Elland Road after Jock Stein went back to Scotland when his wife could not settle south of the border.

Jock's Away

This time there was no cloak and dagger departure. Stein's wife wished to stay north of the border and Scotland were looking for a new manager following Ally McLeod's dismissal after a disastrous World Cup campaign in Argentina.

Stein, who never signed a contract with United, took the job as his country's manager and took Scotland to the 1982 World Cup Finals. Three years later he was on the verge of taking them to the Finals again when in September 1985 he collapsed and died at the end of a qualifying game against Wales in Cardiff, leaving soccer to mourn the loss of one of the all-time great managers.

Lindley stepped into the caretaker role once again as United looked for a successor to Stein.

They eventually landed Sunderland boss Jimmy Adamson, a man who had turned down the job as England manager during the latter stages of his playing career at Burnley.

Although never capped by England, Adamson was Footballer of the Year in 1962 and was assistant manager to Walter Winterbottom for the World Cup of that year.

When Winterbottom resigned, Adamson was offered the post but declined, believing he lacked the necessary experience. He managed Burnley, the club he had served so faithfully as a player, and after a brief spell as manager with Sparta Rotterdam was appointed boss at Sunderland.

With him, Adamson brought another former Burnley man Dave Merrington, his assistant at Roker Park, who opted to stick with Adamson rather than take over his job at Sunderland.

Not surprisingly with all the behind-the-scenes activity, United had made only a moderate start but Adamson got United moving during his early months in office.

John Hawley was proving a bargain goalscorer, Paul Hart and the ever dependable Paul Madeley were rocks in the heart of the defence, whilst Tony Currie hit peak form in midfield.

United went 16 League games without defeat from mid-November and although they faltered at the end, finished fifth to recapture a place in Europe.

They were also tantalisingly close to Wembley.

The FA Cup home ban had virtually made it impossible to make much headway in that

competition and United fell to West Brom after a replay, both games being held at The Hawthorns.

United had more success against Albion in the League Cup, knocking them out at the third attempt in the second round. Impressive wins over Sheffield United, Queen's Park Rangers and Luton followed to put United through the League Cup semi-finals for a second successive year.

It seemed as though they were going to make home advantage count over Southampton as goals by Tony Currie and Ray Hankin built up a 2-0 lead, putting Wembley within sight.

But the Saints staged a late semi-final fight-back to draw level at Elland Road then won the second leg 1-0 as United endured their third semi-final disappointment in as many years.

United, who had already seen Nottingham Forest beat their record of 34 League games without defeat, lost two more landmarks in the final game of the season against Liverpool.

The men from Anfield were already champions when they arrived at Elland Road and a 3-0 win saw them establish a new record points total of 68 and the least number of goals conceded, 16, in a season, beating the previous best set by Leeds United in 1968-9.

Southampton's Terry Curran gets the ball across despite the close attention of Leeds' Paul Hart. Eddie Gray looks on. The sides drew this League Cup semi-final first-leg game at Elland Road 2-2 in January 1979.

Unfortunately bigger disappointments were lying in wait for Leeds.

Adamson's only addition in his first season was Blackburn Rovers Kevin Hird, who was signed for £357,000, a record for an English full-back.

But Adamson was anxious to build quickly on the good start he had made and went into the transfer market in a big way in summer 1979, even though United were to register a record loss of £820,363 on the 1978-9 season.

Adamson's first departure had been David Stewart to West Brom for £75,000, a move which confirmed David Harvey's status as United's number one. Adamson also knew that England youth squad goalkeeper John Lukic also had the potential to challenge Harvey for the goalkeeping job in the near future.

Before the end of the campaign Peter Lorimer, who was within sight of John Charles' goalscoring aggregate of 153 League goals, opened a new chapter in his career by joining Canadian outfit Toronto Blizzard in the North American Soccer League for £25,000. Lorimer's power-packed shooting had become a lethal weapon in United's goalscoring armoury from the day he made his League debut as a fresh-faced 15-year-old in 1962.

That was just the start of a massive rebuilding programme which saw England midfielder Tony Currie, a big hero with the fans, go to Queen's Park Rangers for £400,000, with domestic reasons being cited for his wish to return to his native London.

Frank Gray went to Nottingham Forest for £500,000; John Hawley to Sunderland for £200,000 with Wayne Entwistle coming from Roker in return.

Adamson paid United's record fee to snap up Swansea striker Alan Curtis for £400,000, shelled out a further £350,000 to Manchester United for Brian Greenhoff, younger brother of former Leeds striker Jimmy, then wrote out a cheque for £140,000 for Sheffield United midfielder Gary Hamson and a further £100,000 for Blackpool winger Jeff Chandler.

It was a big and expensive turnover of staff and with so many new players around it was not

Kevin Hird signed for Leeds in January 1979 from Blackburn Rovers for £375,000, at the time making him the most expensive full-back in the British game. By the time he moved to Burnley in August 1984 he had made over 175 senior appearances for United, most of them as an attacking midfielder.

surprising that they failed to knit together immediately.

Curtis made a great debut, scoring twice in the 2-2 draw at Bristol City, but this was a rare high spot for United in another season of under-achievement.

Only three wins had been garnered from the first 14 League games and an embarrassing 7-0 Football League defeat at Arsenal made it a miserable start for United.

Adamson was given two months by the board to improve matters but the first game after their ultimatum saw United crash 5-1 at Everton.

Slowly United pulled round as they eased away from the relegation area, but the restless fans were far from happy with the level of performances.

A section of the South Stand had already been closed for a period after missiles were thrown on to the pitch against Manchester City. The Kop was closed for two games in February 1980 after more missiles were thrown during the 2-1 League defeat against Nottingham Forest.

Attendances at the two games in question, Bolton and Brighton, both failed to reach 20,000, losing United vital revenue.

Even when the Kop was reopened, the fans did not flock back in numbers. Although United paraded former Scottish international striker Derek Parlane, signed for £160,000 just before the transfer deadline to lead the attack in place of the injury-stricken Alan Curtis, United's fans were not convinced.

Parlane marked his debut with a goal in a 2-0 win over Southampton, but following successive away defeats at Ipswich and Liverpool, United mustered a crowd of only 14,967 for the visit of Coventry on 22 March 1980.

It was United's lowest League crowd for 17 years and during the game there were vociferous anti-Adamson chants. After a tedious goalless draw hundreds of fans congregated in the West Stand

Above: Liam Brady and Steve Walford have control as Terry Connor moves in at Highbury in January 1980.
Below: Wayne Entwistle gets in a shot. It was Connor, though, who scored the only goal of the match.

car park demanding Adamson's dismissal before the demonstration was broken up by mounted police. A season of great promise had ended in bitter disappointment, the 11th place hardly reflecting the mediocre fare the fans had been served. Supporters deserted the club in their thousands as League games at Elland Road averaged only 22,788.

Even the return to Europe had been a damp squib. After the Maltese part-timers Valetta were predictably beaten, United were outplayed home and away by the Romanian side Universitatea Craiova.

For United's Welsh international Byron Stevenson there was even more European misery as UEFA dished out a four-year international ban on the player after he was sent off in a European Championship game in Turkey – a suspension that was later reduced to two years.

Adamson's Agony
David Harvey, in his testimonial year, had left for Vancouver Whitecaps. and was soon joined at the Canadian club by Ray Hankin in a £300,000 deal.

Yet despite all his wheeling and dealing in the transfer market, the only shaft of light in a gloomy season for Adamson emerged in the shape of John Lukic and Leeds-born duo Terry Connor and Martin Dickinson, all products of United's youth policy.

Goalkeeper Lukic was a young giant, standing 6ft 4in, and made such an impact that he won England Under-21 honours, whilst 17-year-old Connor showed maturity beyond his years as he filled in for Curtis and Hankin, and Dickinson looked a promising defender in the Norman Hunter mould.

Despite intense speculation over his future, Adamson survived the summer and gambled on a spectacular big money signing for the 1980-81 season and win over the fans.

The man he turned to was Sheffield United's Alex Sabella, an immensely skilful Argentinian midfield player who arrived with a £400,000 price on his head from the Blades.

He came to England after the 1978 World Cup which saw his better-known countrymen Ossie Ardiles and Ricardo Villa link up with Spurs in a sensational deal.

Sabella's flair flourished at Bramall Lane and Adamson looked to his ball skills to create openings for an attack which had been given precious little ammunition in the previous season.

When Byron Stevenson fired United into the lead after just 177 seconds of the new season in the home game against Aston Villa, it seemed as though United may get the lift they badly needed.

But Villa fought back to win 2-1 and the next game brought a 3-0 thumping at Middlesbrough. The doom and gloom merchants were predicting a swift end to the Adamson era.

A few games later Adamson bowed to the inevitable and resigned, leaving Maurice Lindley to slip back into his caretaker manager role once again.

A Hero's Welcome for Clarke
This time United turned to former goal-poacher Allan Clarke to dig them out of trouble. Only Crystal Palace were below United with six games gone and Clarke, who had done well in his first managerial role at Barnsley, clearly had a big job on his hands.

From Oakwell he brought Martin Wilkinson as his assistant and Barry Murphy as coach as Dave Merrington departed with Adamson. Confident

Alex Sabella runs through the Aston Villa defence watched by Derek Parlane and Villa's Dennis Mortimer in the first match of 1980-81. Leeds lost 2-1.

Allan Clarke's second game in charge of Leeds and Gary Rowell scores for Sunderland in the Wearsiders' 4-1 win over United at Roker Park in September 1980.

Allan Clarke, a former favourite on the pitch, returned to Elland Road as manager in September 1980.

Clarke said: "I'm a winner. I shall regard myself as a failure if we have not won a major trophy over the next three years."

He continued: "I have told the players that they will be given the opportunity in the next few weeks to show me what they can do and I think they realise what I expect from them in terms of attitude, not only on Saturday afternoons but throughout the week in training."

Clarke received a hero's welcome at his first game in charge at Elland Road – a goalless draw against Manchester United, but the early days were not all plain sailing.

A 5-0 home defeat at the hands of Arsenal was particularly painful. That match saw the 36-year-old Paul Madeley go off injured and it proved to be his last-ever game for United, announcing the end of his one-club career that had taken him over the 700 appearance mark with Leeds and 24 caps for England.

It was also to prove a significant season for another seasoned professional, Eddie

Brian Greenhoff heads off the Leeds goal-line in the 1-0 win over Everton in October 1980. Brother of former Leeds player Jimmy Greenhoff, Brian was a ballboy at Wembley when Jimmy won a League Cup winners' medal with Leeds in 1968. Leeds paid £350,000 to sign him from Manchester United in August 1979. He had already played for England and was capped again while with Leeds, although injury disrupted his career at Elland Road.

Gray, who despite the club's recent lean spell had maintained his excellent form.

Now in his 30s, Gray was switched from his more advanced role to left-back, a position United had struggled to cover since the sale of Peter Hampton to Stoke for £175,000 just before the start of the season.

It was an astute move by Clarke, who had made his priority sorting out United's defence, but up front the goals dried up and so did the fans.

The 14,333 which saw a Carl Harris goal beat Brighton at the end of November was the lowest at Elland Road since United's return to the First Division.

Harris, nominally a winger, finished as top scorer with just ten goals, while his Welsh international teammate striker Alan Curtis returned to his old club Swansea for a cut-price £165,000 after 16 months of frustration.

Despite scoring only 39 League goals, United finished the season in fairly good shape with nine wins and four draws from their final 16 games lifting them into ninth place.

It seemed United had finally turned the corner, but in reality they were about to drive into a cul-de-sac called the Second Division.

The Violent Downward Spiral

CORNERSTONE to Allan Clarke's ambitious plans was England winger Peter Barnes. Clarke shattered United's transfer record by splashing out a then club record £930,000 on a player with an impressive pedigree.

Barnes, a former Young Player of the Year, won the first of his England caps during his early days at Manchester City where he was hailed as one of the game's most talented forwards, a reputation he enhanced at West Brom.

Barnes was not the only international capture by Clarke, as he re-signed former United man Frank Gray after two highly successful seasons with Nottingham Forest.

Gray, the current Scotland left-back, therefore was challenging his elder brother, Eddie, for the number-three shirt, although he was to resume his Elland Road career in midfield.

United also boasted three new directors, Leslie Silver, Bill Fotherby and Maxwell Holmes, plus new sponsors in R. F. Winder, the Stanningley-based electrical engineers whose name adorned United's new pin-stripe kit.

There was certainly a fresh air of optimism around Elland Road, but the bubble was burst on the opening day of the season as United, including their expensive new man, Barnes, crashed 5-1 at newly-promoted Swansea, Alan Curtis getting one of the goals for the Welsh side. The first ten League games brought only one win, an Arthur Graham hat-trick giving Leeds a 3-0 victory over Wolves.

Clarke reckoned his side, now bottom of the First Division, needed more steel so he returned to Forest to snap up another Scottish international, Kenny Burns, for £400,000.

Burns was made skipper on his arrival, replacing Trevor Cherry, who moved from central

Peter Barnes joined Leeds for a club record fee of £930,000, but never reproduced the form he had shown with Manchester City.

Aidan Butterworth and Tottenham's Graham Roberts fight for a high ball at Elland Road in December 1981.

defence to right-back to accommodate the rugged Burns. The Elland Road payroll was reduced with the departure of Jeff Chandler and Alex Sabella. Chandler went to Bolton for £40,000 while Sabella returned to his native Argentina, where he linked up with Estudiantes in a £120,000 deal.

With Barnes struggling to live up to his reputation and Derek Parlane sidelined by injury for five months, United were misfiring up front and in a bid to shake things up, local youngster Aiden Butterworth was given a chance to lead the attack.

United seemed to be inching their way to safety, but a disastrous run of six games without a goal and only one point from a possible 18 – this was the first season of three points for a win – sent them spinning back towards the relegation zone.

Clarke needed to take drastic action and traded defender-midfielder Byron Stevenson for Birmingham's much-travelled striker Frank Worthington.

Worthington, blessed with great skills, had won eight England caps and, although past his peak, he maintained an impressive strike rate for United after scoring the only goal of the game in his second match, at Sunderland.

That brought a rare and precious win, but United could not shake off the habit of losing and the relegation noose began to tighten.

Left: Scottish international Arthur Graham, who scored three hat-tricks for Leeds, stayed at Elland Road for one season after United were relegated. Then a surprise move to Old Trafford revitalised his career.

Right: Terry Connor made a name for himself after coming on as a 17-year-old substitute and scoring the only goal of the game at home to West Brom in November 1979. After his form suffered in a struggling team, he moved to Brighton in March 1983, in exchange for the Seagulls' Andy Ritchie.

Leeds substitute Kenny Burns gets past two Stoke City players in the goalless relegation battle at Elland Road in May 1982.

The relegation dogfight reached a climax on the final Saturday of the season with United and six other clubs battling to avoid the drop.

United looked as they were going to plunge straight through the trapdoor as they trailed 1-0 at home to Brighton, but two goals in a minute late on by Gary Hamson and Kevin Hird gave United victory and seemingly First Division survival.

But slowly news came through that their fellow strugglers had also done well. Birmingham won 1-0 at Coventry, Sunderland beat Manchester City 1-0 and West Brom were 2-1 victors at Notts County.

When the dust settled it was clear that United had to win their final match at West Brom three days later to avoid relegation with Wolves and Middlesbrough.

United were backed by a huge army of fans when their First Division lives went on the line at The Hawthorns.

But despite their vocal encouragement, second-half goals by Cyrille Regis and Steve Mackenzie gave Albion victory.

Even though Albion and Stoke still had to meet, United's death warrant had been as good as signed and trouble brewed on the terraces towards the end of the game. So-called Leeds fans pushed their way to the front to rip down fencing but the police baton-charged the terracing to nip any pitch invasion in the bud.

Fighting spilled over into the streets surrounding the ground as United, who had been plagued by a hardcore of hooligans since the troubles in Paris in 1975, hit the headlines for all the wrong reasons.

Two nights later Stoke beat West Brom 3-0 at the Victoria Ground to guarantee their First Division status and rubber-stamp United's exit visa to Division Two. Clarke and his assistant

Allan Clarke (left) and his assistant, Martin Wilkinson, paid the price for Leeds United's relegation after 18 years in the top flight.

In the penultimate game of the 1981-2 season, Frank Worthington evades the challenge of Brighton defender Gary Stevens. Leeds won 2-1 after going behind.

Martin Wilkinson paid the price for United's relegation after 18 years in the top flight.

First to go was Wilkinson, who quickly got fixed up as Peterborough's manager, whilst Clarke was replaced two weeks later by the highly popular Eddie Gray. Clarke rejoined the managerial circus when he was appointed Scunthorpe's boss and subsequently returned to Barnsley for a spell and was later in charge at Lincoln City.

Enter Eddie the Boss

Gray was made player-manager and his orders were crystal clear – get United back to the First Division as soon as possible. But that was not going to be easy as United's followers had left the club in droves, the wage bill was still high and United were reported to be a record £1.5 million in debt.

Gates would inevitably be lower in Division Two if United failed to get off to a good start, so Gray had to tread warily.

He brought in Jimmy Lumsden, a former United reserve, from Celtic as his assistant and also persuaded Syd Owen, a key part of the backroom staff in Don Revie's day, to join the club as chief scout. Gray started by clipping United's wings. Peter Barnes, after just one season at Elland Road,

A bad knee injury at the end of 1981-2 sidelined Gary Hamson for a long period before he fought his way back into the side. In February 1981 he had received a nine-match ban, a record under the disciplinary points system of the time.

was loaned out to Spanish club Real Betis for a year, whilst fellow winger Carl Harris joined Charlton for £100,000. But there was no wholesale clearout as the rest of the players were given the chance to prove their value.

Despite missing Trevor Cherry (suspended) and Kenny Burns (injured) for the opening day game at Grimsby, United looked impressive in gaining a 1-1 draw, thanks to Terry Connor's goal.

But there was trouble involving Leeds followers both before and after the match with £6,000 damage done to the Blundell Park ground.

United, who had been ordered by the FA Disciplinary Committee hearing into the West Brom violence to publish warning notices in the club programme, found that crowd-trouble rather than football was in the news again.

Chairman Manny Cussins warned that any heavy fine or ground closure could force United to call in the receiver, such was the financial plight of the club.

New vice-chairman Leslie Silver persuaded all Second Division clubs to meet to discuss ways to combat the hooligans, but it did not take long for trouble to spark off again. United had made a good start on the pitch, but it was the aggro off it which continued to dog the club.

There were fights involving United followers at Chelsea, whose match programme front cover urging thugs not to be mugs went unheeded.

Three weeks later Newcastle's former England

In July 1982, Eddie Gray was appointed player-manager as United faced the Second Division.

skipper Kevin Keegan was felled by a ball-bearing thrown from the Kop at Elland Road during United's 3-1 win over the Magpies. Later in the game missiles were thrown by the Newcastle contingent and the referee took the teams off temporarily as a safety precaution.

United took a leaf out of Chelsea's book by devoting the front cover of the programme for the next home game, against Charlton, to spell out their firm views on the yobs who were putting the club at risk.

'The future of Leeds United Association Football Club hangs in the balance.

'This in no way exaggerates the position and must not be taken as an idle threat.

'Despite repeated pleas and warnings, the mindless actions of a minority of the club's so-called followers last Saturday have placed an enormous degree of uncertainty over this great club.

'We know from the comments received in the last few days that many true supporters deplore what took place at the Newcastle game.

'And we would ask for the help and co-operation of everyone who has Leeds United at heart – and we appreciate that this is the majority of our supporters – to help rid the club of the 'scab' element who, although small in numbers, have caused the club so many problems and whose loathsome actions now place the very existence of Leeds United in jeopardy.'

The FA announced that the terraces must be closed for two home games, so the games against Queen's Park Rangers and Shrewsbury were made all-ticket, all-seater games only.

A crowd of just 11,528 saw Clive Allen give Queen's Park Rangers a 1-0 win at ghostly Elland Road, the lowest League attendance there for 19 years – but because it was seating only the gate receipts were equivalent to a 17,000 crowd. A fortnight later a meagre 8,741 turned up to see Kevin Hird save a point for United in a 1-1 draw.

But despite all their anti-hooligan measures, United seemed unable to drive the message home and the following month there was more trouble involving Leeds followers in the seats at Derby as the Rams fought back from 3-1 down to snatch a point.

The trouble at the Baseball Ground triggered yet another FA inquiry and both Derby and Leeds were found guilty of 'failing to exercise proper control over their supporters' with United warned about the future behaviour of their fans.

It was like the Sword of Damocles hanging over the club but the final three and a half months of the season passed without further major incident, much to the relief of the hard-pressed board.

In the circumstances United did well to keep in the promotion race, even though some pruning of the playing staff had gradually taken place throughout the campaign.

Skipper Trevor Cherry accepted Bradford City's offer to be their player-manager and, with former Leeds man Terry Yorath as his assistant, went on to steer City to the Second Division for the first time since 1937.

All Cherry's 27 England caps had been won during his days at Elland Road, where he proved a consistent performer in central defence, full-back and midfield, often in difficult times.

Following Cherry's departure the captaincy was passed back to Kenny Burns once more, but within months he was on his way to Derby, on loan, a deal that eventually became a permanent move.

Others leaving were 'Tom Thumb' midfielder Brian Flynn back to Burnley for £60,000, the much-travelled Worthington off to Sunderland for £50,000, and fellow striker Derek Parlane on loan to Hong Kong club, Bulova.

The biggest surprise was the departure of Terry Connor, the popular Leeds lad who had made such a sensational impact as a teenager. He went to Brighton in a swap deal for Andy Ritchie, an England Under-21 forward, who had once scored a hat-trick against Leeds for Manchester United.

The exodus of some of the club's most experienced players opened the door for several youngsters. With the club in the red, Gray knew that he would have to rely on youth to rebuild the club so defender Neil Aspin, striker Tommy Wright, winger Mark Gavin and midfielders John Sheridan and Scott Sellars – all of them teenagers – sampled first-team football.

Reversing the youth trend was David Harvey, who returned to United from Vancouver after three and a half years. He took a back seat while John Lukic continued to hold down the number-one spot but took over between the posts for the last 13 League games of the season.

Lukic, who set a club record 146 consecutive League appearances, beating the previous best set by Jim Baker in the 1920s, put in a transfer request because he wanted a new challenge.

Gray's response was swift, dropping Lukic and bringing back 35-year-old Harvey.

Of the younger element, Sheridan, only 18, looked the most accomplished with his wide range of passing clinching him a regular place towards the end of the season.

United had begun the season as hot favourites to go up, but faded badly to finish eighth. Although given the huge problems off the pitch the club were probably relieved to get through the season still in business.

Lukic got his wish of a new challenge with

Arsenal in summer, United banking £100,000 for their England Under-21 international, whilst Arthur Graham, who collected ten Scotland caps in his six years with Leeds was a surprise £50,000 transfer to Manchester United and stopper Paul Hart joined Nottingham Forest for £40,000.

The money was reinvested in talent north of the border in Celtic striker George McCluskey (£161,000) and steely midfield ball-winner Andy Watson (£60,000) from Aberdeen.

Gray and Lumsden had already used their contacts in Scotland to tempt Dumbarton's midfielder John Donnelly into signing full-time forms with United in a £10,000 deal.

During the early part of his reign, Gray had converted a £1.5 million loss into a profit of £196,064, thanks to a transfer profit of £320,833. The message was clear, the big-spending of recent years had to stop and more emphasis was placed on the club's youth policy.

Peter Barnes also returned from his sojourn in Spain and was really buzzing in pre-season training to rekindle hopes that he could spark a United revival the second time round.

This time United were backed by Systime, a computer firm just a mile away from Elland Road at Millshaw Park, but the team failed to serve up much hi-tech stuff on the pitch.

They struggled for any kind of consistency and fans continued to stay away in droves.

The low point came at Elland Road in the League Cup when Chester, 92nd in the Football League, beat United 1-0 in front of an 8,106 crowd. United were able to spare their blushes by winning the second leg 4-1 at Chester, only to be eliminated in the next round by Third Division Oxford.

There was no joy in the FA Cup either, Allan Clarke gaining revenge over his old side as

Scunthorpe, struggling in Division Three, knocked United out in the third round after two replays.

United were looking to the cups to generate some much-needed cash but it failed to materialise, so manager Gray had to struggle on knowing he hadn't got the money to add to his young squad.

His plans had been dealt a severe blow when the talented John Sheridan broke a leg at Barnsley and United laboured to cover his absence, sliding towards the relegation zone.

United had to adjust their priorities. Promotion was no longer realistic but the dreaded drop into Division Three for the first time in the club's history certainly was.

'Peter Pan' Lorimer

United went into their home game against Middlesbrough on New Year's Eve 1983 fourth from bottom and with an elder statesman on their bench – Peter Lorimer.

The United veteran, now 37, and a year older than manager Gray, had returned to Leeds after spells with York City and Vancouver Whitecaps where he was player-coach.

Lorimer came on as substitute in that game for George McCluskey, whose two goals had helped United to a 4-1 win to put a dreadful 1983 behind them.

'Peter Pan' Lorimer soon made his influence tell, making just one more substitute appearance before dropping into midfield to make his experience count over the second half of the season.

As he pulled the strings in midfield, the eager young beavers around him did the running and United finally began to take shape.

Only four more games were lost and United rose impressively up the table to a respectable tenth at the end of the season.

The final match of the campaign marked Eddie Gray's farewell United appearance and completed a glittering playing career which had brought him a dozen Scottish caps and over 550 Leeds appearances, both totals that would have been substantially increased had it not been for a succession of injuries in mid-career.

Gray's final match brought a 1-0 win over Charlton, thanks to a Tommy Wright goal.

Wright was one of the new breed of United fledglings who were progressing under the protective wing of the vintage Lorimer, who had

A cramp-ridden Adrian Butterworth scores against Arsenal in the fourth-round FA Cup replay in February 1983. Graham Rix equalised with a spectacular free-kick in the dying moments of extra-time and Arsenal won the next game 2-1.

Goalkeeper John
Lukic, dropped after
asking for a transfer.
In the summer of
1983 he moved to
Arsenal for
£100,000.

surged beyond John Charles' aggregate of League goals.

Neil Aspin finished the season as the regular centre-half, Scott Sellars oozed class on the left-hand side of midfield and former juniors skipper Denis Irwin looked set to hold the right-back position for years to come.

With the hooligans kept in check, Gray considered 1983-4 a campaign of progress after a poor start.

United also had a new head man in the boardroom, Leslie Silver taking over as chairman in place of Manny Cussins, who took Silver's role as vice-chairman.

Cussins remained vice-chairman until his death in London on 5 October 1983, aged 82. Millionaire Manny never admitted to being rich. 'Rich men do not work,' he once said, adding that retirement only turned men into cabbages.

Silver, like Cussins, was a highly successful businessman. He came out of the RAF in 1947 and launched a paint firm with other members of his family with a £250 gratuity and developed it into a thriving business.

Silver became chairman of Silver Paint and Lacquer (Holdings) Ltd and his firm's Home Charm Paint became one of Britain's best-known names.

A former president of the Oil and Colour Chemists' Association, he was awarded an OBE in

June 1982 for services to export and six months later was elevated to the chairmanship of Leeds United.

Gray's team certainly painted a pretty picture as they launched the 1984-5 season with four successive wins to shoot to the top.

With money still in short supply, Gray paraded only one new man in his side, giant centre-half Andy Linighan, a £20,000 purchase from Hartlepool.

Cost-cutting was the order of the day. Coach Barry Murphy and chief scout Syd Owen had already departed, Peter Barnes was sold to Coventry for £60,000 to add to the £40,000 Gwyn Thomas had fetched when he moved to Barnsley.

United's super start, triggered by a flurry of goals by the quicksilver Wright, proved an illusion and they spent much of the season on the fringes of the promotion race without thrusting themselves into the picture.

Inconsistency continued to be United's bugbear. At times they were capable of some outstanding football which brought them thumping wins, but on other days the youngsters were muscled out of the action.

In mid-season Gray sprung a few surprises by releasing Andy Watson to Hearts and replacing skipper and goalkeeper David Harvey with £30,000 Mervyn Day from Aston Villa.

Day burst upon the scene in the 1970s with

Leslie Silver, a
prominent
businessman, took
over as United
chairman.

West Ham, with a series of outstanding displays which soon had him earmarked as an England prospect. But he lost his way with the Hammers and after a spell at Orient found himself languishing in the reserves at Villa Park before Gray stepped in to resurrect his career.

The popular Harvey, meanwhile, having taken his United League appearances to 350, was loaned out to Partick Thistle and later played a few games for Bradford City before playing non-League football.

Soccer Shrouded by Tragedy

To add more muscle to his attack in a belated push for promotion, Gray recruited Ian Baird, a robust striker from Southampton for £75,000.

Bustling Baird knocked in six goals in his first nine games to give United a mathematical chance of going up as they went into their last game at Birmingham, who had already been promoted.

That game at St Andrew's on 11 May 1985 came on a day of double tragedy for soccer.

It was the day fire at Bradford City claimed 56 lives and crowd trouble reared its ugly head amongst Leeds United followers at Birmingham, where a boy died.

Problems flared at St Andrew's shortly after Martin Kuhl's first-half goal, the only one of the game, was scored at the end where the Leeds supporters were packed.

Somehow a group of Leeds fans got on the pitch and there were skirmishes with their Birmingham counterparts, who had also flooded on to the playing area. The teams were taken off and as the violence escalated, mounted police came on to quell the riot and clear the field.

The second half resumed 30 minutes late and was played out in a tense atmosphere. At the end of the game a wall collapsed under the weight of departing fans and crushed a teenage boy, who became a sad statistic on one of soccer's darkest days.

Ninety-six police were among the injured during the battle of St Andrew's and 110 spectators appeared before Birmingham magistrates the following week.

Mr Justice Popplewell was called in by the Home Secretary to hold an inquiry into the Bradford Fire Disaster and the Birmingham Riot.

Just two and a half weeks later the rising tide of soccer violence exploded at the European Cup Final at the Heysel Stadium between Liverpool and Juventus when 38 fans were killed and over 400 were injured. For United it was back to square one in the war against the hooligans.

The previous season, 1983-4, had seen Leeds enjoy a relatively trouble-free season, but it proved to be the calm before the storm as trouble was reported at Oxford, Huddersfield and Barnsley before the violent climax at St Andrew's put the future of the club at risk once more.

No longer was the talk of United's exciting young talent like John Sheridan, Tommy Wright, Scott Sellars, Denis Irwin and Neil Aspin, it was all about Leeds United thugs.

These were months when it was hard for Leeds fans to lift their heads up high.

Ian Baird joined United from Southampton and soon made his mark with six goals in his first nine games.

Shades of
the Past

UNITED'S punishment for the St Andrew's riot was a £5,000 fine by the FA, who also ruled that all United's away games for the 1985-6 season should be all-ticket.

The latter saw several Second Division clubs kick up a fuss as they lost revenue because all-ticket games failed to attract the same size of attendances as pay-on-the-day games.

United had a huge away support which helped boost the coffers of several clubs, some of whom used to increase prices to squeeze extra cash from United's fans.

In its early days the all-ticket scheme was not 100 per cent successful, but the off-the-field problems were now overshadowed by troubles on the pitch.

As he prepared for the 1985-6 season, Gray sold his younger brother Frank to Sunderland for £100,000. Gray junior later joined Darlington as player-coach and had a short but unsuccessful spell as manager of the Quakers.

Eddie's first spell in management was also coming to a close. United made a dreadful start to the season, failing to win any of their first five League games to put Gray's future at risk.

A run of eight games brought just one defeat and

Gray seemed to have ridden out the storm, but on 11 October 1985 he and Lumsden were sacked.

Gray's 22-year association with the club came to an end at a board meeting which saw a 6-2 vote to terminate his contract. The decision to axe the 38-year-old Gray was not well received, although Gray himself accepted the decision with great dignity.

Some players cried openly after being told of

Billy Bremner returned as manager in 1985 and steered Leeds to the brink of double glory before the side slipped back and he was dismissed in 1988.

the dismissal and skipper Peter Lorimer handed a statement to the board in which the players condemned the timing and handling of the announcement – coming three days after a 3-0 Milk Cup win at Walsall – although pledged to continue to do their best for the club.

Director Brian Woodward, a former United reserve player whose father, Percy, had been chairman, resigned in protest at the sacking, severing a family link with the club which stretched back to 1946.

Coach Peter Gunby was put in temporary charge and chairman Leslie Silver paid tribute to Gray's service, but 14th place in Division Two was not good enough for a club of United's stature, he said.

Silver said: "Undoubtedly reaching this difficult judgement has placed the affairs of Leeds United at a crossroads. With the season less than a third complete there is still a great deal still to be accomplished during the coming months."

The day after the shock announcement, United beat Middlesbrough 1-0 with a Peter Lorimer penalty at Elland Road where fans chanted for the reinstatement of Gray and the resignation of Silver.

Gray later linked up with David Harvey at Whitby Town as a player and later re-emerged as manager at Rochdale and Hull.

Battling Billy's Return

As one legend from the Revie era departed, another arrived in the shape of Billy Bremner, the man who epitomised Leeds United in those glory years.

The fiery human midfield dynamo had entered management with Doncaster Rovers and the appointment of such a well-respected former player took the heat out of the situation at Elland Road.

Bremner became the third successive former United player to assume command at Elland Road in succession to Gray and Allan Clarke and linked up with one of his former Doncaster stars.

Gray had bought Rovers' dynamic England Under-21 midfield international Ian Snodin for £200,000 in the summer and within weeks of Bremner's arrival Snodin was made skipper.

The man whom Snodin replaced as captain, the evergreen Peter Lorimer, was released and teamed up with Harvey and Gray at Whitby Town for a spell. Lorimer had made a massive contribution to United in his two spells at the club which brought him an all-time record 238 goals – 168 of them in the League.

The coffers were hardly bursting at the seams but United took a significant step on the financial front when Elland Road was sold to Leeds City Council for £2.5 million and, in return, the Council granted the club a 125-year lease and unveiled ambitious plans finally being put into practice in summer 1992, to improve the stadium and neighbouring sporting facilities to develop the area into a sporting complex.

Bremner himself was quick to make his own plans, selling defenders Andy Linighan to Oldham for £55,000 and Martin Dickinson to West Brom for £40,000 before buying Aston Villa's Brendan Ormsby (£65,000) and Leicester's David Rennie (£50,000) to form a new central defensive partnership.

More youngsters like Peter Swan and John Stiles, son of England's 1966 World Cup winner Nobby, were given a first-team chance, but generally the team showed no major improvement suffering an embarrassing FA Cup exit at Fourth Division Peterborough and finished 14th.

To add to a fairly traumatic season, the hooligan factor reappeared once again.

Four policemen were hurt as United fans clashed with Millwall supporters at The Den, an incident which prompted the FA to make all Millwall games all-ticket with no tickets for visitors, whilst United fans were banned from all away games.

Enforcing the ban on United's travelling fans proved impossible and after hundreds turned up to see them win at Carlisle and Wimbledon, the FA admitted defeat and lifted the ban after only two games, although the all-ticket ruling remained.

Heroes of Hillsborough

After seeing no marked improvement in his first few months in charge, Bremner rang the changes

Martin Dickinson played as a defender and ball-winning midfielder before moving to West Brom.

in summer 1986 as he prepared for his first season in charge with several of the younger players brought through by Gray sold.

There were comings and goings just about every week at Leeds as Bremner got cracking.

The close season signings included Sheffield United's prolific scorer Keith Edwards for £125,000, Newcastle United defender Peter Haddock for £40,000, experienced stopper Jack Ashurst from Carlisle for £35,000 and winger John Buckley from Bremner's old club, Doncaster, for £40,000.

On the move from the previous squad were George McCluskey to Hibernian and Gary Hamson on a free transfer to Bristol City. Hamson had suffered a terrible time with injuries at Leeds, including three operations in a year, and a

recurring ankle injury was to end his career prematurely a couple of years later at Port Vale.

Some of the youngsters groomed by Gray also moved on. Denis Irwin made the short trip to Oldham for £60,000 where he was soon joined by striker Tommy Wright for £80,000. Scott Sellars, went to Blackburn for £20,000 after asking for a transfer and Terry Phelan went on a free to Swansea. The value of some of them shot up in later years.

The season was only seven games old when mob rule masquerading under the Leeds United banner struck again. The FA had seen an improvement in the behaviour of United fans so decided to lift their all-ticket ban, starting with the trip to neighbours Bradford City.

Valley Parade was still closed after the dreadful fire and the game against United was played at Odsal, the Rugby League and speedway stadium.

The lifting of the all-ticket arrangements for a local derby gave the hooligans a licence to roam free and fighting broke out between the rival factions during the game.

At one stage a fish and chip van was overturned and caught fire – bringing back horrific memories for some Bradford supporters.

The game was held up for 20 minutes and the stadium cleared before the teams came out to play the final few minutes with no fans in the ground.

There was no further addition to the 2-0 score in Bradford's favour. United's directors, anxious to drive the hooligans underground, requested that the all-ticket restriction be reintroduced and the FA agreed.

Genuine fans were pleased with United's good

start to the season and by November, they were in third spot behind Portsmouth and Oldham and looking well-placed for a promotion push.

But United slipped badly in the following weeks, culminating in a disastrous 7-2 defeat at Stoke just before Christmas to set the alarm bells ringing.

Bremner's response was swift. Skipper Ian Snodin was sold to Everton for a club record £800,000 and the money used to buy four new players, winger/full-back Micky Adams from Coventry for £110,000, experienced left-back Bobby McDonald from Oxford for £25,000 and two players from Charlton – Mark Aizlewood, a Welsh international midfielder for £200,000 and lanky striker John Pearson for £72,000.

It was a big risk to take midway through the season but paid off as United gradually gained ground on the leading pack with some stirring displays, particularly at Elland Road.

A season which was threatening to slip away into mediocrity slowly turned into one of great excitement.

United's aim was a place in the top two and direct promotion, but if they finished in the top five would go into the nerve-jangling play-offs.

Each week the door to the First Division seemed to open up a little further while the gates to

Thirty-year-old goalkeeper Mervyn Day enjoyed a 'second' career with Leeds United after Eddie Gray signed him for £30,000 from Aston Villa in February 1985. He was a key figure in United's run to the 1987 FA Cup semi-finals.

Wembley were also being rattled.

Their FA Cup campaign got off to a muted start as they beat non-League Telford 2-1 at West Brom's ground after the FA ruled that Telford's Bucks Head ground could not cope with the feared influx of Leeds fans. Two goals from in-form Ian Baird on a bitterly cold Sunday at The Hawthorns gave United victory in a game which attracted unrivalled police security.

A Mervyn Day-inspired United then won 2-1 at Swindon to set up a fifth-round meeting with First Division Queen's Park Rangers at Elland Road.

Thousands were locked out as Brendan Ormsby's late header put United through to a sixth-round tie at windswept Wigan.

Once again goalkeeper Day proved United's early saviour before superb long-range goals by John Stiles and Micky Adams sent United through to their first FA Cup semi-final in ten years.

Hopes of a place at Wembley were dashed by Coventry in a magnificent semi-final at sun-kissed Hillsborough.

David Rennie thundered in an early header to give United the lead. City were struggling to break United down when Brendan Ormsby made an error which turned the game on its head. Under pressure from Dave

Mervyn Day gathers the ball under pressure from Coventry City's Brian Kilcline in the 1987 FA Cup semi-final. John Pearson is the other Leeds player.

David Rennie of Leeds and Keith Houchen of Coventry in a heading duel at Hillsborough.

Andy Ritchie of Leeds and Coventry's Greg Downs in action during the 1987 semi-final.

Bennett he lost the ball on the byline instead of thumping it clear and Bennett was able to cross the ball for substitute Micky Gynn to fire in the equaliser.

Minutes later Keith Houchen made it 2-1 for the Sky Blues, but Keith Edwards came off the bench to tuck away a late header to take the game into extra-time.

United had played out of their skins, but Coventry had the edge in the extra period and snapped up their first FA Cup Final place with a Bennett goal.

It was hard on United but their display won them many new friends and probably more importantly, there was no misbehaviour from their followers.

Two days later goals by Sheridan and Pearson gave United a 2-0 win at Shrewsbury to step up the challenge for a play-off spot which was achieved three weeks later in some comfort with United finishing fourth.

Derby and Portsmouth were promoted, leaving United, Oldham, Ipswich and First Division Charlton to scrap it out in the Play-offs, which in those days also involved a club in the relegation zone.

Play-off Drama

The play-offs may not have produced the flowing football that United had displayed in the Hillsborough semi-final but the games were truly dramatic.

United were paired with their rivals from across the Pennines, Oldham, who boasted former Leeds players Denis Irwin, Andy Linighan and Tommy Wright in their ranks, all sold by manager Bremner.

Keith Edwards came on as substitute to score a last-gasp winner for United at Elland Road, but that 1-0 advantage was soon lost at Boundary Park when Gary Williams put Oldham ahead.

When Mike Cecere made it 2-0 with only a minute remaining, United were on the brink of defeat, but straight from the kick-off they equalised through super-sub Edwards.

United hung on in extra-time to scrape through on the away-goals-count-double ruling to the play-off final against Charlton, who had eliminated Ipswich. Once more tension and late goals kept the fans on the edge of their seats.

A dour game in London ended with a late Jim Melrose goal giving Charlton a 1-0 win, but in the white hot atmosphere of Elland Road, United levelled the scores when skipper Brendan Ormsby got the final touch to a shot from rookie striker Bob Taylor.

The final game of a long hard season took place at Birmingham on 29 May as United and Charlton fought out another cat-and-mouse battle that shredded the nerves.

Once again late goals decided the showdown.

John Sheridan, who had an outstanding season in midfield, gave United the lead in the first period of extra-time with a superb curling free kick.

But United, who had lost defensive lynchpin Ormsby injured in normal time, could not hang on and fell to two goals from Peter Shirtliff minutes from the end. It was a sickening end to a remarkable season in which United had literally come within minutes of Wembley and promotion.

Echoes of past glories had reawakened interest in United's affairs with Bremner earning an extended contract as he strove to lead the club he loved back to the promised land of the First Division.

Season of Anticlimax

Following their exploits in 1986-7, United were the bookies favourites to go up the following season.

Once again Bremner went into the transfer market to strengthen his squad, adding two players who could play at either full-back or in midfield, Glyn Snodin, brother of former skipper Ian, from Sheffield Wednesday for £135,000 and Aston Villa's Gary Williams for £230,000.

Surprisingly, Bremner sold two of his senior strikers, Ian Baird for £285,000, a fee set by an FA tribunal to Portsmouth, and Andy Ritchie, who had been on a weekly contract, joined the growing contingent of Leeds players at Oldham for the knockdown fee of £50,000.

With Ormsby ruled out for the season with cartilage trouble, Mark Aizlewood took over as captain, but he found himself leading a shot-shy outfit.

Without Baird and Ritchie, scorers of over 80 Leeds goals between them, Bremner relied on the height of John Pearson, Bob Taylor and Keith Edwards for goals.

But only three goals were scored in the opening nine games, two of them by Sheridan grabbing single-goal wins over Leicester and West Brom.

It was a depressing start and United's attacking

John Sheridan takes the ball past Bradford City's Dave Evans at Valley Parade early in the 1987-8 season. The game was goalless.

resources were further diminished when Edwards was sold to Aberdeen for £60,000.

Jim Melrose, whose last-minute winner for Charlton in the first leg of the play-offs helped ruin United's promotion bid, arrived for £50,000 but it was a disastrous move, the player making only three full League appearances before moving on to Shrewsbury for £45,000 later in the season.

Likewise, Liverpool reserve midfield man Ken De Mange arrived for £65,000 but also moved on later in the season, for the same fee, to Hull City.

With a third of the season gone, United looked more like relegation candidates than promotion hopefuls.

Bremner's short term answer to the goal drought was to switch Peter Swan, essentially a reserve centre-half, to the attack, and the ploy worked for several games.

But the season only really took off when proven goalscorer Bobby Davison arrived from Derby and a young baby-faced midfield player called David Batty came on the scene.

Both made their Leeds debuts in the 4-2 home win over Swindon.

Although £350,000 signing Davison netted, it was Leeds-born teenager Batty who proved a revelation.

United hit a hot streak throughout December, winning six games on the trot, culminating in a 2-0 local derby win against Bradford City in front of a remarkably high attendance of 36,004 at Elland Road on New Year's Day 1988.

Just when the sleeping giant of Leeds United seemed ready to

John Sheridan signals the first of a double strike for Leeds at Bootham Crescent in October 1987. United had been held 1-1 by York at Elland Road but won the second leg of this League Cup tie 4-0 before going out to Oldham in the next round after a replay.

reawake, United went into another deep sleep and lost contact with the leading pack.

Even the return of Ian Baird from Portsmouth for £180,000 could not kick-start United back into the promotion race and they finished a disappointing seventh.

It had been a season of anticlimax following the great campaign of 1986-7 and although some youngsters had been given a run out, too many of Bremner's signings had disappointed.

Bobby Davison was a proven goalscorer when he joined Leeds from Derby County for £350,000 in November 1987.

Time Runs Out for Bremner

Despite the feeling of anticlimax, United fans continued to back the club to the hilt and season ticket sales reached £500,000 for the 1988-9 season.

To strengthen his side for the next campaign, Bremner recruited a couple of players from Portsmouth. With Brendan Ormsby struggling for full fitness, Bremner picked up Pompey centre-half Noel Blake on a free transfer and winger Vince Hilaire for a fee.

United offered £70,000 for Hilaire, a former England 'B' and Under-21 international, whom Portsmouth rated at £270,000 and an FA tribunal ruled that Leeds should pay £190,000 for the player.

Blake and Hilaire's first away game in Leeds colours saw them return to Fratton Park, but it was far from a happy one. Not only did United crash 4-0 but another former Pompey old boy, Ian Baird, was sent off.

Only one of the first six League games was won and although they scraped a 2-1 Littlewoods Cup win at Peterborough, it was not enough to prevent the axe from falling on Bremner's reign.

"The board felt it was time for a change," said chairman Leslie Silver.

Out with Bremner went his assistant Dave Bentley and chief scout Dave Blakey, who had been with Bremner in his days at Doncaster, and coach Peter Gunby was put in temporary charge of team affairs.

Bremner was later to rejoin Doncaster for a spell and although he had not quite fulfilled the promise shown in 1986-7, he had restored some pride in the club.

Said Silver: "I don't think there are many people with as much feeling for this club as Billy.

"Leeds United has often been labelled a 'sleeping giant' in football circles and certainly our magnificent supporters have backed the club fully in the last few seasons.

"They deserve the best and so far we have been unable to reward them with First Division football.

"Under Billy's guidance we came within a whisker of promotion two seasons ago and also reached the semi-final stages of the FA Cup and we all had hopes of building on those near-misses.

"Unfortunately, we again missed out and we must now find the right man to arouse that 'sleeping giant and take the club back to its rightful place among the game's elite."

That man proved to be someone fairly close to home – Howard Wilkinson, manager of Yorkshire neighbours Sheffield Wednesday.

Howard's Way

HOWARD Wilkinson's arrival was a major surprise. Leeds were second to bottom of the Second Division while Wilkinson's Sheffield Wednesday were in the top half of the First Division.

It spoke volumes for the stature of Leeds and the persuasive nature of the board that United were able to snap up a manager of Wilkinson's calibre on a four-year contract.

He had already taken both Wednesday and Notts County into Division One and now aimed to make it a hat-trick with Leeds.

As a player, Wilkinson trod an ordinary path. After failing to make the grade as an amateur with Sheffield United, he crossed the city to join Wednesday in June 1962 and played on the wing for the England youth team.

A promising career seemed in prospect, but after only 22 Football League appearances in four years at Hillsborough he moved to Brighton in July 1966.

In six years with the Seagulls he made over 100 League appearances without hitting too many headlines.

In 1971, Wilkinson joined Boston United, a Northern Premier League club, as player-coach, then player-manager. After gaining a degree in physical education at Sheffield University, he taught for two years at his old school in Abbeydale, Sheffield, and became FA regional coach in that city. By this time Wilkinson's coaching ability was well known in the highest circles and was appointed manager of the England semi-professional side, and, in November 1982, the England Under-21 squad.

His long-awaited return to the League came in January 1980 when he was appointed coach to Notts County, eventually succeeding Jimmy Sirrell as manager and played a big part in steering the Magpies to the First Division in 1980-81.

Bigger clubs were now beginning to sit up and take notice of Wilkinson's skills and in June 1983 he returned to his old club, Wednesday, to succeed former Leeds favourite Jack Charlton as boss of the Owls.

He was an instant success at Hillsborough, lifting Wednesday back into the First Division in his first full season and kept the Owls up among the big clubs.

Wednesday would have qualified for Europe but for the blanket ban on English clubs following the European Cup Final Heysel Stadium disaster involving Liverpool and Juventus.

The Owls also had several promising Cup runs, but were unable to make the breakthrough into the big time because the club seemed unwilling to spend. Wilkinson felt he had taken Wednesday as far as he could when Leeds approached the Owls in October 1988 for permission to speak to their manager.

Talks with the United board left Wilkinson in no doubt that Leeds offered far more potential than Wednesday did at Hillsborough.

So Wilkinson, soon dubbed 'Sergeant Wilko' by the Leeds fans, became the eighth man in charge at Elland Road in 14 years. His attention to detail, organisational skills, tactical know-how and hunger to whip his men into tip-top physical shape soon became apparent.

Norman Hunter was axed from the coaching staff as Wilkinson brought in Mick Hennigan, a former teammate from his Brighton days, as coach from Hillsborough.

Wilkinson's first priority was to steer the club away from the relegation zone.

His first signings were £170,000 midfielder Andy Williams from Rotherham and Witton Albion pair Mike Whitlow and Neil Parsley, whom had been on trial at Hillsborough under Wilkinson, for just £30,000.

He also signed on another former Wednesdayite, Carl Shutt, for £50,000 from Bristol

Howard Wilkinson, who joined Leeds as manager in October 1988 and went on to take them to the pinnacle of English soccer.

City in an exchange deal which saw Bob Taylor go to Ashton Gate for £200,000.

Shutt became an instant hero by scoring a hat-trick on his Leeds debut, a 3-0 home win over Bournemouth.

Other departures saw Micky Adams join Southampton for £250,000, Peter Swan go to Hull City for £200,000 and Jack Ashurst to Doncaster Rovers for £10,000.

Wilkinson's arrival worked like a charm as United shot up the table and at one point seemed to be gathering themselves for a late charge for the play-offs before settling for a comfortable mid-table place.

Gordon's Tonic

Once United were safe, Wilkinson began his team-building in earnest in March 1989 with the arrival of Manchester United's former Scotland star, midfielder Gordon Strachan, and England Under-21 defender Chris Fairclough from Tottenham.

Fairclough arrived on loan until the end of the season before the £500,000 deal was concluded while United shelled out £300,000 for the 32-year-old Strachan. Many could not understand why Wilkinson had signed Strachan, whom appeared to be in the autumn of his playing years, but Wilkinson's judgement was spot-on.

Describing the flame-haired little Scot as 'a model professional', Wilkinson had struck one of the bargains of the century.

Just as Bobby Collins, another wee Scot, had proved an influential leader in Don Revie's era, then Strachan was about to repeat the role in Wilkinson s reign.

One of the first things Wilkinson did when he arrived at Elland Road was to remove pictures of the old glory days from the foyer of the main entrance to the club.

Leeds had long lived in the shadow of those great days which were starting to hang like a millstone round the club.

Wilkinson argued it was time that the current Leeds created some history of their own rather than dwell on the past.

Meanwhile, Revie, the architect of those halcyon days was a dying man.

Suffering from the incurable muscle-wasting motor-neurone disease, the Don passed away at his home in Edinburgh in May.

Players from his great side congregated for his funeral in Scotland, while fans covered the gates to Elland Road in scarves and floral tributes.

United chairman Leslie Silver said: "Many heroes have 'feet of clay' under close examination – Don Revie was not one of them. He gave so much to so many. We are all the better for having passed in his shadow."

While United mourned for the past, they began to build for the future.

Silver, managing director Bill Fotherby and the rest of the board sat down with Wilkinson to map out Leeds United's return to the top.

The board agreed with Wilkinson to take 'route one' back to the First Division by breaking the bank and signing star players rather than spend two or three seasons building a side.

Leeds United striker Ian Baird gets up well to power in a header against Hull City at Elland Road in October 1988. Baird scored the goal which gave Leeds their first League victory under Howard Wilkinson. The Hull player on the right is Richard Jobson, who was later to join Leeds.

Local-born David Batty made his League debut when he was only 18, although his first appearance was delayed by a broken ankle.

United reckoned the fans had waited long enough for a return to the top flight, so pinning their faith in Wilkinson's ability to find the right players, got out the cheque book with a vengeance.

Summer Spending Spree

It was a calculated risk which initially left United in the red to the tune of £2 million, but Wilkinson's gambles in the transfer market paid off in spectacular fashion.

The Republic of Ireland international midfielder John Sheridan went to Nottingham Forest for £650,000, where he spent four months in the reserves before being rescued in a £500,000 deal by Sheffield Wednesday.

Former skipper Mark Aizlewood, who had been stripped of the Leeds captaincy and banned for 14 days for making rude gestures to the crowd after being barracked, not surprisingly left for Bradford City in a £200,000 move; another £200,000 saw defender Neil Aspin go to Port Vale and the same fee was received from Bristol City for utility player David Rennie, whilst John Stiles went to Doncaster Rovers for £40,000.

Those deals reaped United around £1 million, but that cash – and considerably more – was used to help build a squad good enough to push for the Second Division title. Wilkinson embarked on a massive spending spree taking his outlay to near the £3 million mark and he recruited experienced players who could stand up to the rigours of the 46-match Second Division campaign.

Mel Sterland had won an England cap when playing under Howard Wilkinson at Hillsborough. Now he rejoined his old boss from Glasgow Rangers, for £600,000.

Carl Shutt immediately repaid a large slice of his £50,000 transfer fee from Bristol City with a hat-trick on his debut, against Bournemouth in April 1989. His value involved an exchange deal which involved Bob Taylor.

The biggest shock was the £600,000 spent on Vinnie Jones, Wimbledon's midfield hard man, whose disciplinary record had earned him the tag 'Psycho'.

A late developer in the game, the controversial Jones had been a driving force in Wimbledon's FA Cup triumph of 1988 and his transfer to Leeds was the big talking point of the summer.

Immensely popular with the fans, Jones' infectious team spirit and willingness to sweat blood for United's cause made up for his lack of some of the game's more finer skills.

In attack, John Hendrie, a winger long coveted by Leeds from his days at Bradford City, arrived from Newcastle United for £500,000.

Wilkinson's other recruits all had international experience. Mel Sterland, who had won his England cap in his days at Sheffield Wednesday under Wilkinson, joined the Elland Road bandwagon from Glasgow Rangers in a £600,000 deal. Another former Rangers man, Northern Ireland centre-half John McClelland, arrived from Watford for £150,000, much-travelled Welsh midfield dynamo Mickey Thomas came for a nominal fee from Shrewsbury and Republic of Ireland full-back Jim Beglin, whose career was cut short by injury, was a free-transfer signing from Liverpool.

Leeds fans responded to all the comings and goings with a big stampede for season tickets – £820,000 of them being sold before the start of the season.

Elland Road was buzzing as United were installed as red-hot favourites to storm to the 1989-90 Second Division championship – but big-spending Leeds were brought crashing down to earth when the big kick-off began.

Injuries forced Wilkinson to leave out Jones and Fairclough for the opening game at Newcastle but despite holding a 2-1 lead through strikers Bobby Davison and Ian Baird inside 30 minutes, Leeds crashed 5-2 with a dire defensive performance as Mick Quinn netted four times for the Geordies.

Four days later Leeds had to rely on a last-minute freak own-goal by Gary Parkinson to beat Middlesbrough 2-1.

United with their batch of new players were taking time to knit together and had to wait until their sixth match for their next League victory – a 1-0 win at Hull.

That seemed to be a vital breakthrough as United began to pile up the victories, and the points.

Goals by Shutt and Fairclough brought a 2-0 win at Middlesbrough in early December to take United to the top of the table.

The following month Ian Baird went to Ayresome Park, to join 'Boro in a £500,000 move, following the arrival at Elland Road of new striker Lee Chapman.

The big powerful Chapman, a £400,000 signing from Nottingham Forest, was another of the ex-Wednesdayites at Elland Road who had played for Wilkinson during his managerial reign at Hillsborough.

Hot on Chapman's trail came another former Wednesday man, experienced striker Imre Varadi for £50,000; Stoke City midfield player Chris Kamara, who opted to join Leeds instead of Middlesbrough, in a £150,000 move. Noel Blake made the reverse trip to Stoke, where Vince Hilaire was already on loan, for £165,000 the following month.

The arrival of Chapman and Kamara proved to be the final pieces of United's promotion jigsaw.

A brave leader of the front line, Chapman's goals proved crucial as Leeds gathered themselves for the final charge to the line with Sheffield United and Newcastle with only two of the three guaranteed to go up automatically.

Kamara was able to cover a variety of positions; a vital factor as Wilkinson was forced to juggle with his line-ups because of a variety of niggling injuries.

Back in the big time

Despite signs of title nerves, Leeds got their act together as they faced championship rivals Sheffield United in front of a season's best 32,727 at Elland Road on Easter Monday.

Leeds, in irresistible mood, swept the Blades aside with a 4-0 victory through Strachan (two goals, one from the spot), Chapman and Gary Speed, an exciting new talent who had emerged

Lee Chapman, who joined Leeds from Nottingham Forest for £400,000 and helped the Elland Road club out of the old Second Division and then to the top of the First.

from the Reserves to keep John Hendrie out of the team.

Speed opened the scoring in the next game at Brighton, but it needed a late own-goal from Ian Chapman to ensure that United would share the spoils in a 2-2 draw.

United, who had been steamrollering sides at Elland Road all season suddenly lost their unbeaten home record when lowly Barnsley sneaked a 2-1 victory, leaving United to win both their final games to guarantee promotion.

Another 30,000 plus crowd at Elland Road saw United get back on to the winning path in their penultimate game of the season against Leicester City – but they left it late.

Mel Sterland clubbed United ahead after 13 minutes with a low angled drive, but United were continually thwarted by City goalkeeper Martin Hodge as they chased the killer second goal.

Instead, Leicester broke out and scored with a spectacular long-range drive from midfield man Gary McAllister, who was to join United in the summer.

Nerve-ends were fraying when Strachan thumped in a tremendous shot for his 18th goal of the season to send Elland Road into raptures.

But promotion celebrations were put on hold as Newcastle's victory over West Ham meant that Leeds, Newcastle and Sheffield United had all to play for on the final day of the season.

Victory at Bournemouth would make Leeds champions, but Sheffield United, at Leicester; and Newcastle, at relegation-threatened Middlesbrough, were waiting to pounce.

Gordon Strachan, the Scottish international signed from Manchester United just before the March 1989 transfer deadline. He was the inspirational skipper of the Second Division title, his form earning him an international recall.

Lee Chapman in action during the vital Easter Monday game against Sheffield United at Elland Road in April 1990.

Bournemouth, also fighting to avoid the drop, would not be a cakewalk but buckled in the intense heat under continuous United pressure.

Bournemouth skipper Kevin Bond had already

clipped a Jim Beglin cross against his own post when Wilkinson's latest signings combined to get the goal which sent United back into Division One after an absence of eight years.

Chris Kamara made space down the right to curl in the perfect centre which Lee Chapman powered into the net with his forehead.

Leeds had little difficulty protecting their lead and even though Sheffield United won at Leicester, Wilkinson's men were crowned Second Division champions because of a superior goal-difference.

Newcastle missed out on promotion as they crashed at Middlesbrough, where Ian Baird scored twice to ensure survival for 'Boro and guarantee himself a Second Division championship medal from his old club.

The only blot on a memorable day were the ugly clashes between police and Leeds fans who had turned up without tickets. The tiny Dean Court ground could only hold just under 10,000 and United had been granted 2,200 tickets, although an estimated 5,500 United followers had made the journey to the South Coast for the game which was played over a Bank Holiday.

Police, who made over 120 arrests over the weekend, complained that warnings to the Football League not to play the game over the

Captain Marvel:
Leeds skipper
Gordon Strachan
holds aloft the
Second Division
trophy.

Howard Wilkinson and his happy band of players after Leeds lifted the Second Division title in May 1990.

Bank Holiday weekend were ignored – an error admitted League president Bill Fox.

The troubles took the gloss off United's achievement but there was no denying their right to return to the top division after leading the table since Christmas.

Wilkinson had assembled a side with tremendous character with each and every man playing a key role.

Skipper Gordon Strachan took most plaudits for a series of outstanding individual displays, which, at the age of 33 had forced him back into the international reckoning with Scotland.

In midfield his skills had been protected by the hard-tackling Jones and the rapidly developing David Batty, while goalkeeper Mervyn Day, right-back Mel Sterland and central defender Chris Fairclough had been pillars of consistency in defence.

The fans had also played their part, filling Elland Road week after week to generate an electric atmosphere which many opposition managers reckoned was worth a goal start to United.

Wilkinson's promotion goal had been achieved, but as soon as the final whistle had sounded at Bournemouth he was already making plans for the new season… in Division One.

Title Tightrope

EVEN though Howard Wilkinson was at the World Cup in Italy with the England party in an advisory capacity during the summer, his plans to prepare United for the First Division continued.

United's managing director Bill Fotherby carried out transfer deals on Wilkinson's behalf while Wilkinson was involved in Italia '90.

Fotherby was a busy man as Wilkinson's shopping list cost around £2.5 million, taking his total outlay to over £6 million since taking over from Billy Bremner in October 1988.

First to arrive was 'old boy' John Lukic from Arsenal, who became United's first-ever £1 million player.

Despite the consistency of 35-year-old Mervyn Day, Wilkinson believed he needed to strengthen the goalkeeping department and had no hesitation in bringing Lukic back to Elland Road where his League career had been launched.

Lukic had left United for Highbury in summer 1983 for £100,000 and had collected League and League Cup honours during his spell with the Gunners. Another £1 million was spent on Scotland international midfielder Gary McAllister of Leicester City before lanky defender Chris Whyte arrived from West Brom for a £450,000 fee set by a transfer tribunal. Whyte had begun his career at Arsenal but after a spell playing in America had caught Wilkinson's eye with some stirring displays for West Brom.

Inevitably there was a crop of departures – Mickey Thomas, his days at Elland Road disrupted by injury and illness, headed for Stoke where he was later joined by Vince Hilaire. Former club skipper Brendan Ormsby, his career almost ended by injury, went to Doncaster Rovers on a free transfer.

The biggest summer departure in terms of cash was John Hendrie, who linked up with Ian Baird at Middlesbrough in a £550,000 transfer.

But that move was overshadowed by the

John Lukic returned to Leeds and picked up more honours.

departure of fans' favourite Vinnie Jones just a few weeks into the season.

The arrival of the talented McAllister meant Jones was the odd man out in midfield and, having played in only one of United's opening five games, rejoined his old Wimbledon manager, Dave Bassett, at Sheffield United in a shock £650,000 move. By a strange quirk of fate Jones made his Blades debut against Leeds at Bramall Lane, Leeds finishing 2-0 winners to confirm their fine start to the First Division campaign.

It had begun at Everton where United roared into a 3-0 lead on the opening day of the 1990-91 season with goals by Chris Fairclough, new Welsh international Gary Speed and veteran striker Imre Varadi. Goals by Pat Nevin and John Ebbrell set up a thrilling finish but with John Lukic showing £1 million form United held on for maximum points.

Gary McAllister joined Leeds for £1 million after making over 200 appearances for Leicester City.

The atmosphere was electric as First Division soccer returned to Elland Road three nights later when old sparring partners Manchester United were fortunate to escape with a point from a goalless draw.

Leeds, whose style had sometimes been blasted by London-based critics during their Second Division championship-winning campaign, were winning over new fans with their brand of attacking soccer. Their form throughout November and December was magnificent and on New Year's Day travelled to Anfield confident of shooting down mighty Liverpool.

But United were outplayed by the mighty Reds 3-0 and any hopes of a shock Championship bid gradually disappeared over the second half of the season as United ran into a fixture pile-up.

The congestion had been caused by United's three-pronged attack on the Cup front.

In the FA Cup they were paired with Arsenal in the fourth round after eliminating Barnsley in a replay.

The battle with the Gunners went to four epic matches before Arsenal edged United 2-1 in the third replay at Elland Road after seven hours of high quality football.

Although Arsenal failed in their bid for FA Cup success, losing to Tottenham in Wembley's first-ever semi-final, they went on to become worthy champions.

Whilst tussling with Arsenal, United were also embroiled in the Rumbelows League Cup, thrashing Queen's Park Rangers 3-0 away and destroying Aston Villa 4-1 at Elland Road on the way to a two-leg semi-final showdown with Manchester United.

Despite a Chris Whyte goal at Old Trafford, Leeds lost 2-1 to goals by Lee Sharpe and Brian McClair to set up the prospect of a tremendous second leg at Elland Road.

Leeds gave it their all but were unable to crack a resolute Manchester defence and were hit on the break in the final minute by Sharpe to wreck their Wembley hopes.

That bitter blow had come only three days after missing another possible Wembley outing when Wilkinson's overworked side were beaten 3-1 at Everton in extra-time in the Northern Area Final of the much-criticised Zenith Data Systems Cup, going out 6-4 on aggregate.

Weary Leeds were in danger of seeing their season collapse, but they pulled themselves together and recovered to provide some marvellous entertainment in the closing weeks of the season to finish in fourth place.

Chapman's Milestone

Striker Lee Chapman finished with 31 goals in all competitions better than anyone else in the top division. He even achieved the rare feat of scoring a hat-trick against Liverpool and finishing on the losing side! It came on 13 April, in front of Elland Road's biggest League crowd of the season, 31,460.

By half-time, many of those fans wanted to go home as Liverpool had built up a 4-0 lead. But United dug in with a remarkable late rally sparked by Chapman's hat-trick – and a harshly disallowed goal – to end an astonishing game 5-4 losers.

Back in the big time: Leeds United striker Imre Varadi powers in a volley during United's 3-0 win over Norwich City at Elland Road in September 1990.

Back on the international scene was Gordon Strachan, who not only earned a Scotland recall but was also named as skipper by national team boss Andy Roxburgh and played alongside team-mate Gary McAllister in midfield.

The inspirational Strachan, who was still out-running young players at the age of 34, reckoned his banana-based fibre diet had helped prolong his career.

Strachan was at the hub of many of United's attacking moves and followed in the footsteps of Bobby Collins, Jack Charlton and Billy Bremner by being named as the Footballer of the Year.

Although they had nothing to show for it in terms of silverware United's return to the First Division had been a roaring success.

They played entertaining football and tremendous strides had been made off the field to clean up the club's image which had been so badly damaged through the 1980s, the decade of decay.

Gordon Strachan followed in the footsteps of Bobby Collins, Jack Charlton and Billy Bremner when he was voted Footballer of the Year in May 1991.

David Batty keeps close to Paul Gascoigne at Elland Road in September 1990. Spurs beat United 2-0.

Carl Shutt celebrates scoring Leeds' second goal against Everton in December 1990.

Chapman crowned a superb season in a last-day thriller at Nottingham's City Ground, where United went down 4-3 to Brian Clough's team.

Chapman, playing against his former club, scored twice to reach a career tally of 200 League and Cup goals – and was rewarded in the summer with an England 'B' appearance against Iceland.

England 'B' honours were also gained by Mel Sterland and John Lukic, but young David Batty went one step better.

Batty, 22, was now a fully-fledged England international following a series of stirring displays which earned him United's Player of the Year Award.

Former Leeds schoolboy star Batty, worked his way through the England Under-21 and 'B' sides to win his first full cap when coming on against the USSR as substitute and went on the England tour of the Far East.

Another youngster to discover international form was Gary Speed, whose sparkling displays on the left-hand side of midfield earned him a regular place in the Welsh side managed by Leeds old boy Terry Yorath.

Lee Chapman, watched by Gary Speed and several Arsenal defenders, sends a header over the bar in the first replay of the marathon fourth-round FA Cup tie in 1991.

Rod Wallace (centre) signed from Southampton for a club record £1.6 million. Tony Dorigo (left) came from Chelsea for £1.3 million. Steve Hodge (right) joined Leeds from Nottingham Forest for £900,000.

Those dark days seemed light years away as United dusted off the cheque book once again.

Leeds lost £2.5 million in their first season back in Division One to add to the £3 million lost in the Second Division championship-winning campaign. The loss was down to the big incoming transfers but other figures reflected the big boom at Elland Road.

The club's total income for the year ending July 1991 totalled £7.3 million, double the previous year. Match receipts were £1.8 million, season ticket sales brought in £2.7 million whilst TV and other broadcasting payments were £821,639.

The Leeds board anticipated the loss and were not frightened to hand more cash for Wilkinson to spend.

Big Spender Wilkinson

Wilkinson was a great advocate of pre-season preparation and in summer 1991 added more

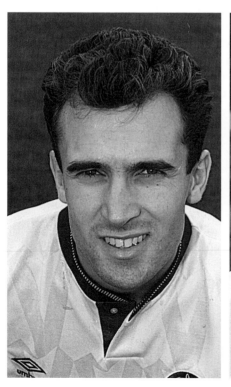

quality to his squad in the shape of Tony Dorigo, Rod Wallace and Steve Hodge.

The cost was astronomical but with 20,000 season tickets sold, bringing in £3.5 million, the United board felt it well worth the money as they strived to bring the title to Elland Road.

The club's transfer record was shattered with the signing of £1.6 million England Under-21 striker Rod Wallace from Southampton with his twin brother, Ray, a full-back valued at £100,000.

Their elder brother, Danny, had already won full England honours with Southampton before joining Manchester United.

Rod was signed to add pace to the Leeds attack, while Ray was expected to be used as a squad player.

Australian-born Dorigo was snapped up from Chelsea for £1.3 million and had already been capped by England. He first attracted international attention with Aston Villa, winning Under-21 caps, but it was not until he moved to Stamford Bridge that he broke through into the full England side.

Midfielder Hodge was also an experienced England international, winning 24 caps in a career which saw him play for Aston Villa, Tottenham and Nottingham Forest, where he had two spells, before joining United from the latter in a £900,000 transfer.

Wilkinson also returned to his old stamping ground at Hillsborough to sign two young Sheffield Wednesday reserve defenders, Jon Newsome and David Wetherall in a surprise £275,000 package.

As two Wednesdayites arrived at Elland Road, another moved on in the shape of lanky striker John Pearson, who was sold to Barnsley for £135,000 after 127 appearances for Leeds – 60 as substitute – having previously been on loan with Rotherham.

There were also big developments at the Elland Road ground with work nearing completion on a £1 million seating extension in the south-east stand corner of Lowfield and the South Stand while construction started on a banqueting suite and reception area in the West Stand car park.

Plans were on the drawing board to demolish the old Lowfields Road Stand at the end of the 1991-2 season and replace it with a 17,000 all-seater stand – the largest cantilever span in Europe.

But the excitement of the summer activity was tempered by the news that Republic of Ireland international defender Jim Beglin was forced to quit at the age of 28 because of a long-term knee injury. Wilkinson had built an expensive and formidable squad which looked capable of keeping up with the front runners. But his plans were thrown into disarray when the opening game at Crystal Palace was postponed because building work at Selhurst Park had not been completed in time.

Elland Road, home of Leeds United. Plans were under way to build the largest cantilever span stand in Europe.

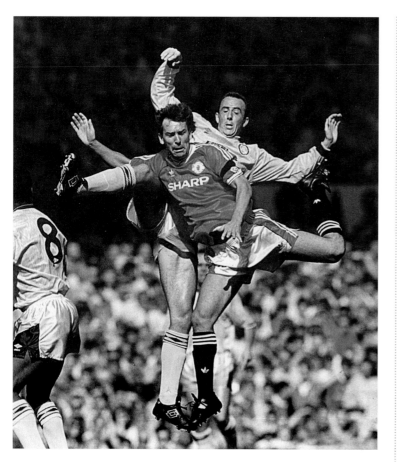

High-flying Bryan Robson of Manchester United and Gary McAllister of Leeds United in action during the 1-1 draw at Old Trafford in August 1991.

After ten League games only Leeds and Manchester United remained unbeaten but Leeds' run ended, rather ironically, in their rearranged game against Crystal Palace when they were beaten 1-0 in injury time.

At that stage of the season Manchester United had already been installed as hot title favourites by the bookies, topping the table with 26 points from ten games – six points ahead of Leeds, who had already played a game more.

Leeds responded with a 4-3 win over Sheffield United and a 4-2 success at Notts County to emphasis their scoring ability and another four-goal haul – a 4-1 live televised triumph at Aston Villa in November had the critics singing the praises of Wilkinson's aces.

That marvellous display at Villa Park took Leeds to the top of the First Division for the first time since they last won the title in 1973-4.

United were ticking over so well that Wilkinson felt able to sell utility player Chris Kamara to Luton for £150,000 in November. Later in the season Glynn Snodin joined Hearts, midfielder Andy Williams went to Notts County for £200,000, Mike Whitlow and reserve player Simon Grayson moved to Leicester for a combined fee of around £250,000, whilst Mervyn Day and Imre Varadi linked up with Luton on loan.

As Christmas approached Leeds United and Manchester United were clear at the top and continually pulling away from the rest of the pack.

While the rest of the First Division enjoyed the big kick-off, United were left kicking their heels, but soon made up for lost time with an impressive start to the season which included a 1-0 home win over Liverpool with a Steve Hodge goal, their first over the Anfield club since 1973-4.

Just to add spice to this heady brew both draws

David Batty scores against Manchester City at Elland Road in September 1991. Leeds won 3-0.

for the FA Cup third round and the quarter-finals of the Rumbelows Cup paired the deadly rivals from either side of the Pennines together at Elland Road.

Titanic Clash – in Triplicate

To add to the coincidence the two United's were scheduled to meet in a League game at Elland Road immediately before the two cup clashes to provide an astonishing triple header which

gripped the soccer public's imagination.

The race for the title was shaping into a fascinating battle.

Boxing Day saw Alex Ferguson's men from Old Trafford enjoy a thumping 6-2 win at Oldham, whilst Leeds handed out two late goals to bottom-of-the-table South-ampton, who left Elland Road with a surprise 3-3 draw.

In-form leaders Manchester came to Elland Road three days later in search of the win that would put clear daylight between themselves and Wilkinson's warriors.

The corresponding League game at Old Trafford earlier in the season had finished 1-1, Lee Chapman's early header being cancelled out three minutes from time by a close-range strike by Bryan Robson.

This time it was Leeds who left it late, Mel Sterland scoring from the penalty spot to ensure the big game finished 1-1, Neil Webb having opened the scoring for the visitors.

Gary Speed and David Batty celebrate a goal by Speed against Tottenham Hotspur at Elland Road in December 1991.

Lee Chapman scores one of his hat-trick goals in the 6-1 hammering of Sheffield Wednesday at Hillsborough in January 1992, when Leeds moved back to the top of the old First Division.

Leeds recovered their poise by opening the New Year in fine style with a 3-1 win at West Ham, whilst Manchester inexplicably collapsed 4-1 at home to Queen's Park Rangers in a televised game.

Psychologically, Leeds seemed to have the edge as the two teams prepared for their Rumbelows Cup quarter-final clash the following week.

Leeds, who had eased past Scunthorpe and Tranmere in the early rounds, had put on another away-day spectacular to thump Everton 4-1 in the fourth round to set up a mouth-watering tie against the Red Devils.

Elland Road erupted when Gary Speed fired Leeds ahead in the first half, but gradually Manchester assumed control and finished 3-1 winners.

This time it was Leeds' turn to bounce back after such a big body-blow and they did it in tremendous style in front of the cameras at Hillsborough.

It was Wilkinson's first game back at Hillsborough since joining Leeds and he went into a crucial League game against a bubbling Owls side without injured skipper Gordon Strachan.

Wednesday were also missing star striker David Hirst, but even his presence would not have stopped Leeds as they stormed to a 6-1 victory to roar back to the top of the table.

Lee Chapman led the way with a hat-trick, Tony Dorigo put away a spectacular long-range free kick

and towards the end substitute Mike Whitlow headed in the fifth before Rod Wallace ran through for the sixth to give Leeds their biggest way win in the League since thumping Blackpool 7-3 in 1930.

The Hillsborough triumph, the biggest-ever win recorded on live television (football televised live was not the all-consuming matter it is today), really got Leeds fired up for their third-meeting with Manchester United three days later.

Leeds, boosted by their tremendous performance at Sheffield began like a house on fire but were caught on the break just before half-time when teenage winger Ryan Giggs escaped down the left and knocked in the cross for his Welsh colleague Mark Hughes to score with a simple far post header.

Despite several near misses Leeds could not find an equaliser and crashed out of the FA Cup. To rub salt into their wounds top scorer Lee Chapman was taken off with a broken wrist just before the end.

The pendulum of power had seemingly swung across to Old Trafford, but the games were starting to pile up for Alex Ferguson's men, while Leeds were left with just the League title to aim at.

At first the men from Old Trafford did not seem as though they were going to buckle, but as the finishing line approached Leeds had two vital ingredients – points in the bag and on loan French star Eric Cantona.

On-loan Eric Cantona, who joined Leeds after Sheffield Wednesday dithered over signing him, in action on his debut, against Oldham Athletic at Boundary Park in February 1992.

Lee Chapman is on target again. The big striker scored another hat-trick, against Wimbledon in March 1992, after recovering from a broken wrist.

Ooh-Aah Cantona!

Cantona arrived at Elland Road almost by accident. He came to England with a reputation of being the bad boy of French football, having quit Nimes and had a trial with Sheffield Wednesday.

While the Owls dallied over what to do with Cantona, Wilkinson took a risk by signing the French international striker on loan without having seen him play.

It was a calculated risk and one which paid dividends as the skilful Frenchman added fresh impetus to United's title bid.

He scored on his home debut – as a substitute in a 2-0 win over Luton – a match in which Chapman marked his come-back with the other goal after missing four games.

Chapman grabbed a hat-trick in the 5-1 thumping of Wimbledon, Cantona and Rod Wallace getting the other two – but United's joy was short-lived as Manchester United had won at Sheffield United.

With eight games remaining, Leeds topped the table by two points, but Manchester United had three games in hand and remained hot favourites to take the crown.

The odds on the Red Devils were slashed still

Chapman, Wallace and McAllister in celebratory mood during the 5-1 win over Wimbledon in March 1992.

further when Leeds managed only draws with Arsenal and West Ham before crashing 4-0 at Manchester City.

Leeds clawed their way back to the summit on 11 April with a 3-0 win over Chelsea, substitute Cantona scoring a magnificent solo goal at the end to wrap up the points.

The popular Frenchman was an instant hero on the terraces where the fans thundered out their booming 'Ooh, Aah Cantona' chant with gusto.

Manchester, who beat Nottingham Forest 1-0 at Wembley that weekend to lift the Rumbelows Cup, were still expected to sweep to the title as they had games in hand.

But whilst Leeds kept plugging away, the Old Trafford team frittered away one of their games in

Gary McAllister celebrates his success from the penalty spot late in the game against Coventry City in April 1992.

hand. They now led by two points with one game in hand.

Leeds had three games left – Coventry (home), Sheffield United (away) and Norwich (home) – whilst Manchester had Nottingham Forest (home), West Ham (away), Liverpool (away) and Spurs (home). On 20 April, Leeds did not kick-off against Coventry until tea-time, and fans at Elland Road had their ears glued to the live radio commentary from Old Trafford where Forest pulled off a 2-1 win to avenge their Rumbelows Cup Final defeat and put the cat amongst the championship pigeons.

Leeds held their nerve to beat the Sky Blues 2-0 with a Chris Fairclough header and a late Gary McAllister penalty to leapfrog their Mancunian rivals.

Alex Ferguson's team, facing four crucial League games in eight days, wasted their game in hand with a sensational defeat at bottom-of-the-table West Ham, leaving Leeds in the driving seat.

Champions on Sunday

Both sides had two matches remaining – if Leeds won both they would be champions, but should they slip then Manchester United or even Sheffield

Jon Newsome (centre), Chris Fairclough (left) and Gary Speed (11) celebrate after Newsome had put Leeds ahead 2-1 at Bramall Lane, in the Championship-decider.

Leeds celebrate
Rod Wallace's freak
equaliser against
Sheffield United at
Bramall Lane.
Players (left to right)
are Strachan,
Speed, Wallace and
McAllister.

Leeds United pictured with the Football League championship trophy before the final home game of the season against Norwich City in April 1992.

Wednesday, who had come with a late run, could snatch domestic soccer's biggest prize.

The Sheffield United-Leeds and Liverpool-Manchester United games had been switched to Sunday, the Bramall Lane clash kicking-off at noon and the battle at Anfield starting three hours later.

With Wednesday only able to draw at Crystal Palace the previous day, then the title would go either to Elland Road or Old Trafford.

In a season of twists and turns, few could have envisaged the drama of Sunday, 26 April as the final page of the Championship chapter was written.

Leeds were put under enormous pressure in the early stages by the Blades, who shot ahead through Alan Cork.

Nervous Leeds grabbed a freak equaliser on the stroke of half-time when a defensive clearance cannoned off Gary Speed then Rod Wallace into the net.

Sheffield goalkeeper Mel Rees was injured in the melee and Leeds cashed in after the interval when the hobbling goalkeeper failed to

reach a Gary McAllister cross leaving full-back Jon Newsome, in for the injured Mel Sterland, to head home. Tragically, Rees never played again. Diagnosed with cancer in the summer, he died in May 1993, aged 26.

Leeds' joy lasted only a few minutes as the game threw up another bizarre goal, John Pemberton's cross-shot being jabbed into his own net by Lee Chapman. But with 13 minutes left another weird goal moved the title closer to Elland Road.

Leeds skipper Gordon Strachan and Gary McAllister with the championship trophy.

Brian Gayle, struggling to clear in the high wind, scooped the ball up and back into his own area. As Eric Cantona and Rod Wallace came in for

the kill, Gayle could only nod the ball gently over his stricken goal-keeper Rees.

The 3-2 win meant that Manchester needed to win at Anfield to keep their flickering hopes alive.

Ian Rush's early goal put Liverpool in command and three minutes from time Mark Walters killed off the Old Trafford title dream to complete a 2-0 win which made Leeds champions for the first time in 18 years.

The title race may have become known as the one which Manchester lost rather than Leeds won – but Leeds had shown tremendous nerve and character at the end.

Wilkinson's team may have had their luck at Bramall Lane, but over the season showed they had the one ingredient that is inherent in all champions – consistency.

"Never in my wildest dreams did I think the League Championship would be possible so soon," said Wilkinson, who had not even bothered to watch Manchester's demise live on television at Anfield.

Immediately before the final carnival game against Norwich at Elland Road – a 1-0 win for Leeds before 32,673 spectators – skipper Gordon Strachan received the Championship trophy. Howard Wilkinson, meanwhile, the Manager of the Year, was already plotting for the new campaign.

He had already achieved one life's ambition, winning the League Championship, and now was preparing to have a crack at the other – winning the European Cup.

The draw gave Leeds a hard tie with German champions Vfb Stuttgart, but Wilkinson strengthened the squad further by paying a club record £2 million for Arsenal and England midfielder David Rocastle, whilst Scott Sellars returned from Blackburn for £800,000.

League champions Leeds finish the 1991-2 season with a flourish as Rod Wallace beats Norwich City goalkeeper Mark Walton to give United a 1-0 win.

Eric Cantona joined Leeds almost by accident but played a huge part in their League Championship triumph. He was just as surprisingly transferred to Manchester United.

Wilko and Out

UNITED'S return to the European Cup after a 17-year absence proved to be eventful, but ultimately disappointing.

Having failed to start in any of United's opening eight games of the 1992-3 season, big money signing David Rocastle did begin United's first-round game at Vfb Stuttgart.

Everything was going according to plan up to the hour mark but Howard Wilkinson's side seemed to lose concentration and the Germans took full advantage with striker Fritz Walter scoring twice in four minutes. When Andreas Buck added the third eight minutes from time it seemed as though United's progress in the competition was as good as over.

But United produced a memorable second leg comeback in one of Elland Road's great European nights.

Needing an early goal United got it with Gary Speed's left-foot volley as Wilkinson's attacking line-up flooded forward in waves. They threw caution to the wind but were caught out when Buck equalised on the night after a rare German raid.

Within four minutes Gary McAllister made it 2-1 with a penalty and Eric Cantona cranked up the pressure with a 66th-minute goal.

Lee Chapman headed in with 10 minutes left as Leeds turned up the heat, knowing another goal would put them through.

Creaking Stuttgart sent on Swiss international Adrian Knup and Jovo Simakic in the dying minutes to hold on to their fragile lead and somehow the visitors survived United's late barrage.

The tie finished 4-4 with Buck's away goal proving decisive leaving brave United to take the plaudits for a magnificent display.

But it transpired that in their panic to get on their substitutes, Stuttgart coach Christophe Daum had finished up with more than the permitted four foreign players on the field.

UEFA immediately launched an inquiry and ruled that Leeds should be awarded the second leg 3-0 and that the teams should play-off at Barcelona's Nou Camp Stadium.

Only 7,400 were in the vast Catalan bowl to see United triumph 2-1 thanks to substitute Carl Shutt's 76th-minute winner, just seconds after coming on.

That set up what was termed the 'Battle of Britain' against Glasgow Rangers, hailed as one of the best-ever sides to come out of Scotland. At Ibrox, Gary McAllister silenced the passionate 'Gers crowd with a stunning first-minute volley.

Leeds United's Brian Deane challenges West Ham's goalkeeper Ludek Miklosko at Elland Road in August 1993. United won 1-0.

But the volume was back on full blast when John Lukic lost the flight of the ball from a corner and punched it into his own net. Worse was to follow before half-time when Ally McCoist grabbed Rangers' second. United were still in the tie but Mark Hateley, later to join Leeds briefly on loan, lashed in a great third minute drive from 25 yards at Elland Road to virtually settle the tie.

McCoist added another in the second half after a fine break down the left and Cantona's 85th-minute goal was a mere consolation as Rangers cruised through 4-2.

Shock transfer

Within days, Cantona, the catalyst of United's title success the previous season, was surprisingly transferred to arch rivals Manchester United for a bargain £1million.

It was a major shock to Leeds fans who had seen the mercurial Frenchman open the new campaign in blistering style. He scored a marvellous hat-trick at a sun-kissed Wembley as The Whites beat Liverpool 4-3 to lift the Charity Shield. A few weeks later he smashed in a another treble at Elland Road – United's first in the new Premiership – as Tottenham Hotspur were thrashed 5-0.

But there were persistent rumours that Cantona had an uneasy relationship with Wilkinson and some of his teammates and when Alex Ferguson asked about Cantona's availability the French star was on his way to Old Trafford.

While Cantona went on to inspire the Red Devils to title and cup-winning success, Wilkinson's Leeds put up a feeble defence of their Championship crown.

Although Leeds lost only one League game at Elland Road they failed to gain a single win on opposition soil as they slipped to a lowly 17th place and found little solace in either the FA Cup or League Cup, tumbling to early exits.

But it was not all doom and gloom. United's youngsters won the FA Youth Cup for the first time in the club's history.

To top it all they beat a Manchester United team including the likes of David Beckham, Paul Scholes, Gary Neville, Nicky Butt, Robbie Savage and Keith Gillespie over two legs in the Final. They won 2-0 at Old Trafford with goals from Noel Whelan and Jamie Forrester.

Gary Speed and Carlton Palmer make life difficult for Arsenal's Ian Wright at Elland Road in August 1994.

The diminutive Forrester added a spectacular overhead kick and skipper Matthew Smithard completed the 2-1 victory in front of 31,037 at Elland Road.

England Under-18 internationals Forrester, Whelan, Robert Bowman, Mark Tinkler and Kevin Sharp all tasted senior football during the course of the season.

They also played a handful of games each in an improved 1993-4 season but it was another youngster, Gary Kelly, who was to make the biggest impact.

Initially a striker, he was given his debut by Wilkinson at right back on the opening day of the season when new recruit David O'Leary, the legendary Arsenal defender, also made his first Leeds appearance.

United's last-gasp equaliser in a 1-1 draw at Manchester City was scored by Brian Deane, whom Wilkinson had secured from Sheffield United for a club record £2.7 million in the summer.

Deane had taken over up front from Lee Chapman, who had scored 80 goals in his three years with Leeds before his cut-price move to Portsmouth.

O'Leary was unable to make much impact on the pitch during the campaign because of injury, but his influence was to be felt in a big way a few years later.

Lightning fast Kelly was a major success and went on to play in the 1994 World Cup for the Republic of Ireland.

With the solid Tony Dorigo on the opposite flank, United possessed just about the best full-back pairing in the Premiership.

Deane's goal return was disappointing but speedy striker Rod Wallace hit a hot streak, finishing with 17 Premiership goals. The previous season he had earned a call-up for the England squad's trip to Spain only to be ruled out through injury and the chance never arose again to play for his country.

While Wallace's England career failed to get off the ground, United's popular England midfielder David Batty was another shock departure from Elland Road.

When Kenny Dalglish offered a record £2.75 million to take him to Blackburn, Leeds allowed him to go despite the protests of fans.

David Rocastle's unhappy stay at Elland Road ended when he was involved in a £1 million transfer swap with Manchester City's David White.

Rocastle had been unable to recapture the fine form he displayed at Arsenal which earned him 14 England caps. Sadly, he was to die of cancer, at the age of 33 on 31 March 2001.

Despite a shock FA Cup home exit against Oxford, Wilkinson's team got themselves back to something like decent form and finished fifth just outside a place in Europe.

Ground improvements

Attendances also picked up to become the third largest in the Premiership, largely thanks to the opening of the £5.5 million 17,000 all-seater stand on the Lowfields Road side of the ground.

The new stand was officially opened in January 1994 by the Lord Chief Justice, Lord Taylor of Gosforth, the man who had produced the in-depth report on the Hillsborough disaster.

Ground improvements continued with the building of the North Stand on the site of the old Kop and was to become the Revie Stand. The work did not go unnoticed and the FA named Elland Road as one of the venues for the 1996 European Championships.

Wilkinson also cast his eyes on the international scene, recruiting four internationals in summer 1994.

England midfielder Carlton Palmer was signed from Sheffield Wednesday for £2.6 million and Northern Ireland defender Nigel Worthington followed the same path from Hillsborough, signing for Wilkinson for the third time in his career.

Both men's qualities were well known to the Leeds boss, but he did take a gamble by snapping up two South Africans, defender Lucas Radebe and striker Phil Masinga for £250,000 each. Both played their parts as squad players in another useful season but it was another African, Tony Yeboah, who propelled United back into Europe.

As United entered 1995 they were a solid, if unspectacular, outfit but short on goals. Brian Deane was a willing and able performer, but not a penalty box predator. Phil Masinga, despite a remarkable extra-time hat-trick which knocked Walsall out of the fourth round of the FA Cup, was still feeling his way in the Premiership, while Wallace's goal output had fallen away.

Wilkinson's answer was to pay German club Eintracht Frankfurt a record £3.4 million for Ghana hot-shot Tony Yeboah, who had been in dispute with the Bundesliga club.

Yeboah patiently built up his fitness for a month in the reserves before Wilkinson gently introduced him to the Premiership.

His first goal came after coming on as substitute in the 3-1 FA Cup fifth round defeat at Manchester United. And he was soon in his Premiership stride, snaffling a dozen goals from just 16 starts, including a clinical finisher's hat-trick in a 4-0 win over Ipswich.

Yeboah inspired United's late charge to the finishing tape while last minute winners by Carlton Palmer in successive matches at Elland Road against Aston Villa and Norwich put United within touching distance of Europe.

A 3-1 home win over Crystal Palace and a 1-1 draw at Tottenham, courtesy of a fine Deane solo goal, saw United finish fifth again which was enough to capture a place in the UEFA Cup.

The title went to Blackburn, with ex-Leeds star David Batty playing a key role, while the season also saw United wave goodbye to one of their most influential players of recent times, Gordon Strachan. Probably Wilkinson's greatest signing at Leeds, he had helped them to both the Second and First Division titles when in the autumn of his career.

Eventually, time, and a niggling back injury, caught up with him and in January 1995, at the age of 38, he retired from first-team football after six years with Leeds and joined Ron Atkinson as assistant manager at Coventry.

There he made a brief playing comeback before taking over from Atkinson and is now in charge at Southampton.

Stylish central defender Chris Fairclough, who played with Strachan in those successful seasons, also moved on in the summer, joining Bolton Wanderers.

Star of Africa

Yeboah lit up the start of the 1995-6 campaign in spectacular fashion.

His two goals on the opening day of the season brought a 2-1 win at West Ham followed by a 1-0 home win against Liverpool thanks to the Ghanaian's stunning volley.

The star of Africa then gave United a remarkable reintroduction to European football with all three goals in their 3-0 win in Monaco.

Eleven days later Yeboah hit another treble as United triumphed 4-2 at Wimbledon and Wilkinson's team were being talked of as potential title winners. But the campaign was to turn sour despite United reaching their first Wembley Final for the first time in 23 years.

Yeboah's goals dried up and United gradually slid down the League table after being humbled 8-3 on aggregate by Dutch side PSV Eindhoven to go crashing out of the UEFA Cup at the second round.

Wilkinson brought in Swedish international striker Tomas Brolin for a club record £4.5 million from Italian side Parma to join Yeboah in attack, but the partnership never really hit it off.

Brolin continually struggled to find full fitness while Yeboah and reserve striker Phil Masinga were away on international duty in the African Nations Cup.

As a short term measure Wilkinson turned to old favourite, 36-year-old Lee Chapman, but he was sent off on his first game back – a 2-0 win over West Ham – and was substituted as United crashed 5-0 at Liverpool after Gary Kelly was ordered off.

United, who had moved on David White to Sheffield United, were way off the pace in the League but were making some headway in the cups.

Derby, Bolton and Port Vale were eliminated as United reached the FA Cup quarter-finals before losing 3-0 at Anfield after a 0-0 draw at Elland Road.

But by then they had already booked a place at Wembley in the Coca-Cola League Cup. After

Gary McAllister curls the ball past Birmingham City's defenders in the 1995-6 Coca-Cola League Cup semi-final second-leg game at Elland Road.

Tony Yeboah celebrates his goal against Birmingham in the 1995-6 Coca-Cola League Cup semi-final at Elland Road.

overcoming Notts County, Derby, Blackburn and Reading, inconsistent United were paired with Second Division Birmingham City.

After falling behind to Kevin Francis' 27th-minute goal, Wilkinson's men fought back with a second-half equaliser from Yeboah and grabbed the winner when former Leeds hero Chris Whyte scored a 73rd-minute own-goal.

Such was United's poor League form that no Leeds supporters were booking their London hotels until after the second leg against the Blues at Elland Road.

Birmingham frustrated Leeds for long periods but once Masinga put Leeds ahead they rammed home their advantage with further goals from Yeboah and Deane to seal a 5-1 aggregate victory and a League Cup Final place against Aston Villa.

Disaster at Wembley

The sides were expected to be evenly matched but United took their poor League form on to the big stage and were outclassed by a fluent Villa who cruised to a 3-0 win.

Frustrated Leeds fans vented their fury by booing Howard Wilkinson as he made his way to the tunnel at the famous old stadium at the end of a bitterly disappointing day.

Wilkinson later admitted he had considered resigning but opted to tough it out.

"I am no quitter. I have never run away from a problem in my life and I don't intend running away from this one," he said defiantly.

Yeboah was not to play for United again that season because of injury, while Brolin became more disillusioned as he was only named as substitute for the showpiece Final.

One of the few bright spots in the Wembley debacle had been the display of 18-year-old winger Andy Gray, son of Frank and nephew of Eddie.

He was one of several youngsters blooded by Wilkinson during the course of the season along with Harry Kewell, Mark Ford, Ian Harte and Alan Maybury as United's more experienced players failed to deliver the goods.

Rumour was rife of dressing room discontent and was fuelled by Carlton Palmer's criticism of teammates after the League Cup Final nightmare.

Six successive defeats equalled United's worst League run since 1946-7 and after finishing a disappointing 13th in the League it was clear that Wilkinson would have to go back to the drawing board in the summer.

There were also changes at the top level with 71-year-old Leslie Silver, who had been on the board since April 1981, stepping down as chairman and managing director Bill Fotherby, who had an increasing influence in bringing several United business deals to a head, taking over. Robin Launders became the new chief executive and members of the Caspian Group plc were added to the boardroom.

There was no summer break for the Elland Road administration staff as the ground hosted three European Championship games featuring Spain against Romania, Bulgaria and the eventual winners, France.

The new-look Elland Road had earned its spurs the previous year when a sell-out crowd witnessed a thrilling 3-3 draw between England and Sweden in the first home international played outside Wembley for 30 years.

It had been a dress rehearsal for Euro 96 and generally regarded as FA acknowledgement for the vast improvements that had taken place at the ground with the opening of the vast East Stand.

England, under Terry Venables, reached the semi-finals of Euro 96 beating Scotland 2-0 on the way in a match which saw Gary McAllister miss a Wembley penalty shortly before Paul Gascoigne netted England's second goal.

Within weeks McAllister left Leeds to join old teammate Gordon Strachan, who was now manager at Coventry City and had earlier taken Leeds youngster Noel Whelan to Highfield Road.

McAllister was one of three members of the Championship-winning team of four years earlier to leave Elland Road during Wilkinson's team-rebuilding.

Goalkeeper John Lukic, now approaching the veteran stage, returned to Arsenal as cover for former Leeds youth team member David Seaman, on a free transfer, while Gary Speed lined up with his boyhood heroes Everton in a £3.5 million move. Between them they had amassed 1,000 appearances in United's colours but the exodus did not end there as Phil Masinga went to Swiss club St Gallen for £500,000, Nigel Worthington went to Stoke on a free while the futures of Tony Yeboah and Tomas Brolin were uncertain.

Neither big-money signings Yeboah or Brolin were in the starting line-up when United drew 3-3 in a thrilling opening to the 1996-7 season at Derby. Wilkinson had four new faces at the Baseball Ground. In goal was ex-Crystal Palace man Nigel Martyn, for whom United had paid a British record £2.25 million for a goalkeeper.

Lee Sharpe, Manchester United's former England winger, had arrived for £4.5 million, while stoking the fires in the engine room was Lee Bowyer, who became Britain's most expensive teenager when the Leeds board wrote out a cheque for £2.6 million for the Charlton youngster.

With Yeboah nursing a knee injury and Brolin still in limbo, Wilkinson turned to the scoring instincts of Liverpool legend Ian Rush. The 34-year-old was no longer required by the Anfield club for whom he had netted a staggering 346 League and Cup goals but Wilkinson believed Rush would provide the goals to get United back up the League.

Wilkinson pays the price

After the collapse of United's form the previous season, Wilkinson was anxious that his new men knit together from the word go.

After the promising display at Derby, they were beaten 2-0 at home by Sheffield Wednesday, but bounced back with wins at home to Wimbledon and at Blackburn.

However, Eric Cantona, the man he had sold to Manchester United at a give-away price returned in triumph for Alex Ferguson's reigning champions in September 1996. Despite missing a penalty Cantona did score as Wilkinson's team were humbled 4-0 in front of their own fans.

It confirmed that the gap between Leeds and the cream of the Premiership was vast and Wilkinson paid the price with his job.

Chairman Fotherby said: "It was a very sad day for me personally but we felt we needed a new impetus. It was my decision and one of the hardest I've ever had to make."

The move brought mixed feelings for many Leeds fans as many felt Wilkinson, the man who had reshaped the club out of the doldrums into the 1991-2 Division One champions, deserved better and more time if his new-look side, who were blighted by injuries, were to progress.

Others felt Wilkinson had lost the backing of many fans at Wembley the previous March and not really regained their confidence since.

Wilkinson certainly made his mark at Elland Road and the club was much stronger when he left than when he arrived. He had delivered the First and Second Division titles, a League Cup final appearance, European football, Charity Shield success and the club's first Youth Cup triumph in an eight-year period.

His skills were recognised by the Football Association and he was appointed to the new role of technical director, later running the England Under-21 team. He also led out the full England side for the 0-0 draw with Finland in a World Cup qualifier at Wembley after the resignation of Kevin Keegan in October 2000, and remains a highly respected figure in the game.

Gunner Graham Takes Charge

FORMER Arsenal boss George Graham was the man charged with restoring success to Elland Road.

The former Scottish international midfielder, dubbed 'Stroller' in his playing days was a hard task master who had brought the Gunners tremendous success. Under his guidance the Highbury club won both the Championship and League Cup twice, the FA Cup and European Cup Winners Cup to become the most successful manager in modern times at the club.

But his managerial career was clouded by the infamous 'bung' affair which led to a 12-month ban from the game and his departure from Highbury's famous marble halls.

Several clubs had made overtures to Graham to get back into the game but it was only when the Leeds job became available that he stepped back into management.

He inherited a lengthy injury list at Elland Road and went about his work with the relish of a mechanic stripping down a second-hand car.

His reign got off to a remarkable start with a goal after just 51 seconds by Andy Couzens at Coventry but the Sky Blues tore up the script as goals by John Salako and former Leeds man Noel Whelan gave Gordon Strachan's side a 2-1 win.

Graham's back-to-basics tactics didn't make exciting viewing. He was determined to tighten United's defence and soon brought in utility player Gunnar Halle, who was poised to be Wilkinson's last signing before Wilko was axed, from Oldham and £1 million Dutch defender Robert Molenaar.

With goalkeeper Nigel Martyn in outstanding form and South African skipper Lucas Radebe developing into an excellent man-marker, United were becoming a hard side to beat under Graham.

Reserve centre-half Mark Jackson was given a run in midfield as a blocker while Ian Rush, who endured a 16-game run, the longest of his career, without a goal, also found himself on the right-hand side of midfield.

United kept 23 clean sheets in all competitions but managed a meagre 28 Premiership goals. A frustrated Yeboah, suffering from lack of full fitness and service from midfield didn't enjoy Graham's defensive tactics and ended his love affair with the United fans when he tore off his shirt and threw it at the dug out when substituted by Graham in the 1-0 defeat at Spurs in April.

Derek Lilley, a £500,000 striker from Morton, and Bastia's £275,000 French winger Pierre Laurent were recruited but neither made a significant impact as Leeds ground their way to 11th place without anyone netting double figures.

Future prospects

United were dull and efficient at senior level but youth coach Paul Hart's exciting crop of teenagers played some fluent attractive football.

Players like Harry Kewell, Jonathan Woodgate and goalkeeper Paul Robinson all played their part in winning the FA Youth Cup for the second time in four years, beating Crystal Palace 3-1 on aggregate in the Final with goals by Wes Boyle and Matthew Jones earning a 2-1 win at Elland Road and Lee Matthews netting the only goal at Selhurst Park. Former United centre-back Hart left for Nottingham Forest in the summer while Graham started to bring in his own players to replace several of Wilkinson's buys.

Out went Tony Dorigo to Italian club Torino, Ian Rush (Newcastle United), Carlton Palmer (£1 million, Southampton), Brian Deane (£1.5 million, Sheffield United), while Yeboah and Tomas Brolin, who had been loaned out for a season to Grasshoppers, were frozen out and joined Hamburg and Parma respectively.

After having their fingers burnt by short-term big-name signings, wheeler-dealer Graham seemed the perfect man to reconstruct a younger United squad.

With David O'Leary elevated to assistant manager, United entered 1997-8 with a good deal of optimism.

Midfielder David Hopkin, who had scored Crystal Palace's late Wembley play-off winner at the end of the previous season was, at £3.5 million, the most expensive summer recruit.

The classy Dorigo's left-back slot went to Rangers' Scottish international David Robertson while the versatile Alf-Inge Haaland came in from Nottingham Forest for £1.6 million, the fee being set by an independent tribunal.

A pair of players from Portuguese clubs completed Graham's summer spree – midfield man Bruno Ribeiro from Vitoria Setubal and the exotically-named Jerel Floyd Hasselbaink, a £2m striker from Boavista.

"He can be the new king of Elland Road," said Graham of Hasselbaink, who became universally known as Jimmy.

A native of Surinam, he harboured ambitions to play for Holland, where he was brought up and felt Leeds would be a good showcase of his talents.

He had netted 27 goals in Portugal in 1996-7 but Leeds fans questioned whether such a relatively unknown player would be able to repeat such statistics in the Premiership.

George Graham took over at Elland Road and his reign got off to a remarkable start.

Jimmy's goals

They soon got their answer. He smacked in a debut goal in the 1-1 home draw with Arsenal and quickly captured the hearts of the United faithful with his fierce shooting.

After a shaky start to the season, which included successive Premiership home defeats against Crystal Palace, Liverpool and Leicester, United got into their stride and moved swiftly up the table.

The dour tactics of the previous season were replaced by flair football with 22-goal Hasselbaink at the sharp end.

There were several top drawer performances – the 5-0 triumph at Derby among them – but the match of the season was in November when, trailing 3-0 at home to Derby after 33 minutes, United roared back to win 4-3 with Lee Bowyer's last-minute winner to move into fifth place.

That was where Graham's new-look side was to finish at the end of the campaign to recapture a place in the UEFA Cup.

In addition to Hasselbaink, the emergence of exciting Australian winger Harry Kewell, the defensive qualities of Radebe and increasing influence of Bowyer in midfield suggested brighter times ahead for Leeds, particularly as a young group of reserve players won the Pontins League for the first time in 61 years.

Lee Bowyer celebrates his last-minute winner in the sensational fightback against Derby County in November 1997.

Harry Kewell, the exciting young Australian who came to prominence under George Graham's managership.

The disappointments were the injury troubles sustained by Robertson, but that opened the door for Ian Harte, Gary Kelly's nephew, that gave United a most unusual family full-back combination.

The cups provided little solace as Reading pulled off a shock fourth-round win in the Coca-Cola League Cup at Elland Road and Wolves also won on Leeds soil to deny United a place in the FA Cup semi-finals.

In the same month of that Wolves defeat, United had their greatest escape.

They were due to fly home after a 3-0 defeat at West Ham when an engine exploded and caught fire on take off at Stansted Airport, forcing pilot Captain John Hackett to make a crash landing. His actions and those of David O'Leary, who coolly helped evacuate the aircraft, undoubtedly averted a major disaster as the travelling party escaped with only minor injuries. United didn't exactly get off to a flying start in 1998-9 as newspapers were reporting that Tottenham wanted Graham to replace Christian Gross as manager.

In summer, Graham had brought in another Dutchman, Clyde Wijnhard, to partner Hasselbaink in attack at Leeds while Rod Wallace moved north of the border to join Glasgow Rangers. However, it was widely known that Graham wished to return to London for personal reasons and, when Spurs came sniffing round, the lure of the capital proved too much. On 1 October, after several weeks of speculation, Graham was installed as manager at White Hart Lane on a four-year contract reputedly worth £6 million.

Leeds chairman Peter Ridsdale, who had replaced Bill Fotherby at the top, fought to keep Graham, who had signed a three-and-a-half-year contract with the club the previous December.

Graham had spent £14 million during his time at Elland Road and it was undoubtedly a huge blow for Leeds at a crucial time in their season. Ironically, Graham's last Premiership game in charge of Leeds was a 3-3 draw at Spurs.

Initially, Leeds turned to Leicester City's Irish boss Martin O'Neill as their first choice. However, the Foxes' board fended off United's overtures and O'Neill eventually opted to stay in the East Midlands, although he later moved North of the border with Celtic where he enjoyed great success.

O'Leary's Super Start

UNITED, who had just started their UEFA Cup campaign, eventually picked a man from within their own ranks – David O'Leary was to be their new manager.

Many thought coach O'Leary would follow George Graham to Spurs, but after it was clear that first-choice Martin O'Neill was staying at Leicester, O'Leary became the obvious choice.

United had been under the impression that O'Neill had a clause in his Leicester contract which allowed him to speak to other clubs should another managerial offer be forthcoming.

While United were pursuing O'Neill, O'Leary and coach Eddie Gray were put in charge of team affairs at Elland Road.

Ironically, their first game was against Leicester at Elland Road – O'Neill's team inflicting a first Premiership defeat of the season on United with a 1-0 win.

Despite the result, the groundswell of popular opinion among United fans was for O'Leary to be given the job.

It would be a gamble to ask O'Leary as, despite his vast experience as a player at domestic and

Leeds United staff line up for the start of the 1999-2000 season.

Michael Bridges celebrates his goal against Middlesbrough early in the 1999-2000 season. 'Boro goalkeeper Mark Schwarzer is helpless.

Harry Kewell (10) has just scored against Roma in March 2000.

international level, he had no managerial experience.

With former Leeds boss Gray ruling himself out of a return to management, O'Leary emerged a better bet the longer O'Neill took to make up his mind about a move to Leeds.

O'Leary quickly showed that he was his own man and immediately rang the changes in his first Premiership away game – a 1-1 draw at Nottingham Forest which saw United play more than half the match with ten men following the dismissal of defender Danny Granville, a pre-season signing from Chelsea.

Granville was one of three players handed his full Leeds debut by O'Leary at the City Ground. Jonathan Woodgate and midfielder Stephen McPhail were the other new faces and both went on the make a big impact, particularly Woodgate,

who made his England debut at the age of 19 against Bulgaria at the end of the season.

Three days after earning his first point at Nottingham, O'Leary flew out to Italy with his team to face Roma in the UEFA Cup second round. But he was unable to take charge of his team as he had incurred a one-match ban during United's penalty shoot-out victory against Portuguese side Maritimo on the island of Madeira for comments made to the referee about the home side's theatrical 'diving'.

United were given little chance against Roma but, with Gray directing operations from the touchline, they put on a mature performance and were unlucky to come away with a 1-0 defeat.

Again they had a man sent off, Bruno Ribeiro, but matched the Italian giants for skill and steel in the Olympic Stadium. The performance impressed

Leeds chairman Peter Ridsdale and his directors and following a 0-0 home draw with Chelsea on 25 October, 41-year-old O'Leary was installed as manager on a two-and-a-half year contract with Gray as his assistant.

Despite a brave effort, United bowed out of the UEFA Cup after being held 0-0 by Roma at Elland Road, while they were also unluckily beaten 2-1 by O'Neill's Leicester in the Worthington Cup fourth round.

Smith's stunning start

O'Leary was not afraid to give youngsters a shot at the big time and one of them – Alan Smith – grabbed his chance in spectacular style.

He came off the bench at Anfield with United trailing 1-0 and scored with his first touch after 79 minutes to trigger an amazing 3-1 win as Jimmy Floyd Hasselbaink netted two late goals.

United's young guns were playing an exciting brand of football and O'Leary's stock rose still further when Leeds-born David Batty, 30, rejoined the club from Newcastle for £4.4million.

But the popular midfielder endured a nightmare second debut for Leeds, getting booked after five minutes in the 2-0 win over Coventry and sustaining a rib injury which restricted him to just a handful of appearances for the remainder of the season.

Despite Batty's absence, United were flying and collected seven successive Premiership victories in a blistering spell from from mid-February to April.

They comfortably finished fourth to qualify for the UEFA Cup again and were tipped in some quarters to make a serious Championship challenge in 1999-2000. Hasselbaink finished the campaign with 18 Premiership goals, Lee Bowyer hit nine from midfield, while young Smith fired in seven from just 14 Premiership starts.

Nigel Martyn was rock-solid in goal, Ian Harte had established himself as the first-choice left-back with a penchant for scoring spectacular free-kicks, while Lucas Radebe was outstanding at the heart of a defence which lost Robert Molenaar and £1 million Austrian international Martin Hiden for most of the campaign.

But the man most observers were raving about was 21-year-old Harry Kewell, a left-sided attacking player blessed with tremendous skill and pace, who finished third behind Arsenal's Nicolas Anelka and Liverpool striker Michael Owen in the PFA Young Player of the Year Award.

O'Leary's revolution continued apace in the summer with David Wetherall, Gunnar Halle and Lee Sharpe all joining neighbours Bradford City while Clyde Wijnhard also moved within Yorkshire to Huddersfield for £750,000.

One man United would like to have kept, but who wanted to go, was leading goalscorer Jimmy Floyd Hasselbaink, who threatened to strike if he didn't get a move after having a transfer request rejected.

United opted to take the £12 million offered by Spanish club Atletico Madrid for the Dutch international whose profile had increased substantially in his two years at Elland Road.

The key to United's 1999-2000 season would be finding someone to fill Hasselbaink's goalscoring boots. The answer came in the shape of England Under-21 international Michael Bridges, a £5.6 million buy from Sunderland, who opted for Elland Road ahead of Spurs.

At the other end of the pitch Charlton full-back Danny Mills (£4.3 million) and Chelsea centre-back Michael Duberry (£4.5 million) were recruited while Norwegian Under-21 midfielder Eirik Bakke was picked up for just £1.75 million from Sogndal.

The season was barely a few weeks old when Coventry accepted a £4 million bid for striker Darren Huckerby, who had done well on his visits to Elland Road in the past including a hat-trick for the Sky Blues. The player turnover continued with Bruno Ribeiro joining Sheffield United for £500,000 and reserve striker Derek Lilley being off-loaded to Oxford.

Billy's statue

But amid all the building for the future, United were able to take time out on the opening day of the season to honour a legend by unveiling the Billy Bremner statue on the corner of Elland Road and Stadium Way.

The dynamic Scottish hero, who died in December 1997, aged 54, was the driving force on the pitch during the Don Revie era and his nine-foot high bronze statue has become a focal point for many United fans.

After the unveiling, Bremner's ashes were scattered at the Kop end of the ground attended by Billy's widow, Vicky, and other family members.

The game that day, a 0-0 draw with Derby, was followed by a 3-0 win at Southampton thanks to a stunning hat-trick by Bridges.

United were up and running and the absence of Hasselbaink was not missed as record signing Bridges finished a thrilling season with 19 Premiership goals.

Goals were flying in from all angles and United pieced together a run of ten successive wins in all competitions with a 2-1 victory at Watford on October 3 sending United to the top of the table.

Their free-flowing attacking football won them international acclaim and they entered the new

Leeds players emerge into the cauldron against Galatasaray, shielded by riot police in March 2000.

Millennium jostling with old rivals Manchester United for the Premiership leadership.

O'Leary, anxious to maintain the momentum, persuaded chairman Peter Ridsdale to get the cheque book out again to add 28-year-old Black-burn winger Jason Wilcox to his improving squad for £3 million.

Within a few weeks Wilcox was back in the England squad while Kewell and Bridges were paired in attack for a spell with Kewell, rapidly approaching superstar status netting in six consecutive matches – one short of the club record jointly held by Peter Lorimer and John McCole.

Turkish nightmare

But United's League form was just starting to waver in the spring when the club was rocked to its foundations when two fans, Christopher Loftus and Kevin Speight were stabbed to death just before United's UEFA Cup semi-final against Galatasaray in Turkey, United had stormed through the early stages of the competition with their attacking football earning respect throughout the continent.

The first round draw paired them with Partizan Belgrade, but the first leg was switched from war-torn Yugoslavia to Holland, United winning 3-1 and completing the job with a Huckerby goal at Elland Road for a 4-1 aggregate win.

The Moscows of Lokomotiv and Spartak were next to fall to Leeds with the latter proving a particularly stiff test.

Lokomotiv were thumped 7-1 on aggregate but the first leg of the Spartak match was postponed because sub-zero temperatures in the Russian capital meant the pitch was unplayable. Much to Spartak's annoyance the game was switched to

Sofia in Bulgaria where a Kewell goal gave United hope in a 2-1 defeat.

The return was a tense battle with United squeezing through on the away goals ruling thanks to a late winner by skipper Lucas Radebe.

That set up a fourth-round meeting with Roma, the big-spending Italians, who had knocked United out the previous season. This time a Nigel Martyn-inspired Leeds held on for a 0-0 draw in the Olympic Stadium and Kewell's stunning goal at Elland Road put them through to a quarter-final with Slavia Prague. The Czech side were outclassed as Leeds won 3-0 at home while Kewell's goal from Stephen McPhail's pass ensured there would be no major recovery in the second leg. However, United lost in Prague 2-1 and that saw the start of a dip in form which was accelerated by the tragic events in Turkey.

Galatasaray's fans had a fearsome reputation and United expected an intimidating atmosphere at the Ali Sami Yen Stadium, darkly dubbed as 'Hell', But nothing could prepare the club or its fans for the horror that was about to unfold.

Before the game in Istanbul the two Leeds fans lost their lives after being stabbed in the city centre. United had to make a quick decision but chairman Ridsdale, left in a no-win situation, opted to go ahead with the game.

"I believe it was the only decision that could be taken," he said.

Relations between the two clubs became further strained when no minute's silence was held and the Galatasaray players didn't wear black armbands as a mark of respect to the dead supporters.

As United players bonded together in a circle just before the kick-off, the Leeds fans on the

Floral tributes were laid outside Elland Road to remember the two Leeds supporters killed in Turkey.

terraces turned their backs on the field in memory of their two dead friends.

The Turkish fans pumped up the volume and a shell-shocked Leeds were 2-0 down by half-time to goals from Hakan Suker and the Brazilian defender Capone. Subdued United recovered some of their composure with Bridges, Kewell and McPhail all going close but the result simply didn't seem important.

At home there was a tidal wave of emotion as the new Billy Bremner statue and the Elland Road gates turned into a floral shrine to honour Kevin Speight and Christopher Loftus.

With the second leg still to be played, it was clearly a volatile situation and Leeds were given the right to prevent Galatasaray fans from attending the return leg.

The Turks were not happy with that and felt that if United could not guarantee their safety then the game should be switched to a neutral venue.

United responded by saying that they would consider withdrawing from the competition if the game was switched to a ground other than Elland Road. The war of words ended when the Turkish champions were allowed to take a limited number of visiting dignitaries to Leeds with Galatasaray announcing that 11 members of an anti-terrorist squad would be accompanying them.

On a highly-charged and emotional night, Leeds fell behind to an early penalty by Romanian star Gheorgi Hagi and despite a couple of goals by the ever-improving Eirik Bakke, had to settle for a 2-2 draw. To complete a sour night PFA Young Player of the Year Kewell was sent off – quickly followed by the Turks' Emre Belozoglu, who missed their penalty shoot-out victory over Arsenal in the goalless Final in Copenhagen.

At least United had avoided a seventh successive defeat and managed to pick up the shattered pieces of their season to remain unbeaten in their final five Premiership matches.

Because UEFA Cup games were played on Thursdays, United often found themselves playing catch-up in the Premiership by playing games on Sundays.

However, every side kicked off on the final day of the Premiership together with United needing to match Liverpool's last-day result to finish third behind champions Manchester United and Arsenal and claim a Champions League spot in Europe the following season.

Leeds wrapped up their campaign with a 0-0 draw at West Ham, Liverpool lost 1-0 at Bradford where United old boy David Wetherall scored the winner. It was the final twist in an astonishing season.

European Dreams

NO ONE at Elland Road was quite prepared for the sensational impact United were to make in the Champions League. First of all they had to play in the qualifying round knowing that defeat would see them drop into the UEFA Cup.

But they got through, winning both legs against TSV 1860 Munich, and shocked all the pundits by going all the way to the semi-finals of the world's hardest club competition.

But before a ball was kicked in anger, O'Leary once again honed his squad in the summer.

David Hopkin linked up with the Leeds contingent at Bradford City for £2.5 million and was joined at Valley Parade five months later by Robert Molenaar for £500,000.

The popular Alf-Inge Haaland was appointed skipper on his arrival at Manchester City for £2.8 million and Martin Hiden returned to Austria for £500,000 with SV Salzburg. But the imports were far more expensive as United paid out around £18 million in total for Celtic striker Mark Viduka (£6 million), French midfielder Olivier Dacourt (£7.2 million) from Lens and £4.2 million for Liverpool's versatile Dominic Matteo. Victory over TSV 1860 Munich guaranteed United £10 million in the group stages of the Champions League but when they were drawn with Barcelona, AC Milan and Turkish side Besiktas, few gave United any hope of progressing further.

That theory gained credence when United crashed 4-0 in the opener at Barcelona. But United bounced back to beat AC Milan with a late Lee Bowyer goal, thrashed Besiktas 6-0, drew 0-0 in the return leg in Turkey, where injury was to rule Michael Bridges out of action for the best part of two years, to set up a mouth-watering clash with Barcelona.

Bowyer's early goal looked like it would be enough to give United the victory they needed to go through to to the next stage but World Footballer of the Year Rivaldo scored an injury-time equaliser to keep his team in the competition.

The Brazilian superstar had been thwarted time and time again by England Under-21 goalkeeper Paul Robinson, who was standing in for the injured Nigel Martyn, but the youngster was beaten by Rivaldo's well-placed shot in the fifth minute of injury time.

It left United needing a draw in Italy to qualify as runners-up up to hosts AC Milan and made it with a 1-1 draw.

But the draw didn't make things any easier as United found themselves up against Real Madrid, Lazio and Anderlecht in the second phase.

Rio grand

With the exciting Champions League run generating plenty of cash, O'Leary moved into the transfer market to snap up West Ham's England international Rio Ferdinand for £18 million, a world record for a defender. A month later

Mark Viduka in celebratory mood against Besiktas in September 2000.

Robbie Keane, the Republic of Ireland striker who was with Inter Milan, joined on loan for the rest of the season after the clubs agreed a £12 million deal to take place in the summer.

Those two big deals led to the sale of Darren Huckerby, who had been sparingly used in his time at Leeds, to Manchester City for £3.5 million, and young midfielder Matthew Jones to Leicester for £3.2 million. Jones, who had come up through the ranks to make the full Welsh side, had done well the previous season but was finding it increasingly difficult to break into the first team.

Leeds had already played two matches in phase two by the time Ferdinand and Keane arrived at Elland Road. They lost their first match – just as they had in the first phase – losing 2-0 at home to Madrid. But a stunning goal by Alan Smith, brilliantly set up by Mark Viduka, gave United a highly unexpected 1-0 win in Rome against Lazio to split the group wide open.

O'Leary knew the back-to-back games with Anderlecht, would hold the key to their progress. United, who welcomed back David Batty to European action after a lengthy lay-off, fell behind midway through the second half but levelled with an Ian Harte free-kick and snatched victory in the 87th minute through Lee Bowyer.

It had been a remarkable effort by Bowyer, who alongside teammate Jonathan Woodgate, was in the midst of a high-profile court case at Hull Crown Court. That hearing collapsed in March as the jury were considering their verdicts and a re-trial ordered by the judge.

Woodgate, Bowyer, reserve team striker Tony Hackworth and two friends of Woodgate, had denied attacking a student after a night out in Leeds, while Michael Duberry had pleaded not guilty to perverting the course of justice.

Young Hackworth was soon cleared of any involvement and moved on to Notts County, but Bowyer, despite being unable to get to United's Thorp Arch training centre, continued to play for Leeds.

Woodgate and Duberry, both labouring with injuries, didn't turn out for the second half of the season with Woodgate struggling to come to terms with the impact of being in the media spotlight as the lengthy court case unfolded.

But Bowyer, despite it, was near unstoppable and won the club's Player of the Year Award. However, even he could not leave Hull in time to make it to Brussels to face Anderlecht. In the event, United didn't need him as they produced a sparkling display to rout the Belgians 4-1 to qualify for the quarter-finals with two more group games to play.

Spanish Armada

Real Madrid luckily edged United 3-2 in the Bernabeu Stadium with the aid of a 'handball goal' and a crazy bounce off the pitch past Nigel Martyn and Lazio held a scratch Leeds side 3-3 at Elland Road but United were already looking forward to their quarter-final showdown with Spanish side Deportivo la Coruna.

United hit the heights again with a magnificent 3-0 home win in the first leg with goals by Ian Harte, Alan Smith and new skipper Ferdinand to virtually book their semi-final place. They endured a real battering in Spain but hung on to go through despite a 2-0 defeat.

Lying in wait were another Spanish side, Valencia, who had been beaten in the previous season's Final by Real Madrid.

Although United made most of the running and went closest to scoring, Valencia were happy with a 0-0 draw at Elland Road.

United were still in the hunt, but were dealt a major blow when Bowyer was ruled out on

Alan Smith gets the ball past the Lazio goalkeeper Peruzzi and into the net in November 2000.

Lee Bowyer scores against Anderlecht in February 2001.

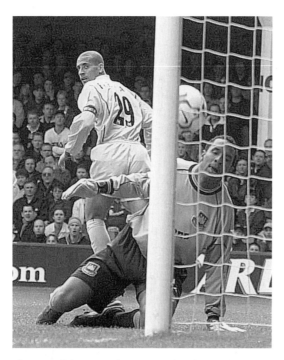

Looking back... Rio Ferdinand's goal against his old club, West Ham United, in April 2001.

the eve of the game by UEFA who slapped a three-match ban on him for allegedly stamping on Juan Sanchez in the first leg – even though the referee saw nothing wrong with the challenge.

Ironically, Sanchez scored the opener in Valencia, knocking the ball past Nigel Martyn with his arm. United would regain control of the tie if they could find an away goal but just after half-time Sanchez struck again and Gaizka Mendieta quickly added the third. To compound United's misery Alan Smith was sent off for a two-footed tackle in the dying seconds.

It was an unhappy end to United's incredible Euro-odyessy but their fans had enjoyed some memorable nights both at Elland Road, and in some of Europe's finest stadia, against the cream of the continent. United tied up their domestic season with eight wins from their last nine matches to finish fourth.

It was not quite enough to gain re-admission to the Champions League as those slots had gone to champions Manchester United, runners-up Arsenal and Liverpool, who had pipped Leeds by one point for the coveted spot as O'Leary's team paid the price of poor form in December and January.

Viduka's finest hour

However, the Premiership highlight had come against Gerard Houllier's men in November as United fought back from 2-0 down to win 4-3 with Mark Viduka, back from duty with the Australian Olympic team scoring all four goals – the first United player to do so since Allan Clarke sank Burnley 30 years earlier.

Clarke and Co had been part of a tremendous era in United's proud history – now O'Leary's

young marauders were carving out their own chapter in the Leeds United story.

Expectations were high within Elland Road as several pundits tipped them to be the major challengers to break Manchester United's stranglehold on the Premiership crown in 2001-2.

O'Leary's young squad had gained in experience and, given a clean bill of health, appeared genuine contenders.

Injuries had restricted the likes of Harry Kewell, David Batty and Lucas Radebe from making much of an impact in 2000-01, Michael Bridges hadn't appeared at all and the ongoing court case had restricted Jonathan Woodgate to just 14 Premiership starts.

O'Leary added no new names to his squad in the summer apart from completing the signing of Robbie Keane from Inter-Milan.

United's season began well as they headed the pack by October with England's Nigel Martyn and Rio Ferdinand in excellent form at the back. Their first away game saw a rare victory at Arsenal but United finished with nine men as both Lee Bowyer and Danny Mills were sent off.

Unfortunately ill-discipline was to cost United dear as they frittered away points and were once again resigned to not having Bridges or Radebe at their disposal, the South African defender being injured while attempting a comeback in a reserve game against Sunderland.

Plans disrupted

Mark Viduka's goal output dried up, Harry Kewell was unable to find his top form consistently while a succession of niggling injuries, added to the longer term ones, plus self-inflicted suspensions, disrupted the team pattern. United simply lost their way and the Woodgate-Bowyer resumed court case was lurking in the background.

Woodgate didn't start a Premiership game until Boxing Day – just days after being found guilty of affray and being sentenced to 100 hours community service. He was acquitted of the more serious charge of causing grievous bodily harm with intent.

Bowyer was cleared of both charges after the nine-week trial and Michael Duberry found not guilty of perverting the course of justice.

A friend of Woodgate's, Paul Clifford, was found guilty of grievous bodily harm and affray and sentenced to six years in prison. Another of Woodgate's pals, Neale Caveney, was also ordered to do 100 hours community service after being convicted of affray, but cleared of the more serious assault charge. Bowyer and Woodgate's England careers had been put on hold during the course of both trials but there was considerable media

The Leeds United bench look grim at Ninian Park during the FA Cup third-round match against Cardiff City in January 2002.

speculation about whether the FA would want coach Sven-Goran Erikkson to select them for the national side.

Leeds was chosen to host a friendly against Italy in March, but neither player was chosen in the England squad with Woodgate being told that he would not be considered until after the 2002 World Cup.

Bowyer, whose form under normal circumstances would undoubtedly have earned long overdue recognition at national level, is still waiting for his first senior cap. Nigel Martyn and Danny Mills both started the England game at Elland Road and new signing Robbie Fowler netted England's goal in a 2-1 defeat.

Fowler had made the surprise move from his hometown team, Liverpool, for £11 million in December and was quickly among the goals – including a hat-trick in the 3-0 win in Woodgate's comeback game at Bolton.

His signing came a couple of months after England midfielder Seth Johnson had been recruited from Derby for £7 million. But Johnson, like so many Leeds players during a frustrating season, soon joined a posse of stars in the treatment room.

It was a similar story in Europe as United rarely hit the heights against mediocre opposition in the UEFA Cup but got past Maritimo, Troyes, and Grasshoppers of Zurich before being paired with Dutch champions PSV Eindhoven in the quarter-finals.

United emerged from a bad run of form to dominate a 0-0 draw in Holland but paid the price

for not taking their chances in the return leg when Eindhoven scored the only goal of the game in injury time. There was not even any solace in the domestic cups. A Keane hat-trick was the highlight of a 6-0 thumping of Leicester in the League Cup at Filbert Street but Chelsea won 2-0 at Elland Road in the next round.

It was even worse in the FA Cup as United became the biggest giants of the year to fall as they slumped to a 2-1 defeat at Second Division Cardiff City in a match blighted by violence by home supporters after the final whistle. That defeat was the start of 10 games without a win and effectively killed off any hope of a return to the Champions League. That run included a 0-0 draw at struggling Everton where some of the travelling support turned on coach Brian Kidd, the former Manchester United number-two to Sir Alex Ferguson.

O'Leary immediately laid the law down to fans in an effort to stop the club from imploding and the situation was nipped in the bud but the free-flowing football and results were still hard to come by. Such was United's plight that they applied to join the Intertoto Cup as insurance in case they didn't qualify for Europe.

To crown a miserable few weeks, Woodgate had his jaw fractured after horseplay among friends on a night out in Middlesbrough, and was ruled out for the last four games of the season.

United's big name stars like Kewell, Viduka and Dacourt were constantly linked in the media to big-money moves abroad because of United's failure to qualify for the Champions League.

Robbie Fowler joins the celebrations at Filbert Street in March 2002 when United won 2-0 against bottom-of-the-table Leicester City.

Although United's future continues to look bright, the club are looking to move away from Elland Road.

After consultation, supporters backed a blueprint to move from Elland Road and construct a state-of-the-art 50,000 capacity stadium just on the south side of the A1-M1 link road, near Templenewsam.

United's board said that it would be possible to build the new ground at no cost to shareholders as it could be funded by the sale of Elland Road and sponsorship naming rights.

However, United's failure to qualify for the Champions League had hit the club's finances hard and they would have to sell players before bringing in new ones.

'El Tel' in Charge

There was much speculation over which players would be leaving but it was a surprise when the first departure became manager O'Leary.

Despite investing heavily, his side had under-achieved throughout 2002 and on 27 June, the Irishman paid the price with his job.

There was intense speculation that Martin O'Neill – who had been the preferred choice before O'Leary's appointment four years earlier – would be top of United's list. But ten days after O'Leary's departure, former England coach Terry Venables accepted the job of leading United to long-overdue success.

The 59-year-old Londoner was a former England coach who took the national side to the semi-finals of Euro '96.

A former star player with Chelsea and Tottenham, he won a couple of full international caps and forged a colourful managerial career.

He cut his teeth in the cut-throat world of management with Crystal Palace and QPR, having played for both clubs, and took them to the Second Division titles in 1979 and 1983 respectively.

In May 1984, Venables headed to Spain and took Barcelona to the League title in his first season in charge, followed by a European Cup Final appearance the following year.

Dubbed 'El Tel' by the media, the high-profile Venables returned to his old club Tottenham as manager and lifted the FA Cup in 1991 – 24 years after playing in a Spurs Cup Final-winning side. His glory days at White Hart Lane ended in 1993

World Cup call-ups

Despite the speculation, United did finish fifth to once again qualify for the UEFA Cup – a fair achievement given the club's lengthy injury list and off-the-field problems.

The campaign ended on an upbeat note for several of the United squad when skipper Rio Ferdinand, Nigel Martyn, Robbie Fowler and Danny Mills were included in the England squad for the 2002 World Cup, while Robbie Keane, Ian Harte and Gary Kelly were in the Republic of Ireland party. Keane proved a late-goal hero as the Irish progressed beyond the group stages in the Far East. Mills and Ferdinand were outstanding as England went to the quarter-finals where they lost to Brazil.

Indeed, in the days following England's dismissal, speculation was rife that Ferdinand's performance had added millions to his value and that he was the target of other clubs, at home and abroad.

after a very public row with Spurs chairman Alan Sugar.

Spurs' loss was England's gain and Venables took over as manager of the national team, just missing out on a place in the European Championship finals on penalties.

He then worked with the likes of Harry Kewell and Mark Viduka as Australia's coach. Although Venables won his first 12 games in charge, the Socceroos missed out on the World Cup finals on away-goals in a play-off. He returned to England for a second brief spell in charge at Palace and later had a stint at Portsmouth before helping Middlesbrough preserve their Premiership status in 2001.

He was on only a short-term contract at the Riverside and returned to being a TV pundit,

seemingly lost to the game at the top level until United came in with an offer Venables himself described as 'irresistible'.

Although Lee Bowyer's much-publicised move to Liverpool foundered and the player returned to Elland Road, United fans saw Rio Ferdinand move to Manchester United for a record fee of £30 million. The transfer speculation dragged on for a week or two before Ferdinand finally made the move.

It was disappointing but Leeds fans seem to be set for exciting times under the leadership of Venables, the charismatic Cockney, whose first signing was midfielder Nicky Barmby from Liverpool for £2.76 million. Then former Lazio midfielder Paul Okon joined Leeds to become the sixth Australian on United's books.

New Leeds manager Terry Venables, pictured at Elland Road in July 2002.